REPENT
AND TURN TO GOD

RECOUNTING ACTS

BABU IMMANUEL

WIPF & STOCK · Eugene, Oregon

Wipf and Stock Publishers
199 W 8th Ave, Suite 3
Eugene, OR 97401

Repent and Turn to God
Recounting Acts
By Immanuel, Babu

ISBN 13: 978-1-55635-950-7
Publication date 7/1/2011
Previously published by Himm International Ministries, 2004

REPENT
AND TURN TO GOD

RECOUNTING ACTS

Dedication

Affectionately dedicated to
My dear wife Usha
and
daughter Aparajitha

CONTENTS

FOREWORD

It is a pleasure for me to write this foreword to this very stimulating work by Dr Babu Immanuel. Dr Immanuel's presentation of Luke's theology of mission is both well argued and insightful. Without a doubt, all who are interested in the mission of the Church will profit considerably from what he has to say.

Dr Immanuel's basic thesis is that in Luke's theology of mission, there are two fundamental elements – the miraculous and the proclamation of the Gospel of Jesus Christ. Further, when these two elements are present in a given situation, the outcome is generally that people convert to faith in Jesus Christ. So conversion is another fundamental point of interest for Luke.

Dr Immanuel's approach to Luke's narrative in the Book of Acts is that of literary and narrative analysis. By carefully examining the narrative and Luke's literary techniques, he identifies various aspects of Luke's theology of mission. Of these, most important is the conviction that God is the Sovereign Lord of history, including the progress of the Gospel. An important implication of this conviction is that the Gospel is of universal significance – that is, it is meant for all. God's saving purpose is universal in its scope.

The sovereignty of God, especially over the events described in Luke's narrative in the Books of Acts, is brought out in several ways. To begin with, Luke draws attention to the scriptural prophecies that were fulfilled not only in the life and ministry of Jesus, but also in the events narrative in Acts. Secondly, Jesus himself foretold the progress of the Gospel to the 'ends of the earth'. Thirdly, God authenticated these events and happenings by 'signs and wonders' performed not only by Jesus but also by those who bore witness to him in the Early Church. And besides, Luke narrates how, at various crucial points, the Church was guided supernaturally even as the Gospel progressed towards the 'ends of the earth'.

However, Dr Immanuel is particularly interested in the miraculous and its role in Luke's narrative and he centres in particularly on its authenticating function. In the Gospel of Luke, Jesus' proclamation of the Kingdom was accompanied by the miracles that he performed. Similarly, in the Book of Acts, miracles, signs and wonders accompany and support the ministry of the Apostles and their associates. Doubtless, for Luke, the miraculous element in the ministry of Jesus and the Apostles and their co-workers was God's own endorsement of the latter. However, it is also clear that in Luke's narrative, the miraculous has further significance. More often than not, the miracles performed served to catch the attention of the audience. But their somewhat numinous and inexplicable nature provokes curiosity and enquiry, which in turn provides an opportunity for proclamation of the Gospel. So while the signs and wonders that were performed on their own might lead merely to amazement and fear, when they were accompanied by the proclamation of the Word, people turned to the Lord in faith.

So Dr Immanuel turns his attention to the apostolic proclamation of the Gospel in Luke's narrative and, particularly, on passages in which the speeches are associated with miraculous happenings. On the basis of his analysis, he observes, first of all, that the apostolic proclamation of the Gospel focuses on God's acting in and through Jesus. This, of course, is fully consistent with Luke's overall conviction that God is the Sovereign Lord of history, including the progress of the Gospel. Besides, the speeches support and bolster the thrust of the narrative by revealing the true significance of the flow of events. Further, on occasion the proclamation is intended to bring the audience to review and revise their perception of past events – especially those relating to Jesus of Nazareth. This is important, for the responses demanded from the audiences to the apostolic witness are repentance, faith and turning to God, and miracles alone are unlikely to elicit such responses. It is only when the miraculous is accompanied by an interpretation that points to the true identity of Jesus as Lord and Saviour that people turn to him in repentance and faith.

A related theme is the universal scope of God's plan of salvation. This is reflected in Luke's arrangement and presentation of his material and in the role that the Spirit plays in his narrative. In the course of his story, the Spirit – and salvation - is given not only to Jews but to Gentiles as well. In some cases, this is in spite of human prejudice and opposition. It is clearly the will of God that it is so, and wherever the miraculous accompanies the proclamation of the Gospel in creative synergy, people turn to the Lord in faith.

So Dr Immanuel turns finally to consider the possible implications of his study and findings. Some of these are self-evident: The mission of the Church is God's universal mission. He calls his people to participate in mission and he sustains them in and empowers them for the task. However, there are other questions that arise: To begin with, What is the significance of the somewhat open-ended conclusion of the Book of Acts? Does it imply that the mission is on going – that is, that it is one and the same mission down through the Church age? And if that is so, what can we derive from Luke's narrative as normative in the Church age? Are there any indicators regarding what is and what is not intended to be normative? Further, a particularly relevant question that arises in many contexts around the world today is, To what extent does conversion to faith in Jesus involve discontinuity with past religious loyalties? For example, how does communalism in the Church and discrimination that is based on ethnic loyalties stand up in the light of Luke's narrative?

In the contemporary context, the charismatic/Pentecostal wing of the Church is arguably the fastest growing. If that is so, another question that arises from this study is: Is the conjunction of the proclamation of the Gospel and miracles normative? Or was it because the proclamation of the Gospel that Luke writes about was apostolic that it was authenticated by the miraculous?

All in all, this is a timely and useful contribution to the theology and practice of mission, and I have every confidence that it will be received well by all who are interested, in one way and another, in the mission of the Church.

Brian C. Wintle

Bangalore, India

July, 2004

ACKNOWLEDGEMENTS

This is a slightly modified version of my PhD Dissertation accepted by the University of London. It is inevitable, therefore, that the production of work of this nature owes a great deal to the support and guidance of others. Therefore, I owe a huge debt of gratitude to all those who have helped in the course of this study, whether financially, intellectually, or through emotional support.

First of all, my thanks are due to Dr. David Samuel, the Director of TAFTEE, who not only encouraged me to study further but also initiated the whole process. I can never thank Prof. Judith Lieu, my principal supervisor, enough. But for her superlative guidance, constructive criticisms, and encouragement my work would not have taken this final shape. I am also immensely grateful to Dr. Edward Adams, my other supervisor, who helped clarify my thinking on many points. My thanks are also due to Prof. Francis Watson, for his initial guidance and to Dr. Douglas Campbell, for reading through portions of my writing and offering helpful comments. I am very grateful to Prof. James D.G. Dunn (Durham University) and Prof. Christopher Tuckett (Oxford University), my external examiners, for approving my work and also for their incisive comments.

My heartfelt thanks to the Langham Research Scholarship Trust, the Theological Trust of King's College, the Goodenough College, and to St. Paul's Church, Howell Hill, Surrey, who together funded the entire programme. Had it not been for their sustained financial assistance, this work would not have been possible at all. My special thanks to Mr. Peter De Leyser, Mr. George S. Hughes and Mr. Ralph Spittle of St. Paul's Church, who helped with the initial editorial work. I am very grateful to Brian Brock and Russell Wilcox, who, from time to time, edited my writing. I am thankful to my good friends Dr. Ashley Null, Kelly and Tabitha Kapic, Eric Flett, Christopher and Hannah Roberts, and

John and Sarah Thomas, and the Rice family of St. Paul's Church, Howell Hill, for all their support, warmth, and camaraderie.

My heartfelt thanks also go to Mr. Michael Keong for suggesting that this study should be published and organising it with the First Printers, Singapore. I am also grateful to HIM International Ministries Inc. for coming forward to publish this work. Above all, I am hugely indebted to Usha, my dear wife for all her encouragement and for being a fellow pilgrim in this journey.

ABBREVIATIONS

AB	Anchor Bible
ACNT	Augsburg Commentary on the New Testament
AES	*Archives Européennes de Sociologie*
AJT	*Anglican Journal of Theology*
ANRW	*Aufstieg und Niedergang der Römischen Welt*
ASR	*American Sociological Review*
Beginnings	F.J. Foakes Jackson & Kirsopp Lake (Eds.), *The Beginnings of Christianity*, 5 Vols., (London: Macmillan, 1920-1933).
BJRL	*Bulletin of the John Rylands Library*
BTB	*Biblical Theology Bulletin*
CBQ	*Catholic Biblical Quarterly*
EQ	*Evangelical Quarterly*
ET	English Translation
ExpTim	*Expository Times*
FRLANT	Forschungen zur Religion und Literature des Alten und Neuen Testaments
BDAG	Frederick William Danker (Rev. & Ed.), *A Greek-English Lexicon of the New Testament and Early Christian Literature*, (Based on Walter Bauer's German Edition; Chicago/London: University of Chicago Press, 2000).
HTR	*Harvard Theological Review*
ICC	International Critical Commentary
Int.	*Interpretation*
JAAS	*Journal of Asian and African Studies*
JBL	*Journal of Biblical Literature*
JBR	*Journal of Bible and Religion*
JJS	*Journal of Jewish Studies*

JRH	*Journal of Religion and Health*
Journ.Rel.Hist.	*Journal of Religious History*
JSNT	*Journal for the Study of New Testament*
JSNTSup.	Journal for the Study of New Testament Supplement Series
JSOT	*Journal for the Study of Old Testament*
JSOTSup.	Journal for the Study of Old Testament Supplement Series
JSR	*Journal of Social Research*
JSSR	*Journal of the Scientific Study of the Religion*
JTS	*Journal of Theological Studies*
L & S	H.G. Liddell & R. Scott (Comp.), *A Greek-English Lexicon*, (Revised by Henry Stuart Jones; Oxford: Clarendon, [1845] Reprint 1968).
LCL	Loeb Classical Library
NovT	*Novum Testamentum*
NovTSup.	Novum Testamentum Supplementary Series
NTS	*New Testament Studies*
OTP	James H. Charlesworth (Ed.), *The Old Testament PseudepiGrapha*, 2 Vols., (London: Darton, Longman & Todd, 1985).
RSR	*Religious Studies Review*
SA	*Sociological Analysis*
SBL	Society of Biblical Literature
SBLDS	Society of Biblical Literature Dissertation Series
SBLMS	Society of Biblical Literature Monograph Series
SBLSP	*Society of Biblical Literature Seminar Papers*
SE	*Studia Evangelica*
SJT	*Scottish Journal of Theology*
SNTSMS	Society of New Testament Studies Monograph Series
ST	*Studia Theologica*
TCGNT	Bruce M. Metzger, *Textual Commentary on the Greek New Testament*, (London/New York: United Bible Societies, 1971).
TDNT	Gerhard Friedrich (Ed.), *Theological Dictionary of the New Testament*, (Tr. Geoffrey W. Bromiley; Grand Rapids: Eerdmans, 1964).
TWNT	Gerhard Kittel, *Theologisches Wöterbuch zum Neuen Testament*, (Stuttgart: Kohlhammer, 1953-79).
WUNT	Wissenschaftliche Untersuchungen zum Neuen Testament

NOTES FROM THE PUBLISHER

The circumstances under which this book was brought to us for publishing were much more than coincidental. The sort of circumstances one normally shares over a cup of coffee or tea. For one such as I, my own conversion into the Faith in God and in Christ corresponded with initial meetings with the author. So, when asked if there would be any interest in publishing his book, I felt that it was only a divine purpose that could have brought the author and I together. And I believe that there is too, a divine purpose for this book. But the *raison d'etre* of HIM International Ministries Inc., is not based on one sole purpose, namely, the publication of this book. I believe that from this first project entrusted upon us, would be the first sign of well springs from which God's love will be showered upon the world. Indeed, HIM International Ministries Inc., though recently incorporated, humbly begs to stay on it's course and remain in obedience to everything that God will want this organisation to do. At this time, I can only say that it will be a format of ministry very much unlike others. It will be one that only God can put together. *Repent And Turn To God* takes on the salvific theme and brings us back to basics amidst developments in Christian theology and Christian practice. I sincerely hope that it is one that will bring us back to the heart of our Heavenly Father.

And to all those, whose hands this book falls on, to God be the Glory.

Michael Keong MBA(Australia) FCPA(Australia) FCCA(United Kingdom) CPA(Singapore)
Founder
HIM International Ministries Inc.,

Perth, Australia

Repent And Turn To God we believe will be the first of many books that HIM International Ministries Inc. will publish. It is presented as a scholarly work and those unacquainted with New Testament Greek may perceive difficulties in benefiting from it. The perception need not be entirely true. The author is no mean academician that leaves you befuddled with one obscure technicality after another. Indeed, the author has demonstrated that writing lucidly is not incompatible with writing scholarly. When I read the book, it was easy to visualize a teacher gently prodding me on as in a one to one tutorial, taking me from one level of understanding to another, and genuinely concerned for me not to miss a point. I hope it will be your experience too. Although teachers, preachers, pastors and academicians are likely to be more comfortable with it, the message of the book is presented clearly for anyone who is a serious student of the Bible. Nevertheless, we apologize that the Greek words used are not transliterated and the English equivalent given. The reprints will make up for this, as it is our intention to make the book accessible to readers not acquainted with New Testament Greek.

An important message that the book brings convincingly to us is that the pattern of conversion stories in Acts is an inextricably intertwined complementarity of "The miraculous phenomenon (the doing) + Missionary discourse (proclamation)". John Calvin was quoted as saying that "it is a holy knot that may not be dissolved". In popular parlance, it is like 'love and marriage, you can't have one without the other!' What then are the implications for Christian missions? Has Luke, the "missions strategist" given us a blueprint for Christian missions? Is it a *sine qua non* for successful missionary endeavors to accord "Christian proclamation a position of functional primacy over the miraculous"?

The "Theo-Christocentric" view of Luke is another important perspective to consider for missionary endeavours. To quote from the author, "Luke's message in his missionary discourses is this: God has revealed himself fully and normatively in Jesus by exalting him as the Lord and Messiah. Therefore, the only way to be saved or be forgiven of sins is to believe in him or to call on his name or to turn to him." It is God who causes people to turn to Him in the act of conversion. The miraculous events themselves are acts of God, which are "one of the means" causing people to turn to Him. However, the completion of the turning to Him requires the "acts of proclamation" which "originates from God's own providence and advances" through the human medium of the apostles.

Luke's vision, as the author argues, is a worldwide mission. God purposes to bring salvation to all people, without "excludedness," "The Christian witness is part of God's universal redemptive purpose. It is willed by God (Acts 11:21), envisioned by Jesus (Acts 1:8), empowered and guided by the Spirit (Acts 2:1-13), and implemented by Jesus' followers." The universality of God's redemptive purpose for mankind and the complementarity of proclamation and the miraculous we hope will stir the heart of His followers not just to "go" to the mission field, wherever that may be for the reader, but also to "make" disciples.

To him who sits on the throne and to the Lamb be praise and honour and glory and power, for ever and ever! (Revelations 5:13). Amen.

Nelson Choo M Counselling (Australia) BA (Hons)(Singapore) B Theology (Hons) (Australia) Dip Theology (New Zealand)
Founder
HIM International Ministries Inc.,

Perth, Australia

1

PROLOGUE

INTRODUCTION

Next to the speeches in the book of Acts[1], the so-called conversion stories represent the most important formal grouping, consisting of over one-quarter of its narrative material.[2] This is evident from the fact that there are twenty-two accounts and five summary statements showing the various means and components by which people turn to God (e.g., miracles, missionary discourses, etc). The following table shows them all.

	The Miraculous	Discourse	Response Demanded	Audience Response
2:1-42	2:3-4	2:14-36,40	2:38-40	2:41
3:1-4:4	3:1-10	3:12-26	3:19	4:4
5:12-16	5:12	—	—	5:14

Summary: 6:7: "The word of God continued to spread; the number of the disciples increased greatly…a great many became obedient to the faith."

8:4-25	8:6-7,13	8:12	—	8:12
8:26-40	8:29,32	8:35	—	8:38
9:1-19 22:1-16 26:9-18	9:3-4,10-16	—	—	9:15; 22:15; 26:16

---

1 The scope of this study is limited to the book of Acts.

2 Robert A. Black cited in David Lertis Matson, *Household Conversion Narratives in Acts*, (JSNTSup. 123; Sheffield: Sheffield Academic Press [SAP], 1996), 11.

Summary: 9:31: "The church throughout Judea, Galilee, and Samaria had peace and was built up. Living in the fear of the Lord and in the comfort of the Holy Spirit, it increased in numbers."

	The Miraculous	Discourse	Response Demanded	Audience Response
9:32-35	9:32-35	—	—	9:35
9:36-42	9:36-42	—	—	9:42
10:1-11:18; 15:7-11,14	10:3-6,10-16	10:34-43	—	10:47-48 11:11,14
11:19-21	—	11:20	—	11:21
11:23-24	—	11:23	—	11:24

Summary: 12:24: "The word of God continued to advance and gain adherents."

	The Miraculous	Discourse	Response Demanded	Audience Response
13:4-12	13:8-11	—	—	13:12
13:46-49	—	13:16-47	—	13:48
14:1 —	14:1	—	14:1	
14:8-18	14:8-10	14:15-17	14:15	—

Summary: 16:5: "The churches were strengthened in the faith and increased in numbers daily."

	The Miraculous	Discourse	Response Demanded	Audience Response
16:11-15	—	16:13	—	16:15
16:25-34	16:26	16:31-32	16:31	16:33,34
17:1-4—	17:3	—	17:4	
17:10-14	—	—	—	17:12
17:16-34	—	17:22-31	17:27,30	17:32,34.
18:1-11	—	—	—	18:8
19:11-20	19:16	—	—	19:18

Summary: 19:20: "The word of the Lord grew and prevailed."

Evidently, the number of conversion stories and the conversion summaries tabulated above, point to the prominence of the conversion motif in Acts.

Despite the unmistakable prominence of the conversion stories, only few scholars have identified conversion as one of the major themes in Acts. Some earlier studies have focused solely on defining conversion in Acts. Further, recent studies, particularly from the social sciences, have tended to interpret conversion in general as a modern development by explaining it as a sociological phenomenon in terms of re-socialisation, or as a psychological process, or as a cultural factor. The emphasis of these explanations, however, being the definition of conversion, the operative or the substantive questions of our inquiry are first, "how does conversion take place in the story? Second, how do the constituent parts of apostolic testimony function together in effecting conversion?"

Each of these questions directs our attention primarily to the different means of conversion enumerated in the stories listed above. Sometimes it takes place through the combination of a miraculous phenomenon and a speech.[3] Sometimes, the audience turns to God or comes to believe in him either solely through a miracle or solely through a (missionary) speech. Besides these particularised means of conversion, Acts also simply states that people were added to the Lord or that they turned to God. These types can be neatly structured and classified broadly into five categories as follows:

a) The combination of Miracle and Discourse

i) *Detailed Stories*

Miracle	2:1-13	3:1-10	10:1-6, 9-13	14:8-10
Reaction	2:6-7a, 12-13	3:10b	10:7-8, 14-16	14:11
Discourse	2:14-36, 38-40	3:12-26	10:34-43	14:15-17
Conversion	2:41 (3000)	4:4 (5000)	10:44-48	—
Audience	(Jews)	(Jews)	(Cornelius' Household)	(Lystrans)

ii) *Short Stories*

Event	8:6b-7	8:26	16:25-26
Reaction	8:8	8:27	16:27
Discourse (Summaries)	8:5,12,35	8:35	16:31, 32a
Conversion	8:12a,c	8:36-38	16:33c, 34b
Audience	(Samaritans)	(Ethiopian Eunuch)	(Philippian Jailer)

3 The phrase 'miraculous phenomenon' is used in the study as a convenient umbrella term denoting any supernatural occurrence in the book of Acts, such as miracles, signs, wonders, healing, visions, angelophanies, heavenly voices, and the like. It is not used in the study in any philosophical sense.

b) Miracles only

Event	5:12-16	9:1-19 22:1-16 26:9-18	9:32-35	9:36-42	13:4-12	19:11-20
Reaction	5:11				13:12	19:17
Conversion	5:14	9:18	9:35	9:42	13:12	19:18
Audience	(Jews)	(Saul/ Paul)	(Lydda/ Sharon)	(Joppa)	(Sergius Paulus)	(Ephesians)

c) Speech/Proclamation

Proclamation	11:19-21	11:23-24	16:11-15	17:1-4	17:22-31
Conversion	11:21	11:24	16:15	17:4	17:34a
Audience	(Hellenists)	(Hellenists)	(Lydia &) Household)	(Jews)	(Athenians)

d) Conversion Summaries

Summary	13:46-49	14:1	17:10-14	18:1-11
Conversion	13:48	14:1	17:12	18:8
Audience	(Gentiles)	(Jews/ Gentiles)	(Beroeans)	(Corinthians/ Crispus' Household)

e) Summary Statements

6:7; 9:31; 12:24; 16:5 and 19:20.

Such a classification and structural arrangement of the conversion accounts in Acts makes obvious the different groups of conversion stories that lay out various emphases that could be singled out for further investigation.

The above texts, however, highlight prominently one type of conversion story that occurs so often that it could be called a 'type-scene'. There are about seven such stories (Group 'a' above). The purpose of this book is to study only those stories where a distinct narrative pattern of conversion stands pronounced, i.e., "The Miraculous Phenomenon + Missionary Discourse = conversion".

Type-scenes are basic situations recurring a number of times in a narrative.[4] As literary techniques, they report a series of identical or similar events,[5]

[4] R.C. Tannehill, *The Narrative Unity of Luke-Acts. A Literary Interpretation*, 2 Vols., (Philadelphia: Fortress, 1986/1990), 1.170.

[5] Mark A. Powell, *What is Narrative Criticism?*, (Minneapolis: Fortress, 1990), 39.

particularly for reasons of emphasis, and the task of considering the significance of an event.[6] The conversion type-scenes singled out above (Group 'a') provide the operative question for this investigation: "How does the conversion take place in the present story?" It will become progressively clear in the study that for Luke this question is pivotal for two reasons: a) almost all the conversion accounts in Acts ask this question at least covertly, and b) it is bound up with Luke's position that God is the author of conversions in Acts.

Furthermore, the Group 'a' of the conversion stories raises the following important questions: "Why are the miraculous and the Christian proclamation juxtaposed in these stories? What is the connection between them? What makes an event 'miraculous' for Luke? Why is it important to him? What narrative functions does the miraculous perform? Why does Luke interpose his narratives with missionary speeches? Why do they appear together with the miraculous? What literary roles do they play within the conversion stories? How do the miraculous and the proclamation function together in Christian witnessing in achieving the results enumerated above? Why is the conversion ratio very high where the miraculous and the missionary discourses function together? How does this affect the overall development and the purpose of the book of Acts?" The express purpose of this study is to answer these questions by investigating the literary roles the miraculous and the missionary discourses play, both respectively and together in Christian witnessing in the book of Acts.

What immediately follows is a brief review of scholarship to trace how the theme of conversion has been interpreted by other disciplines, in order to situate the present study within scholarly discussions on the subject and to locate its distinctive contribution.

SCHOLARSHIP ON CONVERSION

New Testament Scholarship on conversion in Acts

Scanning previous scholarship on the theme of conversion in Acts encounters two realities. First, the body of literature is miniscule; second, it focuses primarily on the definition of conversion, or it assumes it as a *prima facie* part of Acts. For example, taking cues from sociological approaches to conversion, B.R. Gaventa proposes a tripartite model of conversion:

---

6 Ibid., 39-40.

> "In addition to those experiences that grow out of the past (alternations), and those that result in an affirmed present at the expense of a rejected past (conversion), there are experiences that we may call transformations."[7]

Acknowledging the difficulty in using the term conversion to represent all kinds of experiences,[8] and making use of other imageries such as new birth and new life to denote experiences that cannot be strictly called conversion,[9] Gaventa suggests three more types: Alternation, Pendulous Conversion, and Transformation.[10] *Alternation* is a change emerging out of an individual's past. For instance, in Acts 8, the Ethiopian Eunuch has been worshipping in Jerusalem; has been reading the book of Isaiah; and is keen to hear the good news about Jesus from Philip, resulting in his baptism. Therefore, the Ethiopian Eunuch's conversion did not require the rejection of his past, but flowed naturally from his past experience. Similarly, Cornelius was devout, God-fearing, charitable and prayerful (10:2). Even God himself recognised this (10:4). Therefore, Gaventa concludes, Cornelius' conversion comes in recognition of his previous religiosity. *Pendulous Conversion* is rejecting past convictions and affiliations for an affirmed present and future. In Acts 9, Paul swings from being a persecutor to an ardent preacher of the Gospel and is persecuted as a result. Paul's conversion here is pendulous, in that it represents a reversal in his activity. *Transformation* reinterprets the past in light of a new perception about God and the world and new circumstances. It is a "change of perspective in which some newly gained cognition brings about a changed view of understanding—a re-cognition of the past."[11] In Galatians 1:11-12 Paul admits that because of revelation, he has come to see that Jesus was indeed the Messiah. However, this does not sever his relationship with his past. Rom. 9:1-5 indicates a continuation of ties with his fellow Jews. The revelation of Jesus does not demand the rejection of the past, but its reinterpretation. One merit of Gavanta's argument here is that she points out the difficulty in using the term conversion as a composite term to explain every experience.

The most important lacuna in Gaventa's argument is the absence of the means of conversion. In her treatment of Pentecost and the Cornelius story, she does not point out the roles played by the supernatural phenomena (the descent of the Spirit and the parallel-visions) and the addresses delivered by Peter on both these occasions. An analysis of the functions of the miraculous and the

---

7 B.R. Gaventa, *From Darkness to Light. Aspects of Conversion in the New Testament*, (Philadelphia: Fortress, 1986), 13.

8 Ibid., 96, 148.

9 Ibid., 130-45.

10 Ibid., 148-49.

11 Ibid., 11.

conversion speeches both respectively and collectively is crucial to understanding these stories.

The other literary work that deals in some detail with the phenomenon of conversion in Acts is by D. L. Matson. Taking the mission of Jesus in the third Gospel as a precursor to the apostolic mission in Acts, Matson studies the household conversion accounts in Acts. In his work, he devotes one full chapter to the conversion of Cornelius' household.[12] But he almost totally ignores the role of the visions that led Peter to Cornelius' house and the fact that the earlier visions and their internal recapitulations, i.e., within the main narrative itself (10:1-48), provide a starting point for Peter's missionary speech at Cornelius' place (10:34). Importantly, Matson does not consider at all the crucial role that the discourse and the internal and external recapitulations, i.e., outside the main narrative (11:1-18; 15:7-21), of the visions play in the overall Cornelius narrative. He ignores the fact that if Cornelius' household conversion is the end, the miraculous (visions) and the speech are the definite means to that end.

Besides the above-mentioned works, Leo O'Reilly's work on the "*Word and Sign in the Acts of the Apostles*"[13] draws some implications of the word and the signs, particularly for the understanding of Luke's theology of the word. He correctly points out that the signs confirm the word and (occasionally) lead people to faith.[14] Importantly, however, in his theological analysis of Pentecost[15], he does not clearly point out how the word and sign are related within the text, nor what literary roles they play together in the conversion of the masses. Further, he does not show that the descent of the Spirit is the connecting link in all the sections of Peter's Pentecost address, fulfilling a prophecy (2:16-21), linking it to the passion and the resurrection of Jesus (2:22-33), and confirming and resulting from Jesus' exaltation as the Lord and Messiah (2:34-36). Therefore, it provides an opportune moment to invite people to repent and be baptised (2:38-41).

Elizabeth Schüssler Fiorenza, conversely points out the role played by miracles as a *means* of attracting people in the early church and converting them. In the Graeco-Roman world, the wandering preachers and missionaries *attracted* their audience by demonstrating the exceptional nature of their message through

---

12 Matson, *Household Conversion*, 86-134.

13 L. O'Reilly, *Word and Sign in the Acts of the Apostles: A Study in Lucan Theology*, (Analecta Gregoriana 243; Roma: Editrice Pontificia Universita Gregoriana, 1987).

14 Ibid., 192-200

15 Ibid., 15-121.

miraculous deeds. Therefore, the success of the early Christian mission was predominantly due to the audience's attraction to the miracles and exorcisms performed by the Christian missionaries and apostles. For instance, Paul and Barnabas heal a paralytic in Lystra (14:8-18). The miracle impressed the Lystrans so much that they exclaimed: "*The gods have come down to us in human form!*" (14:11). Therefore, Fiorenza claims,

> "The strong emphasis of Acts on miracles...indicates...that Luke attempts to picture the Christian missionaries and apostles more as miracle workers than as itinerant philosophers of the time." [16]

Fiorenza's observation that the miraculous attracted people to the church, leads well into the theme of our investigation, as it is accurate, but only partially. Whereas, for Fiorenza miracles are an end in themselves, as will be demonstrated in the study, Acts presents miracles first, only as one of the 'means' by which people turn to God, and secondly, they function mostly in conjunction with the missionary discourses.[17] The latent principle—sometimes explicit and sometimes implicit—in the conversion accounts selected for this investigation is that the miraculous functions as an entry point into the missionary discourse and is well integrated into it so that they both function together in a complementary fashion. Missionary discourse both expounds the 'miraculous' event and invites the audiences, either explicitly or implicitly, to respond to proclamation.

The scholars discussed above are the only few who study the phenomenon of conversion in Acts. Therefore, given this dearth of material, there is room for further exploration of this theme.[18] It is hoped, therefore, that this inquiry into the literary functions of the miraculous and the missionary discourses in Acts, both respectively and collectively, will enable us to see their role in Christian witnessing.

---

16 E.S. Fiorenza, "Miracles, Mission, and Apologetics: An Introduction", in Elizabeth S. Fiorenza (Ed.), *Aspects of Religious Propaganda in Judaism and Early Christianity*, (Notre Dame/London: University of Notre Dame Press, 1976), 10-16, esp. 12. This point is also noted by Ramsay MacMullen in *Christianizing the Roman Empire (A.D. 100-400)*, (New Haven/London: Yale University Press [YUP], 1984), 26-30.

17 The term 'discourse' in the investigation denotes simply the spoken word, whether briefly or elaborately, in monologue or dialogue.

18 The Study of Paul J. Achtemeier ("The Lukan Perspective on the Miracles of Jesus: A Preliminary Sketch" in C.H. Talbert, (ed.), *Perspectives in Luke-Acts*, (Edinburgh: T.&T. Clark, 1978), 153-67; also in *JBL*, 94, (1975), 547-62) does advert to the complementary relationship between preaching and miracles, particularly in the ministry of Jesus in Luke's Gospel.

Besides the above stated scholarly works specifically on the theme of conversion in Acts, in recent times there has also been a growing interest in the theme of conversion, particularly to Christianity, in a variety of academic disciplines, such as sociology, psychology, and anthropology.[19] Therefore, before examining Luke's conversion motif in Acts, the following section briefly reviews the modern scholarship on this phenomenon in order to provide disciplinary foci, to discover the broad conceptual framework that conditions these different disciplines, and also to locate Luke's distinctive contribution.

MODERN SCHOLARSHIP

Sociology

Sociology interprets conversion as the development of a new conception of self, as a phase in socialisation, and also as a shift in group identification. Within this larger conceptual framework, Lofland and Rodney Stark propose a seven stage model of conversion[20]: a) an experience of acute and persistent tension b) within a religious problem-solving perspective, which helps the individual c) to define oneself as a religious seeker, d) to encounter the new religious movement at a crucial turning point in life, e) to form an affective bond with the other converts of the new religious group, f) to forego extra-cult attachments, and g) to interact intensively with the new religious movement. When such conversions take place in terms of re-socialisation or transition into another religion, the most effective way of sustaining them, Berger and Luckmann suggest, is the *plausibility structure*—a social base that supports and helps the convert to continue in the converted state.[21] A religious community is such a plausibility structure. For instance, Saul could have become Paul in the aloneness of religious ecstasy, but he could remain Paul only in the context of the Christian community that recognised him as such and confirmed the new being in which he located his identity.[22]

Further, the conversion experience itself may be partly moulded by expectations of what it is about. Therefore, Lofland and Skonovd present six motifs of

[19] For a very detailed annotated bibliography on conversion from a disciplinary point-of-view, see Lewis R. Rambo, "Current Research on Religious Conversion", *RSR*, 8, (1982), 146-59.

[20] Lofland and Stark, "Becoming a World-Saver: A Theory of Conversion to a Deviant Perspective", *ASR*, 30, (1965), 862-75.

[21] Peter L. Berger & Thomas Luckmann, *The Social Construction of Reality. A Treatise in the Sociology of Knowledge*, (Harmondsworth: Penguin Books, 1971), 177-82. See also Karl Olav Sandnes, *A New Family: Conversion and Ecclesiology in the Early Church with Cross-Cultural Comparisons*, (Bern/Berlin/Frankfurt: Peter Lang, 1994), 14.

[22] Berger & Luckmann, *Social Construction*, 177-78.

conversion[23]: *Intellectual* (Self-conversion without any actual encounter with the devotees of the respective religion); *Mystical* (Involves visions or feelings that provide the impetus to convert); *Experimental* (Slow, gradual experiment with the new religious belief and a transformation of religious identity, behaviour, and worldview); *Affectional* (The interpersonal relationship within the religious group that support the new convert); *Revivalist* (Experiences involving strong emotions), and *Coercive* (Brainwashing, programming, mind control, persuasion, and thought reform).

Sociological approaches also suggest that conversion involves a complex network of various social, relational, and circumstantial factors. Rambo, for instance, presents a 'holistic model of conversion'[24] that is influencing and being influenced by a matrix of relationships, expectations, and situations. Therefore, he identifies five types of conversion: a) *defection* (Or apostasy from previous commitment); b) *intensification* (Revitalisation of the previous religious commitment); c) *affiliation* (Transition from no or minimal commitment to full commitment); d) *institutional transition* (Movement from one denomination to another within the same religious tradition), and e) *tradition transition* (Movement from one religion to another).[25] Thus, the sociological approaches conceive conversion as re-socialisation, or as a shift in group identification in order to find a sense of belonging so that the individual's conversion will be sustained by the community of believers.

The concept of group-affiliation or re-socialisation, propounded by the sociological approaches is relevant to the study of the conversion stories in the book of Acts since in many cases they lead to joining a community at some point.

Psychology

Psychological approaches concentrate on issues such as the definition of conversion, the question of pathology (whether conversion is pathological, abnormal, regressive, a sign of illness or emotional instability), the question of convertible types, and the question of the right age of conversion.[26] William James, for instance, defines conversion as "the process, gradual or sudden, by

---

[23] John Lofland & Norman Skonovd, "Conversion Motifs" *JSSR*, 20, (1981), 373-85.

[24] L.R. Rambo, *Understanding Religious Conversion*, (New Haven/London: YUP, 1993), 7.

[25] Ibid., 13-14.

[26] J.R. Scroggs & William G.T. Douglas, "Issues in the Psychology of Religious Conversion", *JRH*, 6, (1967), 204-16, esp. 206-13.

which a self hitherto divided, and consciously wrong, inferior and unhappy, becomes unified and consciously right, superior and happy, in consequence of its firmer hold upon religious realities."[27] Arthur D. Nock upholds differently William James' focus on the individual and on conversion as a psychological osmosis. He distinguishes between adhesion (acceptance of a religious position to a degree but which required no absolute allegiance) and conversion which is

> "The reorienting of the soul of an individual, his deliberate turning from indifference or from an earlier form of piety to another, a turning which implies a consciousness that a great change is involved, that the old was wrong and the new is right."[28]

Nock, therefore, describes conversion as involving moral judgments and locates it within an individual's psyche. To prove the credibility of his definition, Nock analyses the psychological appeal of the mystery cults that coexisted with Christianity in the late Roman period and points out that "any philosophy of the time that set up a standard of values different from those of the world outside...could serve as a stimulus to a stern life...be something 'like conversion'...."[29] Thus, Nock confines his analysis of the phenomenon of conversion to the inner state of the individual who chooses to belong to a new faith because of a personal spiritual conviction.

Like Nock, Luke also makes use of the concept of 'turning' in his description of some of the conversion stories in Acts (e.g., 3:19; 14:15). The difference, however, is whereas psychological approaches, like Nock's, interpret conversion as a mental process, Luke interprets it as an actual turning to God.

In tandem with Nock's psychological analysis of conversion, Ramsay MacMullen too offers an interior definition of conversion. It is "that change of belief by which a person accepted the reality and supreme power of God and determined to obey Him...."[30] In his historical analysis of the Roman Empire between A.D. 100-400, MacMullen proposes that such a conversion, particularly to Christianity, is motivated primarily by miracles and martyrdom.[31]

---

27 W. James, *The Varieties of Religious Experience*, (London: Longmans, 1902), 186.

28 A.D. Nock, *Conversion. The Old and the New in Religion from Alexander the Great to Augustine of Hippo*, (Oxford: Clarendon, 1933), 7. See Seppo Syrjänen, *In Search of Meaning and Identity: Conversion to Christianity in Pakistani Muslim Culture*, (Helsinki: The Finnish Society for Missiological Ecumenics, 1984), 34, for conversion as an internal moral revolution.

29 Nock, *Conversion*, 173.

30 R. MacMullen, *Christianizing*, 5.

31 Ibid., 26-30a; cf. E.S. Fiorenza, "Miracles and Mission", 12.

However, he calls conversions motivated by miracles as "Low Class" type as opposed to conversions motivated by intellectual quest, which he calls an "Upper Class" type of conversion.[32]

Luke also makes references to the miraculous as playing its part in Acts in people's turning to God (e.g., 9:35-41). However, the fundamental difference between MacMullen and Luke is that whereas MacMullen's observation stems from actual historical situations in the Roman Empire, Luke basically reports miracles as a literary construct with definite literary functions to perform.

In general, what differentiates the phenomenon of conversion in Acts from the psychological approaches is that whereas the psychological approaches see as crucial certain states before and after conversion and explain it purely as a process of moving from one form to another form of consciousness, in Acts 'turning' is towards a definite goal (26:18) or God (3:19; 14:15). Also, Luke does not refer to the mental states of the converts either before or after conversion.

Anthropology

Anthropology presents culture as a powerful force in shaping individuals, groups, and societies. Within this framework, anthropologists explore the ways in which culture either impedes or catalyses transition from one religion to another. Robin Horton, an Africanist, for instance, isolates three main elements which facilitate conversion, particularly to Christianity within the Yoruba tribe[33]: a) the intellectual concepts current in a given society which may be harmonised with, or said to anticipate, Christian concepts; b) focus on the differences between local spirits and (local concepts of) the supreme being; c) the roles of religious and secular leaders. Horton proposes that the religious and secular leaders could become facilitators of conversion to Christianity provided they are open to new influences from outside cultures. Given this possibility, should any missionary group come to augment the indigenous groups' struggle to achieve a broader understanding of their own condition, it would be received more favourably.

In some other societies, as J.W. Pickett suggests, conversion to Christianity is closely connected to social conditions, the programme of education subsequent to conversion, and the role of the indigenous religious leaders in sustaining the

---

[32] R. MacMullen, *Christanizing*, 37-39.

[33] R. Horton, "African Conversion", *Africa*, 41, (1971), 85-108.

state of conversion and propagating the new faith.[34] Therefore, in general, the dynamics at work in conversion, in these societies, are better social conditions, education (primarily Christian education) and a kind of plausibility structure (as Berger and Luckmann suggest). Sustaining conversion was achieved through education, primarily by the native-born clergy and leaders.[35] Therefore, Pickett warns that conversion should not be presented as a kind of 'social dislocation' and Westernisation; it is imperative, therefore, to preserve the social group identity.[36] Similarly, Susan Bayly cautions that in order for the (Christian) conversion movements to have lasting impact in countries like India, it is important that it does not imply obliterating pre-existing beliefs and social ties amongst the new affiliates.[37]

Conclusion

From the above discussion, it becomes clear that the sociological approaches hinge upon the corporate identity and the sense of belonging that the new converts need to sustain them in their converted state. Psychological approaches revolve around the *prima facie* proposition that all conversions involve an interior change. Historical analyses revolve around the primary motivation that leads to conversion and the anthropological approaches imply conversion as a cultural phenomenon that either strengthens or abrogates the indigenous social institutions and religious beliefs.

All said, nonetheless, it is still difficult to identify the core of conversion. Therefore, Rambo suggests, conversion can be only "what a faith group says it is".[38] In the end, three things become clear: a) conversion has multifarious forms; b) it involves wide-ranging factors; c) everything under the term conversion might not mean the same thing everywhere. Therefore, one might ask, "What is an authentic conversion?" Difficulties arise in attempting to discern the fundamental nature of conversion amid the plethora of methods since they deal with real people and actual historical situations, address wider

---

34 J.W. Pickett, *Christian Mass Movements in India*, (Nashville: Abingdon, 1933), 23ff.

35 Ibid., 240-41. See also D. Schreuder & G. Oddie, "What is Conversion? History, Christianity and Religious Change in Colonial Africa and South Asia", *Journ.Rel.Hist.*, 15, (1989), 496-518, esp. 513, for a similar view.

36 Pickett, *Mass Movements*, 331.

37 S. Bayly, *Saints, Goddesses and Kings*, (Cambridge: Cambridge University Press [CUP], 1989), 1.

38 Rambo, *Religious Conversion*, XIV. See also Alan F. Segal, *Paul the Convert: The Apostolate and Apostasy of Saul the Pharisee*, (New Haven/London: YUP, 1990), 6.

issues, and answer different questions. The subject of conversion is indeed very complex to deal with.

It is impossible to be certain whether Luke was aware of such nuances and varied applications and implications of conversion. All the above-mentioned disciplinary approaches to conversion are modern developments. We cannot, therefore, transpose modern concepts naively into Luke's texts. What Luke records in Acts may or may not bear any resemblance to the way in which these disciplines deal with the subject. Therefore, we should focus on the inner world of Luke's *text* that calls for a special attention on its own terms.

THE METHOD OF THE STUDY

Many scholars have written on the sources and traditions behind Luke's writings. For instance, in his seminal study, particularly on the conversion of Cornelius, Martin Dibelius investigates the 'sources' behind the Cornelius account and how Luke treats them.[39] He concludes that "Luke enriched it (the source) by additions...This must have been born in 'tradition'...."[40] The rest of his chapter discusses how Luke deals with this original story. Although earlier methods of this kind have their own merits, it is time now to consider new ways of understanding Luke's writings, particularly in view of recent trends in biblical scholarship that interpret the text in its final form despite the use of sources and traditions, if any. Such trends have been encouraged by the rise of literary criticism, which assumes that the text has its own independent identity and that it can communicate a message through its linguistic components independently of any sources and traditions.[41] Owing to such a shift in the method of reading the biblical text, a new study of the conversion stories is justified.

To achieve our objectives and to answer the questions raised earlier, we employ the type of narrative criticism that focuses on the text in its final form and views it as a self-sufficient unit.[42] Narrative theory is used here primarily for the reason that it provides important tools essential for a clear analysis of

---

39 M. Dibelius, *Studies in the Acts of the Apostles*, (Ed. Heinrich Greeven; Trans. M. Ling; London: Student Christian Movement [SCM], 1956), 109-122.

40 Ibid., 109.

41 See Stephen D. Moore, *Literary Criticism and the Gospels*, (New Haven: YUP, 1989), xv-xix and M.W.G. Stibbe, *John as Story Teller: Narrative Criticism and the Fourth Gospel*, (SNTSMS 73; Cambridge: CUP, 1992), 5-12 for an outline of narrative criticism.

42 On the various types of literary criticism, see M.A. Powell, *What is Narrative Criticism?*, 11-12.

narrative texts. Therefore, we make use of the results of literary analysis of various subjects by scholars such as C.H. Talbert[43], R.J. Karris[44], R.C. Tannehill[45], Mark A. Powell, and D. Rhoads and D. Michie.[46] Apart from these works, the study also borrows from modern literary and film theories and occasionally from Speech-Act theory. Although modern literary criticism encompasses a vast array of systems and methods that are based, in turn, on diverse hermeneutical conceptions concerning language and communication, New Testament narrative criticism can still draw insights from it. Therefore, the inquiry refers to works by W. Booth[47], Wolfgang Iser[48], Seymour Chatman[49], S. Rimmon-Kenan[50], Meir Sternberg[51], Jakob Lothe,[52] Julia Swindells[53], and Rachel May.[54]

Before proceeding further, the study acknowledges that New Testament narrative criticism is basically an eclectic discipline that borrows from modern literary criticism, which is still in its evolutionary stage and that not all cross-disciplinary approaches may fit the biblical texts. Contemporary literary criticism focuses on fiction and poetry and, therefore, not all the categories and approaches of contemporary fiction may be relevant to biblical narratives, especially to those with historical claims. For example, M. Sternberg criticises Robert Alter for applying the term 'fiction' in some sense, to most biblical

---

43 C.H.Talbert, *Literary Patterns, Theological Themes, and the Genre of Luke-Acts*, (Missoula, MT: Scholars, 1977).

44 R.J. Karris, *Luke, Artist and Theologian: Luke's Passion Accounts as Literature*, (New York: Paulist, 1985).

45 R.C. Tannehill, *Narrative Unity*.

46 D. Rhoads & D. Michie, *Mark as a Story. An Introduction into the Narrative of a Gospel*, (Philadelphia: Fortress, 1982).

47 W. Booth, *The Rhetoric of Fiction*, (Harmondsworth: Peregrine Books, 1987).

48 W. Iser, *The Act of Reading: A Theory of Aesthetic Response*, (Baltimore/London: Johns Hopkins, 1978).

49 S. Chatman, *Story and Discourse: Narrative Structure in Fiction and Film*, (Ithaca, NY: Cornell University Press, 1980).

50 Shlomith Rimmon-Kenan, *Narrative Fiction: Contemporary Poetics*, (London: Methuen, 1983).

51 M. Sternberg, *The Poetics of Biblical Narrative: Ideological Literature and Drama of Reading*, (Bloomington: Indiana University Press, 1985).

52 J. Lothe, *Narrative in Fiction and Film: An Introduction*, (Oxford: Oxford University Press [OUP], 2000).

53 J. Swindells, (Ed.), *The Uses of Autobiography*, (London: Taylor & Francis Ltd., 1995).

54 R. May, "The Power of Speech: Dialogue as History in the Russian Primary Chronicle", in Michael Macovski (Ed.), *Dialogue and Critical Discourse: Language, Culture, Critical Theory*, (New York/Oxford: OUP, 1997), 47-64.

narratives.[55] Nevertheless, despite the reservations needed when employing modern literary critical tools to study an ancient text, tools from the study of modern literature can still shed light on the study of ancient literature. Therefore, Alter posits that

> "The Bible, considered as a book, achieves its effect by means no different from...written language...indeed literary analysis must come first, for unless we have a sound understanding of what the text is doing and saying, it will not be of much value in other respects."[56]

Besides borrowing concepts and insights from contemporary literary criticism, the investigation also draws from Luke's Graeco-Roman literary milieu.[57] Since Luke's writings are but fragments of a larger literary enterprise, a reasonable familiarity with the contemporary Hellenistic thought forms might be helpful to illuminate Luke's narratives. However, this study does not attempt to determine mutual influences. It takes the position that the text of the book of Acts is ultimately self-referential and has its own literary identity. Luke's contemporary Graeco-Roman examples have only a referential value for the present study. One advantage of considering Luke's Graeco-Roman literary milieu is that where Luke is ambiguous, these surrounding literary examples might suggest the way Luke's first century readers could have understood his ideas.

Since the term 'literary criticism' can be understood in various ways, we clarify some of the aspects of literary critical method adopted in the investigation to examine some of the conversion texts[58] in Acts, particularly those that result from witnessing through the miraculous and proclamation. While some of these categories may be useful throughout, others may be more useful in certain contexts than in others. Some of these categories will become fully clear in the detailed case studies given later in the book.

---

[55] Sternberg, *Poetics*, 24-35 in response to R. Alter, *The Art of Biblical Narrative*, (New York: Crossroad, 1981), 23-25.

[56] Alter and Frank Kermode (Eds.), *The Literary Guide to the Bible*, (London: Collins, 1987), 2.

[57] On the importance of studying Graeco-Roman literature for New Testament scholarship, see Loveday C.A. Alexander, "The Relevance of Greco-Roman Literature and Culture to New Testament Study" in Joel B. Green (Ed.), *Hearing the New Testament: Strategies for Interpretation*, (Grand Rapids: Eerdmans/ Carlisle: Paternoster, 1995), 109-26.

[58] Here the term 'text' means simply the words of the story as recorded in the 27th edition of the Nestle-Aland, *Novum Testamentum Graece*, (Stuttgart: Deutsche Bibelgesellschaft, 1993). Unless otherwise stated, the English translation follows the *New Revised Standard Version*, (London: Harper Collins, 1998). The term 'text' is also used to denote any written material.

The Text

In line with the tendency of literary criticism to focus on the text itself, this investigation also treats the text as the final referent and the communicator of meaning, for the reason that the text constructs its own unique literary reality and through its words, it discloses the world of a text.[59] Thus, the text functions as the way into perceptions, attitudes, and imperatives contained within it.

Since meaning is embedded primarily within the final form of the text as a unified narrative,[60] the text should be regarded as an entity that is endowed with life. Therefore, we ask, "What is happening in the text? What does the text mean?"[61] In this way, narrative criticism focuses on the message in the text for its own sake.[62] Since the text is modelled as an act of communication between the implied author and the reader, it invites the latter to identify and understand meaning within the text in its final form.

The Implied Author

The text of Acts can be used to infer something about the implied author. It demonstrates that while being well versed in Graeco-Roman literary forms (e.g., prefaces, speeches, etc), the implied author, referred to as 'Luke', is a person of deep Theological and Christological convictions.[63] For him, God is the sole cause of peoples' coming to believe in him; he also intervenes and involves in the human realm. He has acted decisively in the person and work of Jesus (2:22-24,32-36; 3:13-16; 10:36-43; Cf. 4:12) and continues to do so through the apostles by endowing them with the Spirit (2:1-13). God's dealings are, thus, a *sine qua non* of Luke's presentation of the conversion stories. According to him, since everything is preordained by God (2:23), no one can turn to him without his initiative and intervention. In sum, Luke cannot be understood fully apart from his Theocentric and Christocentric perspective. This is Luke's foundational worldview. Thus, the text of Acts

---

59 Paul Ricouer cited on the notion 'world of a text' in Michael Fishbane, *Biblical Text and Texture: A Literary Reading of Selected Texts*, (Oxford: One World Publications, 1998), xi.

60 Cf. Rhoads and Michie, *Mark as Story*, 2-3.

61 Cf. Elizabeth Malbon, "Narrative Criticism: How Does the Story Mean?" in Janice Capel Anderson and Stephen Moore (Eds.), *Mark and Method*, (Minneapolis: Fortress, 1992), 23-49, esp. 23.

62 Powell, *What is Narrative Criticism?*, 8.

63 In course of this study, terms such as Theological, Christological, soteriological, etc. are employed simply meaning Luke's conviction about God, Christ, and salvation, etc. without considering any 'Theological' implications.

opens up before the readers an already constructed convictional world in which they must inevitably enter and let it condition their own approach to what happens in the text.

Moreover, as one who is often external to the story, Luke, the implied author presents objectively what happens in the story. He knows the sequence of the narrative events and the meaning of what happens in them. For instance, he knows that witnessing to the ends of the earth cannot happen before or without the descent of the Spirit (1:4,8; Cf. 2:1-13). Likewise, he knows that Peter's staying with Simon, the tanner (9:43) is significant, in that it foreshadows Peter's visit to and stay with Cornelius (10:48). Similarly, Luke's commentary in the form of summary statements, interspersed throughout Acts, functions as a hermeneutical tool for the reader to understand conversion as an ongoing movement in Acts. To this extent, the text and the implied author condition the way the conversion stories should be read.

Point-of-View

Point-of-view in the study refers to the perspective from which the story is told. A narrative is mediated or filtered through the telling of the implied author or another character. The readers see only what is shown and hear only what is said in the text. It is not possible for them to know the happening in the text in any other way than the implied author's faithful presentation of the details.[64] Thus, point-of-view helps the readers to understand how the narrative is mediated through the telling of the story, to travel with the characters in the narrative and eventually discover the conceptual worldview of the implied author, which, as emphasised above, is thoroughly Theocentric.

Moreover, point-of-view can take place at two levels: a) the hyperdiegetic or the implied author's objective point-of-view and b) the intradiegetic or the point-of-view of a character internal to the story.[65] For example, the Cornelius story is told both from the hyperdiegetic (10:1-48) and intradiegetic points-of-view (11:1-18; 15:7-11). These objective and subjective points-of-view aid the reader towards constructing a total perspective and identifying the full meaning of what is happening in the story.

---

[64] A. Berlin, *Poetics and Interpretation of Biblical Narrative*, (Sheffield: Almond Press, 1983), 43.

[65] On the various levels of narration, see Robert W. Funk, *The Poetics of Biblical Narrative*, (Sonoma: Polebridge Press, 1988), 130-34.

The Reader

As a literary artefact, the words of the text come to life in the act of reading, since reading unfolds the latent meanings of a text. Thus, discovering meaning is the function of the dialectic between a particular reader and a particular text. Therefore, one may ask, "Who is the 'reader' posited here?"[66]

A longstanding concern of scholars has been to identify Luke's reader. What one encounters in the first reading of Acts is that it is addressed explicitly to Theophilus (1:1), whom Tannehill calls the 'overt narratee'.[67] However, from a literary critical point of view, the book of Acts envisages *Ideal Implied Readers* who approach the text with whatever it requires for a meaningful reading, and interaction with the text; they respond to the text in the most ideal way. As literary constructs they are the most important locus of interaction with the story.[68] Since they are expected to read the text according to the norms implicit within the text itself, and respond to them in the most ideal way, the readers are expected to switch to a world dominated by the implied author's worldview.

What, then, does an ideal reading involve? Wolfgang Iser suggests three possible kinds of reading that might constitute an ideal reading. First, *temporal reading*. This is a sequential reading—reading back and forth. While reading forward, the text may demand recalling an earlier event or it may foreshadow an event, which will be narrated later. The purpose of temporal reading is to revise the earlier conclusions in view of new information.[69] Narrative disclosures may complement earlier assumptions, or require their revision, or add to the meaning accrued in the course of reading. Thus, there is a strong reciprocal relationship between the text and the reader, which, in the present investigation is fostered particularly through the theme of conversion.

Secondly, *reading as identification.* Here, the readers might identify themselves with one or more characters within the narrative and assess their own interaction with the story and respond to what happens in the story. For example, while encountering responsive characters in the story such as the believing Jews on Pentecost (3:37ff; 4:4), Samaritans (8:4-25), the Ethiopian Eunuch (8:26-40),

---

66 See Robert M. Fowler, "Who is 'the Reader' in Reader-Response Criticism?" *Semeia*, 31, (1985), 5-23; John A. Darr, *On Character Building: The Reader Rhetoric of Characterization in Luke-Acts*, (Louisville: Westminster Press/John Knox, 1992), 16-36. See also Jack D. Kingsbury, "Reflections on 'the Reader' of Matthew's Gospel," *NTS*, 34, (1988), 442-60.

67 Tannehill, *Narrative Unity*, 2.9.

68 Iser, *Act of Reading*, 34f.

69 Ibid., 148-50.

and Cornelius (10:44-47), the readers have before them different character sketches and definite response patterns to compare. These invite them to identify themselves with one or more characters in the story, assume their position, and become active participants in the story, and locate the most ideal response that commensurates the invitation from the text to repent, believe, and turn to the Lord.

Thirdly, *reading as consistency-building.* Here the readers are invited to put together the different themes that interact with each other in the text to construct a total picture.[70] This is an invitation to reconstruct the world inhabited by the (implied) author and enter into it and build consistency through sequential reading.

Moreover, since the interaction between the readers and the text is dialogical, they may be able to identify the challenges contained in the narrative in terms of new meanings and values. For instance, in the Pentecost account, Luke clearly portrays a situation where the narrative audience is accused of embodying certain attitudes and presuppositions that run counter to God's purposes, which, in Luke's scheme, need to be revised and reconstituted. One of them is the negative assessment of Jesus by the Jews that culminated in his crucifixion. The Jews thought of Jesus as a criminal to be rejected, and crucified (2:23). By juxtaposing this negative evaluation with a positive evaluation of Jesus—God's own attestation (2:22) and exaltation of Jesus as the Lord and Messiah (2:36)—Luke has clearly demonstrated what a positive assessment of Jesus should be, and in the repentance of the narrative audience (2:37ff), what it actually means. Here Luke's readers identify two evaluative patterns—God's and humans', positive and negative. Since they are already within Luke's Theocentric worldview, they are also invited to reaffirm their favourable assessment of Jesus.

The focus of narrative criticism on the reader as the locus of interaction with the story reflects Luke's concern to explain how one should ideally respond to the imperatives embedded in the conversion stories. The text gives only hints about what the ideal response ought to be. It is not always possible to anticipate the response of the actual reader, but the narrative can hint at what it should be ideally by showing the response of the implied readers. In this sense, the

---

[70] Ibid., 119.

implied readers are the points of comparison for the actual readers. Thus, the text should be read from the vantagepoint of the implied readers.[71]

Story and Discourse

By 'story' we mean the narrated events arranged together with the characters[72], while 'discourse', as already stated, basically refers to the spoken word, either brief or elaborate.[73] In other words, they refer to what the readers read (the story) and hear (speeches).

Character and Characterisation

Both in the story and missionary discourses, the actors are presented as the agents who carry out the action.[74] They are sketched or 'characterised' through character indicators, which may take place in two ways. First, a character may be characterised by means of adjectives or abstract nouns, which is known as 'Direct Definition'.[75] For example, Cornelius is characterised by means of certain adjectives perhaps, as an ideal convert (10:1-11:18). Another striking feature in the Cornelius story is that, along with the narrator's objective account of Cornelius' character (10:2), Luke juxtaposes God's own assessment of Cornelius and his piety (10:4; cf. 10:31). This provides a confirmatory pattern for the readers. While reading this, Luke may encourage them to ask, "How does my personal piety count before God? Does God esteem my piety as being worthy of divine approbation?"

While presenting positive characters for others to emulate, Luke also negatively characterises some in Acts, from whom he would expect his readers to dissociate. For example, by presenting characters such as Simon Magus who responded to the proclamation for wrong reasons (8:4-25), Luke wants his readers not to identify with him.

A necessary characteristic of ideal characters, such as Cornelius and Peter, is what they think or say in a dialogue or in a direct speech. This is important for the story since it is not only the author's literary device, but also it is a way of

---

[71] Powell (*What is Narrative Criticism?*, 21) comments: "To the extent that the implied reader is an idealised abstraction, the goal of reading the text 'as the implied reader' may be somewhat unattainable, but it remains a worthy goal nevertheless."

[72] Gérard Genette cited in Lothe, *Fiction and Film*, 6.

[73] Lothe, *Fiction and Film*, 6.

[74] Powell, *What is Narrative Criticism?*, 51.

[75] Lothe, *Fiction and Film*, 81.

shaping the characters in the narrative and disclosing their inner state.[76] Through them Luke attributes the characters an active participation and involvement in the narrative progression. Instead of being mute spectators, through their speeches the characters become active participants in the movement of the story. The readers will, then, be able to interpret these details and construct the mental and emotional frame of the characters in the narrative. This is possible, because the content of the speech is so designed as to express an emotion, to form an attitude, or to elicit a particular kind of response. In the Cornelius story, for instance, the internal recapitulation of Peter's visions and the message of the angel (10:30-33) and its external recapitulation by him (11:13-14; 15:7-11) are essential for the story and for reconstructing its meaning and total picture.

The opposite of 'Direct Definition' is the 'Indirect Presentation'[77], which is a demonstration, dramatisation, or exemplification of a given character rather than naming it explicitly. Peter personifies such a characterisation. Although, he is not described anywhere by any adjectives, he is a preacher *nonpareil* besides being a miracle-worker.

Another factor that shapes the character and characterisation is that a character's actions may be unpredictable, but he/she may develop and change as the narrative progresses. Such a character is called a 'Round Character', the opposite of which is a 'Flat Character' whose characterisation remains constant throughout the story. Therefore, he or she might appear as a type[78], and perform certain functions in the narrative. Again here, Peter epitomises the former and Cornelius, the latter. In the Cornelius story, from being a reluctant preacher to the Gentiles (10:28), Peter develops into a preacher who passionately defends the Gentile conversion as God's own doing before the Jerusalem Council (15:7-11; cf. 11:1-18). By contrast, Cornelius' characterisation remains constant throughout the story (10:2,23). How effectively these categories help the reading of Luke's conversion stories in Acts will also become clear in the case studies in this book.

Plot and Irony

Plot outlines a basic framework for the events happening in the story. It employs the literary technique of 'cause and effect' and explains why the events happen

---

76 Shimon Bar-Efrat, *Narrative Art in the Bible*, (Decatur, GA: Almond Press, 1992), 64.

77 Lothe, *Narrative and Film*, 82.

78 E.M. Forster, *Aspects of the Novel*, (Harmondsworth: Penguin Books, 1971), 75.

as they do.[79] It has already been emphasised so far that for Luke, the basic plot is the narrative world shaped by divine providence within which God is the sole author of the conversions. He initiates and guides the movement and the advance of the apostolic witness to the ends of the earth (1:8; Cf. 28:31). This is tangibly seen in the actual conversions in Acts listed above.

Further, the emplotment can happen at different levels at the same time. Within the main plot, there may be subplots. At the basic level the missionary discourses mention the rejection of Jesus (2:33; 3:13b; 10:39b). At the same time, they also point out that this Jesus is not a simple person to be rejected, but the one attested by God (2:22), the risen one (2:32), the one exalted to the right hand of God, the giver of the Spirit (2:33), and the Lord and Messiah (2:36). He is also God's glorified-servant (3:13a), the Holy and Righteous one (3:14a) and the author of life whom God has raised from the dead (3:15). He is the preacher of the message of peace (10:36) and the Lord of all (10:36) and God's anointed one (10:38b), and judge (10:42; 17:31). Such a functioning of the plot at different levels at the same time also demonstrates the irony of the situation.

Irony results from a disparity of understanding. In any situation in which one person knows or perceives more or less than another, irony must be either actually or potentially present.[80] The irony here is that the readers know and perceive more than the characters in the story do. Repeatedly they observe characters in Acts who lack some of the privileged information that they possess.

Irony also communicates ideas that were not originally seen.[81] The Jews might have thought that Jesus was an ordinary man, to be rejected and crucified, but he is the Messiah. He was attested to the Jews by God (2:22a). He was the human form in and through whom God acted among them (2:22b). But the irony is that those who are supposed to receive him as such, rejected and crucified him (2:23b; 3:13b-15b; 10:39b).

Irony is also seen in the apostolic mission. Those who attempt to oppose God's purpose of worldwide witnessing, unwittingly catalyse its actualisation. In 8:1-3, there breaks out a persecution against the church in Jerusalem, perhaps

---

[79] J. Knight, *Luke's Gospel*, (New Testament Reading; London/New York: Routledge, 1998), 40.

[80] Robert Scholes & Robert Kellog, *The Nature of Narrative*, (London/New York: OUP, 1968), 240.

[81] Cf. William S. Kurz, *Reading Luke-Acts: Dynamics of Biblical Narrative*, (Louisville, KY: Westminster/John Knox, 1993), 144-47.

to curb the growth of the community of believers. However, ironically, "Those who were scattered went from place to place *proclaiming the word*" (8:4). They crossed geographical boundaries and travelled as far as Phoenicia, Cyprus, Antioch and spoke the word there and *proclaimed the Lord Jesus* to the Ἑλληνιστὰς (11:19-20).

Function

A function is "an act of a character, defined from the perspective of its significance for the course of the action."[82] It denotes one factor that determines what makes an event important and what consequences it has for the characters and for the subsequent development of the plot. A kind of function that is relevant for the present study is the 'kernel' function. It "...promotes the action by giving the character one or more alternatives to choose between; it can also reveal the results of such a choice."[83] For example, the parallel visions (10:1-6, 9-13) in the Cornelius story are basically divine commands to Cornelius and Peter to obey. However, they may choose either to obey or not to obey. But if they do choose to obey the divine commands embedded in the visions, they will become active participants in what God is about to do.

LIMITATIONS OF THE STUDY

After stating the problem, the purpose, and some aspects of narrative critical method employed in the study to accomplish its objectives, certain constraints within which this study is made should also be enumerated. First, questions of sources and traditions behind the conversion stories in Acts may be relevant and important, but in light of the method adopted for this study, this investigation does not deal with questions of historicity, sources, and traditions of the conversion stories. It confines itself strictly to the text and what happens there, asking only certain literary questions that the text itself prompts. This is because this investigation assumes that the text has its own identity, existence, and function; it raises its own questions and gives its own answers and creates its own literary world.

Secondly, the present investigation is not an attempt to study all the conversion stories in the book of Acts. Although its scope is broadly limited to Group 'a' of the conversion stories mentioned above, the study is confined specifically to two detailed case studies (Pentecost and Cornelius). The case studies are

---

[82] Vladimir Propp, *Morphology of the Folktales*, (Austin: University of Austin Press, 1968), 21.

[83] Lothe, *Fiction and Film*, 76.

kept to a minimum in order to adequately explain the nuances and the dynamics of the fine balance that Luke maintains between the miraculous and proclamation, their respective roles, and the way Luke makes them operate as an integrated whole in Christian witnessing in Acts. The adoption of this particular reading strategy permits a more narrowly defined course of study and raises the question, "What are the literary functions of the miraculous and the mission discourses in Christian witnessing in its advance to the ends of the earth?" There will also be cross-references to other stories in Group 'a' and elsewhere in order not to limit the principles and conclusions only to these two stories.

The other problem that this study encounters is the problem of definition, particularly the definition of terms such as the miraculous, proclamation, and conversion. Some take, for instance, the term miracle or miraculous either as a commonplace term and therefore, do not see the need to define it,[84] or caution that the term might carry a note of trickery.[85] Chapter 3 will study some of the terms that Luke himself employs and will work towards a possible definition of the 'miraculous' in Acts.

The term 'proclamation' is used in the investigation, not as an abstract concept, but as denoting the act of proclaiming the word in Acts. It includes some direct speeches and summaries, but implying the whole speech that contains certain missionary elements such as a call to repentance (2:37), to repent and turn (3:19-20), to turn (14:15), and believe (16:34).

The other consideration is the text of this study. The second volume of Luke's writings, known as the book of Acts, has been chosen for this study. Although, for the most part scholars have accepted Cadbury's hyphenated term for the two volumes as "Luke-Acts"[86], recent studies now limit the way one can speak about it. Some have questioned the unity of Luke-Acts on various grounds,

[84] For example, Tannehill, *Narrative Unity*, 2.26; Fiorenza, "Miracles, Mission", 10; Jack T. Sanders, *Charisma, Converts, Competitors: Societal and Sociological Factors in the Success of Early Christianity*, (London: SCM, 2000), 98.

[85] Scott McCormick, *Behold the Man: Re-reading Gospels, Re-humanizing Jesus*, (New York: Continuum Publishing Company, 1994), 125.

[86] Cadbury, *The Making of Luke-Acts*, (London: Macmillan, 1927), 8-11. See also W.W. Gasque, *A History of the Criticism of the Acts of the Apostles*, (Tübingen: Mohr, 1975), 309; W.C. van Unnik, "Luke-Acts, a Storm Center in Contemporary Scholarship" in L.E. Keck and J.L. Martyn, (Eds.), *Studies in Luke-Acts*, (London: SPCK, 1968), 15-32, esp. 18; Martin Hengel, *Acts and the History of Earliest Christianity*, (Tr. John Bowden; Philadelphia: Fortress, 1979), 14, 36-37; Gregory E. Sterling, *Historiography and Self-Definition: Josephos, Luke-Acts and Apologetic Historiography*, (Leiden/New York/Köln: Brill, 1992), 332ff.

which need not be elaborated here.[87] This study does not deal with this issue. Since the arguments for and against the unity of Luke and Acts are almost equipoised and the debate still continues, this study generally prescinds from using this hyphenated expression.

The other reason for this abstention is more internal. Since the conversion stories in the book of Acts find an internal unity within Acts itself, they may not simply or fully compare with Luke's Gospel. Although there have been attempts to find parallels between Jesus and his apostles[88], the miracle and proclamation combination in Christian witnessing is predominantly a characteristic of the apostolic mission in Acts.

Moreover, it is only in Acts that the subject of conversion finds detailed expression. However, while the scope of this study is confined strictly to the book of Acts, it does acknowledge the ongoing debate concerning the unity of Luke and Acts, and with an attitude of openness, it will cross-reference the book of Acts from Luke's Gospel where and when necessary, but it will be minimal.

THE STRUCTURE OF THE STUDY

The present investigation is divided into two parts. Part One consists of four chapters. Chapter one introduces the subject of conversion as an important theme in the book of Acts, presents a brief review of present scholarship on conversion, and sets out the method of research employed in the study together with some of its limitations.

Chapter two attempts to establish conversion as one of Luke's dominant themes in Acts. It first studies different terms that Luke employs in the conversion

---

87 See Maddox, *The Purpose of Luke-Acts*, (FRLANT; Göttingen: Vandenhoeck & Ruprecht, 1982), 24, n.14; M.C. Parsons, *The Departure of Jesus in Luke-Acts: The Ascension Narratives in Context*, (JSNTSup. 21; Sheffield: JSOT Press, 1987), 24; idem, "The Unity of the Lukan Writings: Rethinking the Opinio Communis" in Naymond H. Keathley (Ed.), *With Steadfast Purpose: Essays on Acts in Honor of Henry Jackson Flanders, Jr.*, (Waco: Baylor University, 1990), 30-31; Richard I. Pervo, "Must Luke and Acts Belong to the same Genre? in D. Lull (Ed.), *SBLSP* 28 (Atlanta: Scholars 1989), 309-16; M.C. Parsons & R.I. Pervo, *Rethinking the Unity of Luke and Acts*, (Minneapolis: Fortress, 1993). Matson (*Household Conversion*, 17, n.25) too refrains from using this hyphenated expression in light of the given misconceptions inherent in the phrase 'Luke-Acts'.

88 For example, Susan Marie Praeder, "Jesus-Paul, Peter-Paul, and Jesus-Peter Parallelisms in Luke-Acts: A History of Reader-Response" in Kent H. Richards (ed.), *SBLSP 1984*, (Chick, CA: Scholars, 1984), 23-39.

stories in Acts in order to arrive at a possible Lucan definition of conversion. Secondly, it attempts to present the evidence within Acts in a cogent manner to prove that conversion is indeed one of Luke's chief themes, in order to answer the implicit question, "Is the theme of conversion a concern of Luke himself or do scholars merely read it into his narratives?" Although numerous proposals have already been made regarding the purpose of the book of Acts, it is argued below that they have failed to pay sufficient attention to Luke's evangelistic concerns. The attempt here is not to settle the issue of the purpose of Acts or to invalidate the earlier proposals, but only to contribute to the ongoing scholarly discussion on the subject.

Chapter three studies Luke's presentation of the miraculous in Acts, its literary role both independently of and in conjunction with the missionary discourses. This is done in comparison with Graeco-Roman examples, OT, Philo, and Josephus, in order to show Luke's distinctive treatment of the miraculous and how it serves to establish the basis of the study's overall argument.

Chapter four follows the same course as the previous chapter. It first discusses the presentation of speeches in Graeco-Roman literature, particularly the function of the speeches in Thucydides' *History of the Peloponnesian War*. The chapter locates the ways in which speeches function in the OT and in the writings of Josephus. Again, the objective is to investigate Luke's distinctive treatment of his missionary speeches and their literary functions in the book of Acts.

Part Two consists of Chapters 5 and 6 and demonstrate in detail how supernatural phenomena and missionary discourses function together as an effective means of conversion of the masses during Pentecost (Chapter 5) and in the Cornelius story (Chapter 6). In these chapters an attempt is made to establish the mechanics of conversion and importantly, to suggest a clearly discernible narrative pattern of conversion within each story. Chapter seven, the Conclusion, answers the questions raised in the first chapter and in the process summarises the study's findings as well as discussing certain possible implications for further study.

2

REPENTANCE AND TURNING TO GOD AS LUKE'S CONCERN IN ACTS

INTRODUCTION

Chapter one proposed that conversion is an important theme in Acts and established the study's objective as that of investigating the literary roles that the miraculous and the missionary discourses play and of demonstrating the way they function together in apostolic witnessing. However, before proceeding further with this task, it is necessary to be clear as to "What is conversion in Acts? Are there internal pointers within Acts demonstrating that it is one of Luke's dominant themes? If yes, why is he concerned about it?" These questions are particularly important in light of the inadequate manner in which the previous studies have addressed them, simply assuming, as they did, that conversion, whatever that might mean, is present in Acts. D.L. Matson, for instance, in his work on the household conversions in Acts, assumes this as a given factor without either defining it or producing internal evidence that it is a dominant theme.[1] By contrast, this chapter studies closely the book of Acts to find answers to the questions raised above. But before doing that directly, it discusses the difficulty of defining conversion in light of the diversity of terms that Luke employs to convey the idea of 'turning to God."

A NOTE ON TERMINOLOGY

The difficulty in defining the term conversion in Acts is largely due to the different expressions that Luke employs with varying frequency to denote the audience-response to the Christian testimony, both explicitly and by implication. Some of them are: μετανοεῖν (2:38; 3:19; 8:22; 17:30; 26:20), σώζειν (2:47; 4:12; 11:14; 16:31, etc), ἐπιστρέφειν (3:19; 9:35, etc), πιστεύειν (9:42; 16:31,

1 D.L. Matson, *Household Conversion*, passim.

etc), δεχέσθαι τὸν λόγον τοῦ θεοῦ (8:14; 11:1), πείθειν (17:4), βαπτίζειν (2:28), and ζητεῖν τὸν θεὸν (17:27), etc. Luke neither defines nor describes any of these expressions even as abstract concepts. This might simply mean that Luke himself found it impossible to define the core of peoples' experience that could be called conversion. Or this might be his technique to break the monotony, but denoting the same experience. Whatever the case, the varied expressions demonstrate that different experiences in different contexts may or may not refer to the same phenomenon. Conversion might mean different things to different people in different contexts at different times.

Sometimes the term conversion might mean joining a different faith-community or the different mental states that one might experience before and after conversion. Therefore, conversion can function no more precisely than as an umbrella term for a variety of experiences. It varies in form and motifs, and in individual and communal connotation. Therefore, we cannot too naively impose a uniform pattern and significance thereto. This is why, and perhaps considering the complexity of his characters' experiences, Luke himself is unable to employ one single term that can be translated as conversion. However, notwithstanding all these problems, having been left with no such blanket term, the investigation takes recourse to the same term conversion as an eclectic, or a cover term while acknowledging its polysemous nature meaning different things at different times to different people.

The following sections first, study Luke's conversion vocabulary in order to arrive at its working definition in Acts and secondly, explore Luke's material from different angles to answer the questions raised above.

PART I: THE CONVERSION LANGUAGE IN ACTS

Luke's use of different terms in Acts makes the task of defining conversion in Acts problematic. We are, therefore, forced either to use the context to understand these terms or turn to contemporary Graeco-Roman literature or the OT for insights that might shed light on the way Luke's first century readers could have understood his language.

Christian proclamation in Acts meets with divergent responses. For instance, the audience reactions to Paul's preaching in Athens might represent all the narrative audiences' responses everywhere: having heard, some scoffed, others expressed their willingness to hear more, and some joined Paul having become believers (17:32-33). This demonstrates the diverse ways in which the Christian mission was greeted in Acts. But the important point here is that the Christian proclamation in Acts, when heard, necessarily demands, in literary critical terms, the most ideal response which accepts the offer of salvation. In what follows, we briefly consider some of Luke's prominent terms such as μετανοεῖν, ἐπιστρέφειν, πιστεύειν, and βαπτίζειν employed both in missionary speeches and in the narrative sections, either as a demand or as a response language, to arrive at a possible Lucan definition of conversion.

μετανοεῖν

The verb μετανοεῖν generally means to take subsequent note of something, to adopt another view, and therefore to regret and change the prior viewpoint.[2] Xenophon employs μετανοεῖν in the sense of changing one's mind: "...when Cyprus...reduced to obedience a vast number of men...we were...compelled to change our opinion (μετανοεῖν)...."[3] Thus, μετανοεῖν can generally signify a change of mind. To this general meaning, Xenophon himself adds a religious meaning, "Instead of realizing too late that you have grossly sinned against the gods...."[4]

The OT too employs μετανανοεῖν in the sense of changing one's mind or behaviour. It presents the concept of repentance within the context of the covenant between Yahweh and Israel. The people individually and collectively transgressed the law and are in need of reconciliation with God and restoration to God's favour. Therefore, it was demanded particularly of people whose repentance was often merely formalised in cultic actions and as such condemned by prophets as inadequate and empty (Amos 4:6; Hos. 6:4; Isa. 1:10-17). The logic behind such a demand is that God would give the penitent a new heart (Isa. 1:18-19) and would establish a new covenant with them (Jer. 31:31-34). Such penitence was sought through inward contrition accompanied by outward signs of repentance such as confession, lamentation, wearing sackcloth, and offering sacrifices (Joel 2:12-13; Hos. 14:2-5; Ezek. 14:6; Pr. Man. 7-14). Thus, μετανοεῖν in the OT is a sign of inward contrition and the creation of a new heart and the restoration of covenant with Yahweh.

---

2 L & S, 1115.

3 Xenophon, *Cyropaedia*, (I.1.3), (Tr. Walter Miller; London: William Heinemann/New York: The Macmillan Co., 1914).

4 Xenophon, *Hellenica*, (I.7.19), (Tr. Carlton L. Brownson; London: William Heinamann/ New York: G.P. Putnam's Sons, 1918). Cf. BDAG, 640.

A similar religious meaning is found in non-canonical Jewish literature where it means a "change of mind" and "regret". In Josephus' account, when David married Bathsheba, after killing Uriah, her husband, by deliberately exposing him in the battlefront, the prophet Nathan warned him saying, "God would inflict punishments...on account of...wickedness...his own wives should be forced by one of his sons...he should be treacherously supplanted by the same son...the child...born...shall soon die."[5] In response David "said with tears and sorrow that he had sinned...was reconciled to him (God)...he (David) repented of the things he had done..." (*Antiq.*, VII.7.4 (153). Similarly, David repented for sinning against God when he took the census (*Antiq.*, VII.13.1 (318-20). Likewise, Sirach records that miracles should ideally lead to repentance, but they may not necessarily accomplish that. Even after seeing the signs performed by Elisha, "the people did not repent (οὐ μετανόησεν), nor did they forsake their sins...." (48:12-15). Thus, μετανοεῖν, while generally emphasising change in mind and perception and assuming a new viewpoint, in the Jewish tradition it includes a sense of regret for the wrongs committed, particularly against God.

μετανοεῖν in the sense of repenting for a particular sin is also found in Acts. In the opening chapters of Acts, Peter consistently holds his Jewish audience responsible for rejecting and crucifying Jesus (2:36; 3:14); therefore, he commands them to repent (μετανοήσατε, 2:38-40; 3:19)[6] for rejecting and crucifying Jesus, the Lord and Messiah (2:36) and author of life (3:15). Luke extends this invitation to repent in different ways. The Pentecost episode brings out the shock caused by Peter's announcement that the Jesus whom they had rejected and crucified was indeed the Messiah chosen by God (2:37). We have already referred to the irony of the situation. The Temple speech (3:12-26), on the other hand, presents a list of supporting motivations. In response to the exhortation to repent and turn (3:19), the Jewish audience must repent for their rejection of Jesus, their Messiah and turn to God if the promises are to be fulfilled. Their impenitence will result in being excluded from the λαός (3:22-23). Thus, the summons to repentance and to be baptised is for the Jewish rejection of their Messiah (2:38; 3:19).

Similarly, in Samaria, Peter charges Simon Magus to repent of his "wickedness"— thinking that he could buy God's gift with money and trying

[5] Josephus, *Antiquities*, VII.7.4 (152). Unless otherwise stated, all quotations will be from William Whiston, (Tr.), *The Works of Josephus*, (Peabody, MA: Hendrickson Publishers, 1999).

[6] So also C.K. Barrett, *The Acts of the Apostles*, 2 Vols., (ICC; Ed., J.A. Emerton, et al.; Edinburgh: T&T Clark, 1994/1998), 1.204.

to do so (8:22). Thus, sometimes Luke employs μετανοεῖν with audience-specificity. Elsewhere he employs μετανοεῖν with universal perspective expecting both his Jewish audience (3:19), all people everywhere (17:30), and the Gentiles (τὰ ἔθνη, 26:20) to repent for their ignorance. By universalising ignorance, Luke makes repentance a fitting universal response to Christian proclamation.

In the mission discourses in Acts μετανοεῖν is demanded of the audience three times, but with no direct audience-response. The following references show how the narrative audiences responded:

μετανοήσατε (2:38):	"Those who welcomed his message *were baptized*" (2:41). "All who *believed*" (2:44a).
μετανοήσατε...(3:19):	"Many who heard the word *believed*" (4:4a).
μετανόησον (8:22)	Simon pleads for intercession (8:24).

Here there is no word-to-word correlation between the demand in the discourse and the actual audience response in the narrative. In such situations, perhaps Luke expects his readers to assume that the actual audience-response (believing, 2:44a; 4:4a) recorded in the narrative, adequately expresses its repentance. He is seemingly more interested in conceptual equivalence than verbal correspondence. As shown above, the 3000 (2:41) and the 5000 (4:4) believed that Jesus is indeed the Messiah (2:44a; 4:4a). Thus, we may conclude that for Luke *μετανοεῖν generally refers to a change in outlook, a new phase in life marked by a new perception. But in 'religious' sense, it refers to considering a past action wrong, correcting it, and assuming a new way of life.*[7]

Besides this, Luke's juxtaposition of μετανοεῖν with ἁμαρτία in Acts also suggests that he is also keen on employing μετανοεῖν in the sense of repenting of sin in general. It appears in Acts as follows:

2:38	μετανοήσατε...εἰς ἄφεσιν τῶν ἁμαρτιῶν
3:19	μετανοήσατε...εἰς τὸ ἐξαλειφθῆναι...τὰς ἁμαρτίας

By deliberately placing repentance alongside 'sin', Luke shows that he is very much interested in the idea of repenting of sin in general. Therefore, even

7 Segal, (*Paul the Convert*, 6) suggests: "Conversion does involve a radical change in a person's experience."

where they do not appear together explicitly, either of them could be assumed. For example, at Cornelius' house, Peter makes reference to the forgiveness of sins (ἄφεσιν ἁμαρτιῶν) without mentioning μετανοεῖν (10:43).

ἐπιστρέφειν

The second term that Luke employs expecting an appropriate audience-response is ἐπιστρέφειν. In classical and secular Greek, in its philosophical sense ἐπιστρέφειν means, "to turn about, turn around, to turn towards, to turn from an error, to correct, to repent."[8] Epictetus adds a religious sense to this general use: "What is your opinion of piety and sanctity? 'If you wish I shall prove that it is good'…"By all means prove it that our citizens may be converted (ἐπιστραφέντες) and may honour the divine one, and at last cease to be indifferent about the things that are of supreme importance."[9] Thus, ἐπιστρέφειν can mean a change of mind to know the gods and to take seriously things of ultimate importance, to correct, and to cause someone to repent, and hence to convert him/her. It is a new outlook to and new direction in life, turning to piety or the divine. In this sense, μετανοεῖν and ἐπιστρέφειν appear to have parallel functions.

In non-canonical Jewish literature ἐπιστρέφειν stands for causing a person to change belief or conduct, with the focus primarily on the person to whom one turns. Josephus reports that when there was a decline in spirituality and morality in Israel under Amon, his son Josiah, "brought the people to a sober way of living, and exhorted them to leave…their idols...to worship their own God...corrected what they did wrong...brought the people back...to the worship of God."[10] Here, the idea of turning to God is evident.

ἐπιστρέφειν in the Old Testament used both transitively and intransitively, suggests that it means to turn, return, bring/come back, and to restore. Both the individuals and the nation as a whole may '*be turned*' from evil (ἐπιστραφῇ, Jer. 18:8) or from other gods, or they may '*return*' to God (Mal. 3:7) themselves. As seen here, in certain instances an agent is involved in turning people to God; in some other cases, people themselves take the initiative. God's covenant people constantly '*turn away*' from God (Jer. 2:27 [ἔστρεψαν]; 11:10

---

8 L & S, 661.

9 Epictetus, *Discourses*, (II.20.22), (Tr. W.A. Oldfather; LCL; London: William Heinamann/ New York: G.P. Putnam's Sons, 1926). Cf. W. Barclay, *Turning to God: A Study of Conversion in the Book of Acts and Today*, (Edinburgh: Saint Andrew Press, 1978), 20.

10 Josephus, *Antiq*., X.4.1 (47-53, esp. 53).

[ἐπεστράφησαν]), and therefore, the prophets call for a firm resolve on the part of the people themselves to '*return*' (ἐπιστρέψωμεν) to God (Hos. 6:1). Otherwise, they may '*be turned*' (ἐπιστράφητι, 14:1) by God himself.

ἐπιστρέφειν in the OT, then, has two foci: i) God turns people to himself; ii) people turn themselves to God. Together they emphasise a "turning" from evil to God, a process in which both God and the individual (or the whole community) are involved. This is summed up, for example, in Malachi's words, "*Return* (ἐπεστρέψατε) *to me and I will return* (ἐπιστραφήσομαι) *to you...*" (3:7).

Such a turning to God results in certain blessings, namely, the forgiveness of sins and life. This may be emphasised either positively or negatively. Isaiah proclaims that turning to God leads to the forgiveness of sins (Isa. 55:7: ἐπτιστραφήτω...ἀφήσει τὰς ἁμαρτίας). Prophet Ezekiel emphasises the same blessing negatively by emphasising the consequences of not turning to God. If anyone does not take the warning and turn (μὴ ἀποστρέφῃ) to Yahweh, he/she may die (ἀποθανεῖται) (e.g., Ezek. 33:9). Positively it means that turning to God leads to life. Such a blessing is for non-Jews as well. For example, the Ninevites turn away (ἀπέστρεψαν) from their wickedness (Jonah 3:8,10).

Luke's use of ἐπιστρέφειν in Acts resembles the OT understanding of turning from evil and turning to God. ἐπιστρέφειν in Acts has two foci: i) turning from (ἀπὸ) something; ii) turning towards (ἐπὶ) something or someone. ἐπιστρέφειν is *turning from* darkness to light and from Satan *to* God (26:18) and "*turning from worthless things to the living God*" (14:15b). Importantly, however, in 14:15, the turning is used polemically against idolatry and polytheism, involving turning from other gods to the living God whom Paul and Barnabas preach.

In the mission addresses in Acts ἐπιστρέφειν is demanded of the narrative audience twice as follows:

ἐπιστρέψατε (3:19):	"believed" (4:4a)
ἀπὸ τούτων τῶν ματαίων	Sacrifice & Hostility (14:19)
ἐπιστρέφειν ἐπὶ θεὸν (14:15b).	

Here the first one occurs with repentance (3:19), but does not meet with any direct response in the narrative. Luke summarily states that many of those who heard the word "believed" (4:4a) in response to Peter's demand to "repent" and "turn" (3:19). The second occurrence (14:15) meets with mixed response in the narrative. It is hard to say why Luke does this. As stated earlier, we may only assume that Luke is simply interested in attributing to ἐπιστρέφειν a universal significance by a general presentation of what it means to turn to God.

When people turn to God, it results in certain blessings, namely the forgiveness of sins and times of refreshment (3:19; 26:18; Cf. Isa. 55:7), finding a place in the community of believers (26:18) and even physical healing (28:27).

In sum, ἐπιστρέφειν, for Luke, *is a new direction given to life and action, a turning to God, which can be summed up as believing* (4:4a). This takes us to πιστεύειν, Luke's other conversion term.

πιστεύειν

The response of the narrative audience in Acts to the Christian witnessing is sometimes expressed in terms of either believing (e.g., πιστεύειν: 2:44; 4:4), or coming to believe (e.g., πεπιστευκώς: 16:34). The Samaritans believed (ἐπίστευσαν) Philip's proclamation of the good news of the kingdom of God and the name of Jesus (8:12; Cf. 9:42; 11:21; 13:12,48; 14:1; 17:2,34; 18:8, etc.). Thus, believing is a response that takes place almost always in the context of Christian proclamation (16:31,34; cf. 4:4; 15:7; 18:27; cf. 13:48-49). Conversely, it implies that hearing Christian proclamation should lead to believing.

Although Luke employs πιστεύειν as quite a common response to the apostolic proclamation (e.g., 2:44; 4:4; 11:17; 14:23; 16:34; 19:4,9; 26:27), only twice is it demanded of the audience:

"...πιστεύοντα" (implicit demand: 10:43):	Reception of the Holy Spirit (Experience) Baptism (10:44-48).
πίστευσον (16:31): πεπιστευκὼς τῷ θεῷ (16:33b-34).	Baptism

Only in 16:34 does Luke say that the respondent had come to believe in God in direct response to the demand that he should believe on the Lord Jesus (16:31). If we grant that in 10:43, "*everyone who believes*" is an implicit demand, it does not meet with a direct response from Cornelius' household, in terms of verbal correspondence. Luke does not tell us why this is so. As stated earlier, it appears that for Luke, the actual positive audience-response in the narrative differently expresses what is implied in the demand. The descent of the Spirit and baptism in the Cornelius episode, for instance, means that Cornelius believed and obtained forgiveness of sins in the name of Jesus (10:43).

Moreover, the occurrence of πιστεύειν with the dative, εἰς, and ἐπὶ indicates the direction, the object, and the consequences of believing.[11] It means that one is entrusting oneself to an entity in complete confidence. It is believing (in) and trusting; it implies total commitment to the one who is trusted, for instance God or Christ. They appear in Acts as follows:

πιστεύειν with the dative

5:14 πιστεύοντες τῷ κυριῷ
8:12 ἐπίστευσαν τῷ Φιλίππῳ εὐαγγελιζομέν
13:12 ἐπίστευσεν...ἐπὶ τῃ διδαχῇ
16:34 πεπιστευκὼς τῷ θεῷ
18:8 ἐπίστευσεν τῷ κυριῷ

πιστεύειν with εἰς

10:43 πιστεύοντα εἰς αὐτόν
14:23 τῷ κυρίῳ εἰς ὅν πεπιστεύκεισαν
19:4 πιστεύσωσιν...εἰς τὸν ᾽Ιησοῦν

πιστεύειν with ἐπὶ denoting the accusative of God/Lord

9:42 ἐπίστευσαν...ἐπὶ τὸν κύριον
11:17 πιστεύσασιν ἐπὶ τὸν κύριον
16:31 πίστευσον ἐπὶ τὸν κύριον
22:19 κύριε...πιστεύοντας ἐπὶ σέ

As the grammatical constructions show, πιστεύειν involves a new direction and has the Lord, the word proclaimed or the apostolic teaching or God as the object of one's believing.

Also it is obvious that Luke does not give his readers a creed to believe. Instead he directs their "faith" to the word (e.g., 2:44; 4:4; 8:12) or to God/Jesus (e.g., 5:14; 11:17,21; 16:31). The Samaritans, for instance, believed (ἐπίστευσαν)

[11] BDAG, 816-7.

when Philip was preaching the name of Jesus Christ and the kingdom of God (8:12), and, consequently, were baptised (8:12). Moreover, for Luke the result of believing in Jesus is forgiveness of sins (e.g., 10:43; 13:39) and salvation (16:31), etc. Thus, Luke is interested only in showing that *it is Jesus in whom people should believe and that by believing in him they may receive forgiveness of sins and salvation.* This, for Luke, is the sole means of salvation (4:12). In light of this Lucan perspective, the Philippian jailer's question, "*what must I do to be saved*?" (16:30), may not be an isolated one. Even where it is absent, presumably this question is latent. Therefore, the reply of Paul and Silas to this question perhaps is representative: "*Believe on the Lord Jesus, and you will be saved, you and your household*" (16:31). Thus, believing actualises salvation.

βαπτίζειν

Baptism as a response to Christian proclamation is demanded only once in the missionary discourses (2:38). Significantly, however, the three thousand at Pentecost (2:41), the Samaritans (8:12), Simon Magus (8:13), the Ethiopian Eunuch (8:35-38), Cornelius and his household (10:44-48), the Philippian jailer and his household (16:31-34) are all baptised immediately following their conversion, though baptism is not demanded of all of them.

At Pentecost Peter demands that the narrative audience repents and be baptised. In response to this, the narrative audience is baptised (2:41). Obviously, here Luke wants to present baptism as evidence of repentance and believing (2:38; 8:16; 10:48). Also, since in some conversion accounts baptism is administered "*in the name of Jesus*" (2:38; 8:16; 10:48), it is, for Luke, an expression of commitment to Jesus (2:38; 8:16; 10:48).[12]

Moreover, Luke's record of the conversion of the masses, of households, and of individuals, raises questions such as, "Why does Luke record a group of believers in the context of Christian witnessing? Does conversion entail joining a community?" There are views suggesting that baptism in these cases was an initiation into the believers' community. J.D.G. Dunn, for instance, holds that baptism is a "rite of entry into the community of the end-time and expression of the initiate's commitment to that community..."[13] Some others simply take

---

[12] Also J.D.G. Dunn, *Jesus and the Spirit. A Study of the Religious and Charismatic Experience of Jesus and the First Christians as Reflected in the New Testament*, (London: SCM, 1975), 183.

[13] Ibid., 183.

it for granted that baptism means joining a group.[14] Although this is not the main concern of our study, we must briefly discuss the communal connotation of Christian witnessing to answer the questions raised above.

Conversion and Community

Luke records that a community was formed following the conversion of the masses on Pentecost: "*those who welcomed his message were baptized...about three thousand persons were added* (προσετέθησαν)"(2:41; 4:4). It is to this group that the Lord added a great number of those who were being saved (2:47; cf. 5:14; 11:24b). We deduce a communal connotation also from Luke's vocabulary such as προστίθημι, μαθητής, ᾿Αδελφός, πιστεύοντες, and ἡ ἐκκλησία. Although it is not mentioned in each case, Luke might call the togetherness of the believers as κοινωνία (2:42).

Luke records that when the word of God spreads, the number of the disciples also increases (6:7; 12:24) and a group of believers is born.[15] Paul and Barnabas build up the church throughout Judea, Galilee, and Samaria (9:31). This demonstrates a natural proclivity for believers to cluster together.

Moreover, in the context of Christian witnessing Luke records the presence of a group of converts whom he variously calls ᾿Αδελφός, πιστεύοντες, and ἡ ἐκκλησία as shown below:

Terms	Place	
μαθητής	Antioch	11:26
	Derbe	14:20
	Antioch in Syria	14:22-23
	Region of Galatia & Phrygia	18:23
	Achaia	18:27
	Corinth	19:1
	Ephesus	20:1
	Tyre	21:4
	Caesarea	21:16

---

14 Lars Hartman, *"Into the Name of the Lord Jesus" Baptism in the Early Church*, (Edinburgh: T&T Clark, 1997), 127-45; H.C. Kee, *Christian origins in Sociological Perspective*, (London: SCM, 1980), 112.

15 For the ecclesial tendency contained in the word see J. Kodell, " 'The Word of God Grew': The Ecclesial Tendency of Logos in Acts 6:7; 12:24; 19:20", *Biblica*, 55, (1974), 505-19.

’Αδελφός	Wherever Paul and Barnabas proclaimed	15:36
	Antioch	15:40
	Lystra and Iconium	16:2
	Philippi	16:40
	Thessalonica	17:6,10
	Beroea	17:14
	Corinth	18:1
	Achaia	18:27
	Ptolemais	21:7
	Puteoli	28:16
πιστεύοντες	Jerusalem	2:44; 4:4,32; 5:14
	Samaria	8:12,13
	Joppa	9:42
	Antioch	11:21
	Antioch in Pisidia	13:48
	Iconium	14:1
	Philippi	16:34, etc
ἡ ἐκκλησία	Region of Syria and Cicilia	15:41
	Lystra Derbe	16:5

The plurals in the above references such as ‘disciples’, ‘brothers’, etc., are themselves an indication of the presence of a group of believers. Importantly, however, Luke records these groups of believers in the context of Christian proclamation, without any invitation to form a community. Therefore, our hypothesis is that these different groups seem to have evolved as a natural expression of commitment to Jesus in one form or the other (e.g., 2:41).[16] The book of Acts as a whole makes it clear that the main objective of the Christian testimony was repentance and turning to the Lord (cf. 2:38) and not group-formation or re-socialisation. But this does not deny the possibility that conversion might lead to joining a group.

If we grant that community formation or joining a community was not the main objective of Christian witnessing, then, why did the converts tend to form groups after their conversion? Although Luke is not explicit, his records show that on four occasions the disciples/converts are seen together:

---

[16] For more details, see C.J.A. Hickling, “Baptism in the First-Century Churches: A Case for Caution”, in David J.A. Clines, et al (Eds.), *The Bible in Three Dimensions*, (JSOTSup. 87; Sheffield: JSOT Press, 1990), 249-67.

a) Those who repented, were baptised, and believed in Jesus, shared a corporate identity and a sense of belonging together on the basis of their common 'faith' even if they were geographically separated, thereby showing that they belonged to a confessional community.

b) In decision-making situations (1:24; cf. 13:1-3).

c) For social reasons, i.e., to help each other in need so that "*There was not a needy person among them...*" (2:44-45; 4:34a; cf. 4:32-5:11; 6:2).

d) At times of persecution, being together was a sign of solidarity and mutual support (4:23-30; 5:42; 12:12).

These examples do suggest the natural tendency among the believers to be together. However, while showing different communities in different places as representing "One Community" of believers in Acts, Luke does not seem to advocate the idea that Christian witness naturally demanded joining a community as its concomitant sequel, although it might lead to it in most cases. A sense of community seems to have evolved naturally in Acts and not out of any compulsion inherent in Christian proclamation. Community consciousness, or joining or forming a community is a consequence and not the main objective of Christian witness.

Summary

Acts shows that most, if not all, of the missionary discourses demand, either explicitly or implicitly, repentance, turning to God, believing in him or to be baptised. Sometimes the response demanded applies only to a specific audience (e.g., the Jerusalem Jews: 2:38; 3:19) and sometimes universally—all people everywhere (Cf. 17:30). This also keeps in view the various audiences mentioned earlier—Jews, Samaritans, and Gentiles. Moreover, the demand may not meet with direct audience-response in terms of verbal correspondence. But for Luke, the actual audience response in the narrative is a conceptual equivalence to what is demanded in the speech. Luke would expect his readers to assume what is not explicit.

In the conversion stories both μετανοεῖν and ἐπιστρέφειν convey the idea of change and turning. Whatever else it might mean, conversion basically involves a "God-ward Orientation" marked by turning away from idols (14:15), sin, darkness, and Satan to God (26:18). Further the OT concept of both the individuals and the nation as a whole turning or returning to God may be applied to Luke's stories as well, since the different narrative audiences include individuals, households, and masses.

μετανοεῖν focuses more on the decision to turn and break from the past, while ἐπιστρέφειν may broadly signify the turning itself.[17] πιστεύειν conveys the content or the object of one's belief, i.e., God/Jesus, the Lord and Messiah. However, Luke does not clearly say what the converts actually become (perhaps it did not really matter to him), except that they are called the 'believing ones' or 'disciples' or 'brothers' as shown above.

We may now put together all the different expressions discussed above to arrive at a provisional definition of conversion in Acts: "*Conversion is the change in perception and lifestyle effected by repenting and renouncing of all erroneous ways and turning to God. This is actualised by believing on the Lord Jesus.*" The fact that Luke does not define any of his conversion terms suggests that he is not interested in offering definitions, but in emphasising the fact that Christian proclamation does demand a response and the most ideal response is turning to God by repenting and believing on the Lord Jesus.[18]

After working out a possible definition and implications of conversion in Acts, Part II explores some of the internal evidence to the phenomenon of conversion in Acts in order to study it as one of Luke's predominant themes in Acts.

PART II: CONVERSION AS A THEME IN ACTS

The Purpose of Acts

The purpose of Acts has long been the subject of scholarly discussion. More than four decades ago W.C. van Unnik complained that scholars have neglected the issue of the purpose of Luke-Acts.[19] That contention is now obsolete since many theories concerning Luke's purpose in Acts have been propounded and

[17] Cf. Barrett, *Acts,* 1. 203.

[18] Gaventa (*Darkness to Light,* 52-129) also underscores this point. See also R.F. O'Toole, *The Unity of Luke's Theology: An Analysis of Luke-Acts*, (Wilmington, DE: Michael Glazier, 1984), 191-224.

[19] W.C. van Unnik, "The Book of Acts: The Confirmation of the Gospel," *Sparsa Collecta*, I, (Leiden: Brill, 1973), 340-73, esp. 342 (Repr. from *NovT*, 4, [1960], 26-59).

modified in various ways since then.[20] What follows is only a brief review of the various scholarly views on the purpose of Acts to find out the place that they accord to the theme of conversion; it is not an attempt to settle the issue of the purpose of Acts conclusively.

The ongoing scholarly discussion on the purpose of Acts is yet without any definitive conclusion, illustrating the inherent difficulty in settling the issue conclusively. Some, such as Crehan and Stonehouse, suggest that Acts was written to confirm and supplement Theophilus' knowledge about the historical basis of Christianity[21], while some others, such as C.H. Talbert, suggest that Luke's purpose in Acts is to combat a Gnostic understanding of Christianity.[22]

Conzelmann, on the other hand, holds that since the *parousia* was the most important issue in the early kerygma, Luke attempts to rectify the mistaken

---

20 See S. Brown, "The Prologues of Luke-Acts in Their Relation to the Purpose of the Author", *SBLSP 1975*, (Ed. G.W. MacRae; Missoula: Scholars, 1975), 1-14; idem, "The Role of the Prologues in Determining the Purpose of Luke-Acts" in C.H. Talbert, (Ed.), *Perspectives on Luke-Acts*, (Edinburgh: T&T Clark, 1978), 99-111; F.F. Bruce, "Paul's Apologetic and the Purpose of Acts", *BJRL*, 69, (1987), 379-93; J.H. Crehan, "The Purpose of Luke in Acts", *SE*, 2, (1964), 354-68; N.A. Dahl, "The Purpose of Luke-Acts", in *Jesus in the Memory of the Early Church*, (Minneapolis: Augsburg, 1976), 87-98; B.S. Easton, *The Purpose of Acts* ("Theology" Occasional Papers 6; London: SPCK, 1936); Repr. in *Early Christianity: The Purpose of Acts and Other Papers*, (Greenwich, CT: Seabury, 1954/London: SPCK, 1955), 33-118; A. Erhardt, "The Construction and Purpose of the Acts of the Apostles", *ST*, 12, (1958), 45-79; Repr. in *The Framework of the New Testament Stories*, (Cambridge: Harvard University Press [HUP], 1964), 64-102; Earle E. Ellis, "Situation and Purpose of Acts", *Int.*, 28, (1974), 94-98; Eric Franklin, *Christ and Lord: A Study in the Purpose and Theology of Luke-Acts*, (London: SPCK/Philadelphia: Westminster 1975); Maddox, *Purpose*; A.J. Mattill (Jr.), "The Good Samaritan and the Purpose of Luke-Acts: Halevy Reconsidered", *Encounter*, 33, (1972), 359-76; idem, "The Jesus-Paul Parallels and the Purpose of Luke-Acts: H.H. Evans Reconsidered", *NovT*, 17, (1975), 15-46; idem, "Naherwartung, Fernerwartung, and the Purpose of Luke-Acts: Weymouth Reconsidered", *CBQ*, 34, (1972), 276-93; idem, "The Purpose of Acts: Schneckenburger Reconsidered", in W.W. Gasque and R.P. Martin (Eds.), *Apostolic History and the Gospel: Biblical and Historical Essays Presented to F.F. Bruce*, (Grand Rapids: Eerdmans, 1970), 108-22; P.S. Minear, "Dear Theo: The Kerygmatic Intention and Claim of the Book of Acts", *Int.*, 27, (1973), 131-50; R.F. O'Toole, "Why did Luke Write Acts (Luke-Acts)?" *BTB*, 7, (1977), 66-76; A.C. Winn, "Elusive Mystery: The Purpose of Acts", *Int.*, 13, (1959), 144-56; J. de Zwaan, "Was the Book of Acts a Posthumous Edition?" *HTR*, 17, (1924), 95-153.

21 Crehan, "The Purpose", 366; N.B. Stonehouse, *The Witness of Luke to Christ*, (London: Tyndale Press, 1951), 44.

22 Talbert, *Luke and the Gnostics: An Examination of the Lucan Purpose*, (Nashville: Abingdon, 1966), particularly Ch. 7: "The Alternatives"; idem, "An Anti-Gnostic Tendency in Lucan Christology", *NTS*, 14, (1967-68), 259-71. See also H.J. Cadbury in *Beginnings*, II.510; idem, *Making of Luke-Acts*, 315; G.B. Caird, *Saint Luke*, (London: SCM, 1963), 44.

notion of its imminence by explaining its delay.[23] Some others hold that Luke's purpose is to provide an apology, both political and personal. Of the many, B.S. Easton argues that Luke's purpose is to offer a political apology in defence of Christianity so that Rome would accept it as a legitimate religious entity.[24] To accomplish this Luke shows the political innocence of Paul and others (Acts 13-28) and portrays Christianity as the fulfilment of Judaism, and hence meriting the rights of a *religio licita*. Conversely, Walaskay proposes that Acts is an apology for Rome; therefore, it presents Rome in a favourable light to the Christians and the Jews.[25] Thus, the Roman recognition of the innocence of Jesus and Paul has the motif of reverse commendation of the Roman judiciary.[26] In line with the theory of apology and basing his argument on the basis of the parallels between Jesus and Paul, and the various anticipations foreshadowed in the Gospel of the life, work, and thought of Paul in Acts, A.J. Mattill suggests that Acts is an apology for Paul.[27]

Richard Cassidy, on the other hand, proposes the 'allegiance and witness' theory.[28] The author of Acts wants to provide the early Christians with what they needed in order to maintain their own witness by demonstrating the end result of Jesus' constancy in witnessing.[29] Although Cassidy's view correctly points out the importance of the witness motif in Acts, it restricts the theme of 'witnessing' to 'Christianity' itself, as it were. By contrast, the evidence from Acts strongly suggests that Luke's emphasis is more universalistic than sectarian: from "*Jerusalem to the ends of the earth*" (1:8). We will discuss this later in the chapter.

Some other scholars consider Luke's purpose as conciliatory. The old Tübingen school, represented by F.C. Baur and others, proposes that Luke's purpose is

---

23 H. Conzelmann, *The Theology of St. Luke*, (London: Faber & Faber, 1960), 95-136. See also E. Earle Ellis, *The Gospel of Luke*, (London: Oliphants, 1974), 58f.

24 B.S. Easton, *Early Christianity*, 33-48. See also Dibelius, *Studies*, 149; Conzelmann, *Theology*, 138-44; Martin Hengel, *Earliest Christianity*, 60; Fitzmyer, *The Gospel According to Luke*, 2 Vols., (AB; Garden City, NY: Doubleday, 1979/1981), 1.10; H.J. Cadbury, "Some Foibles of New Testament Scholarship," *JBR*, 26, (1958), 213-16.

25 P.W. Walaskay, *"And so we came to Rome": The Political Perspective of St. Luke*, (Cambridge: CUP, 1983).

26 By contrast Walaskay overlooks the corrupt Roman officials such as Felix who expected bribe from Paul to release him (24:26).

27 Mattill, "Schneckenburger Reconsidered", 108-22; idem, "The Good Samaritan", 359-76; idem., "Naherwartung, Fernerwartung", 276-93.

28 R. Cassidy, *Jesus, Politics, and Society: A Study of Luke's Gospel*, (Maryknoll, NY: Orbis Books, 1978); idem, *Society and Politics in the Acts of the Apostles*, (Maryknoll, NY: Orbis Books, 1988), 145-55).

29 Cassidy, *Society and Politics*, 158-70.

to present an adjustment of the original contrast between Jewish Christianity—represented by Peter—and Gentile Christianity—represented by Paul—by showing them no longer as contrasting, but as parallel figures.[30]

Robert Maddox suggests that Luke's purpose is to show that Jesus fulfils the Scriptures regarding the Messiah's role of suffering and resurrection. In light of Jewish belief that they are the λαός, Luke's (Gentile) readers may feel that they are outside the scope of salvation. Therefore, Luke shows that salvation can be fully experienced within the church together with Jews and Gentiles as the legitimate fulfilment of God's promises.[31] Finally, some scholars argue that socio-political factors, rather than theological problems, are decisive in determining Luke's purpose. Philip Esler, for example, argues that Acts is the legitimation of the table-fellowship between the different factions in the church.[32]

What is conspicuously obvious is the total absence of the theme of conversion as one of the dominant themes in Acts. Obviously some of the above proposals may not deny Luke's interest in mission. But why do scholars overlook the conversion motif in Acts? This demands a closer study of Acts to investigate whether or not there is enough evidence to emphasise that conversion is, indeed, one of Luke's main concerns. Therefore, we turn to some features such as the structure of Acts, divine providence, and some literary techniques that Luke employs in Acts, to explore whether these literary evidence establish that conversion is one his *leitmotif*.

The Structure of Acts

It has already been pointed out that the conversion stories in Acts represent the most dominant formal grouping, accounting for over one-quarter of Luke's narrative. The sheer volume of these stories and their spread throughout Acts is the first evidence of its central importance to Luke's overall purpose in Acts. Besides this, as noted earlier in the chapter, Luke's conversion vocabulary and the presence of a community of believers, wherever there was Christian witnessing are also indications that Luke is chiefly concerned about conversion.

The final words of Jesus before his ascension in Acts 1:8 occupies a strategic position in the structure of Acts since, in general, the rest of Acts as a whole

---

30 Cf. Johannes Munck, *The Acts of the Apostles*, (New York: Doubleday, 1973), lv.

31 Maddox, *Purpose*, 187.

32 Esler, *Community and Gospel*, 107.

seems to follow the emphasis embedded in Luke's "Great Commission" regarding the dissemination of the Christian witness. It functions as a herald of a universal mission and as a harbinger of the events that are yet to unfold in the narrative progression of Acts: "*...You will be my witnesses in Jerusalem, in all Judea and Samaria, and to the ends of the earth*."

This commission will be further reinforced if read in the light of Lk. 24:48-49. In the Gospel Jesus promises his disciples the power from on high, while talking about proclaiming "*repentance and forgiveness of sins...in his name to all nations, beginning from Jerusalem*" (Lk. 24:47-49; Cf. Acts 1:8). Thus, the functions of witnessing to the ends of the earth (Acts 1:8) and proclamation to τὰ ἔθνη (Lk. 24:47) become one and the same. Undeniably this makes the witness/proclamation motif a major theme in Acts at the outset.

Acts 1:8 also shows the apostolic witnessing as a movement between Jerusalem and Rome. The movement begins in Jerusalem with Peter's proclamation at Pentecost and ends with Paul proclaiming in Rome (28:31), Jerusalem signifying the Jewish beginning of the apostolic mission and Rome functioning as the precursor to the ends of the earth (Cf. 1:8). Within this movement, the number of converts keeps increasing all the time, seen either in the exact figures given (e.g., 2:41; 4:4) or summarily stated (e.g., 11:21,24).

Further, Luke portrays his conversion stories as a teleological journey with an end in view. The disciples must keep witnessing till their testimony reaches whatever Luke construes as "*the ends of the earth*" (1:8). Therefore, those who were scattered in the aftermath of Stephen's martyrdom and persecution, proclaim the word (8:4; cf. 11:20) travelling (διέρχεσθαι) to places they would never have gone otherwise. Once Paul's missionary journeys take centre-stage from Acts 13 onwards, geography and specific places begin to assume evangelistic significance.

The outward expansion of Christian witness is also built around the following pattern: Christian leaders arise and engage in proclamation; God performs mighty acts, both through and independently of them, to confirm the word with the result that the listeners turn to the Lord (e.g., 11:21). It is important for Luke that this happens everywhere every time. Therefore, even when and where he does not have a detailed conversion account to report, or an exact figure to record, he summarily states that a large number of people did turn to God. Thus, a careful reading cannot fail to notice the important theme of conversion running throughout Acts like a lifeline.

As stated above, the narrative of Acts appears to follow the scheme given in Acts 1:8: Jerusalem (2:1-8-3)—Judea and Samaria (8:4-12:24)—ends of the earth (12:25-28:31).[33] What follows is to show how the very structure of the book of Acts demonstrates that God's eternal purpose is to bring salvation in all its fullness to all peoples. That is why the Christian witness incorporates different people groups—Jews, Samaritans[34], and the Gentiles in its movement towards the end of the earth. The miraculous and the apostolic voices in Acts anticipate this aim.

The first section (2:1-8:3) is about the mission to the Jews; it revolves around the happenings in Jerusalem, where Luke reports three accounts of mass-conversion, two of which result from a combined operation of a miracle and proclamation and the other following a miracle. In addition, this section contains two conversion summary statements. This sets the agenda for the subsequent narratives. They appear as follows:

Story	*Summary*
A)3,000 come to believe (2:1-41)	A) "...And day by day the Lord added to their number those who were being saved" (2:47b).
B) 5000 come to believe (3:1-4:4)	

[33] James M. Scott (*Paul and the Nations: The Old Testament Jewish Background of Paul's Mission to the Nations with Special Reference to the Destination of Galatians*, [Tübingen: Mohr, 1995], 162-79) relates the commission to witness to the ends of the earth starting from Jerusalem to the influences from the Table-of-Nations tradition. Luke T. Johnson (*The Literary Function of Possessions in Luke-Acts*, [Missoula: Scholars, 1977], 16-17) is emphatic that the geographical schema of Acts fulfils Acts 1:8. See also G. A. Krodel, *Acts*, 60. By contrast, Robert L. Brawley (*Luke-Acts and the Jews: Conflict, Apology, and Conciliation*, [SBLMS 33; Atlanta: Scholars, 1987], 28-50) avowedly contradicts this saying that Acts 1:8 is not about the geographical spread of the gospel, but about Luke's legitimation of mission, particularly Paul's.

[34] Luke does not give us any information whether the Samaritans should be viewed as Gentiles or as M.D. Goulder (*Type and History in Acts*, [London: SPCK, 1964], 65) calls them as the heretical and seceded Israel or as Martin Hengel (*Earliest Christianity*, 75) views them as belonging to the 'outposts of Judaism'. The readers knowing the third Gospel might recollect the Jewish antagonism towards the Samaritans. For instance, James and John suggest destroying the Samaritan village which would not receive Jesus (Lk. 9:51ff.). Other stories like the good Samaritan story (10:25ff.) and the story of the ten lepers (Lk. 17:11ff.) indicate a deep-seated animosity between the Jews and the Samaritans.

Story	*Summary*
C) Great number of men and women believers were added to the Lord (5:14)	
	B) "The word of God continued to spread; the number of the disciples increased...and a great many... became obedient to the faith (6:7).

Here, significantly, the first of the conversion accounts (2:1-41) starts only after the descent of the Spirit, thereby, Luke shows the divine origin of the mission of turning people to God. Also at the outset Luke establishes that God is the real author of conversions. This corroborates the point made earlier that Luke's narrative world is designed solely by divine providence, and that in order to be able to understand fully what happens in these events, a proper alignment with his Theocentric worldview is essential.

The second section (8:4-12:24) deals with the mission to Samaria, to the Ethiopian Eunuch[35], Peter's Judean mission, and the progression of the Christian testimony to the principal cities of Judea, namely Lydda and Sharon, Joppa, and Caesarea. In this section too the supernatural phenomena and the discourses function together, resulting in many conversions.

Story	*Summary*
A) Philip's Mission (8:5-40)	
i) Mass-Baptisms in Samaria (8:5-25) ii) The Ethiopian Eunuch baptised (8:26-40)	

---

35 M.D. Goulder (*Type and History*, 65) takes it for granted that the Ethiopian Eunuch was a Jew. This is too quick a conclusion since Luke does not provide us with any information as to his identity. For a very detailed account of Philip's mission to the Ethiopian Eunuch and his identity, see F. Scott Spencer, *The Portrait of Philip in Acts: A Study of Roles and Relations*, (JSNTSup. 67; Sheffield: SAP, 1992), 128-87. After thorough research, Spencer concludes that the Ethiopian Eunuch was a Gentile (Ibid., 173). However, the real questions are "Did Luke think that the Ethiopian Eunuch was a Gentile? To what extent can we transpose our modern knowledge and understanding of, say the Samaritans and the Ethiopian Eunuch, on Luke?"

Story	*Summary*
B) Saul/Paul's conversion/Call (9:1-30)[36]	
	A) "...The church throughout Judea, Galilee, and Samaria...increased in numbers (9:31).
C) Peter's Mission (9:32-11:18) i) The residents of Lydda and Sharon turn to the Lord (9:32-35) ii) Many in Joppa believe in the Lord (9:36-42) iii)Cornelius and household experience the Spirit and are baptised (10:1-11:18)	
D) Mission of the Scattered (11:19-30) i) A great number believe and turn to the Lord (11:21)	
	B) "The word of God continued to advance and gain adherents" (12:24)

The third section (12:25-28:31) shows how, in its march towards the "*ends of the earth*", the Christian witness reaches Rome. The highlight of this section are the three 'missionary journeys' of Paul through many Gentile areas: i) 13:1-14:28; ii) 15:36-18:22 and iii) 18:23-21:27). As the following occurrences show, Pauline mission is full of conversion accounts; at least two of them result from the combined operation of the miraculous and proclamation.

Story	*Summary*
i) Sergius Paulus believes (13:4-12) ii) Gentiles in Antioch believe (13:48) iii) A great number of Jews and Greeks believe (14:1) iv) Many made disciples in Derbe (14:21)	

[36] Despite K. Stendahl's influential article, "Call rather than Conversion" in *Paul Among Jews and Gentiles and other Essays*, (Philadelphia: Fortress, 1976), 7-23, scholarly opinion is divided whether or not Paul's experience should be designated a call or conversion. Recently scholars tend to integrate both, for instance Ronald D. Witherup, "Functional Redundancy in the Acts of the Apostles: A Case Study", *JSNT*, 48, (1992), 67-86. Alan F. Segal (*Paul the Convert*, 6) also takes a conciliatory position: "From the viewpoint of mission Paul is commissioned, but from the viewpoint of religious experience Paul is a convert."

Story	*Summary*
	A) The Churches were strengthened in the faith and increased in numbers daily (16:5).
v) Lydia's household baptised (16:11-15). vi) The Philippian jailer & household baptised (16:25-34). vii) Some of the Jews, a great many of devout Greeks and leading women were persuaded and were allotted to Paul (17:1-4). viii) Many receive the word and believe (17:10-14). ix) Some in Athens join Paul and believe (17:16-34). x) Crispus' household believes and is baptised (18:1-11). xi) Many believe in Ephesus (19:11-20).	
	B) The word of the Lord grew mightily and prevailed (19:20).

Within the narrative of Acts, the proclamation motif that starts from 1:8 comes to a grand finale with Paul in Rome "*Proclaiming the kingdom of God and teaching about the Lord Jesus Christ...*" (28:31), providing a literary *inclusio*. What the narrative flow of Acts shows is that for Luke, conversion is too important a concern that requires nothing less than the heavenly δύναμις promised in 1:8, which is for both miracle working (e.g., 2:22; 3:12; 4:7; 8:13; 10:38; 19:11) and for proclamation (4:33; 6:8).[37]

Acts 1:8 clarifies God's universal purpose and thereby provides a yardstick by which to ascertain all human ventures in spreading Christian testimony. Those who obey Jesus' command to witness operate under the guidance and power of the Spirit; they are God's authentic witnesses. The book of Acts demonstrates that their mission includes those at the "*ends of the earth*" (11:1-18; ch. 15; 21:1=26:32). Therefore, "*the ends of the earth*" in 1:8 is a reference to the universal scope; Rome, standing at the end of Acts, is its precursor.

The narrative aim of Acts is, thus, to highlight the centrality of God's purpose to bring salvation to all people, everywhere. The Christian witness is, indeed, part of God's universal redemptive purpose. It is willed by God (11:21),

[37] So also Barrett, *Acts*, 1.79.

envisioned by Jesus (1:8), and empowered and guided by the Spirit (2:1-13), and implemented by Jesus' followers. Thus, through all these convincing proofs, enumerated above, Luke demonstrates his concern about the universal mission that needs the power of the combined operation of the supernatural and proclamation. It takes nothing less than God's own intervention to fructify this universal mission.

Before we proceed further, we must point out another important development in what we have shown so far. As we notice, most of the conversion stories enumerated above are closely bound up with the reciprocity and complementarity that exists between the miraculous and the proclamation. However, one finer point that comes out of Luke's arrangement of his material is that although the miraculous and proclamation function together, he accords Christian proclamation a *functional primacy*, putting forward strongly that his story has a proclamatory intent, a message to proclaim.

While reading the witness motif in 1:8, Luke's readers might recollect Luke's portrait of Jesus in his Gospel as categorically declaring the purpose of his coming: "I must *proclaim*[38] (εὐαγγελίσασθαι)[39]...for I was sent for this purpose...So he continued *proclaiming* (ἦν κηρύσσων)" (Lk 4:44, 81). Thus, in Luke's eyes, proclaiming good news is an obvious description of Jesus' total mission. Moreover, Luke places greater emphasis on the divine mandate of Jesus' mission of proclamation: "*I must* (δεῖ) *proclaim...I was sent for this purpose*" (Lk. 4:41).[40] Thus, proclamation is a divinely mandated mission. Luke's conversion motif, therefore, is primarily bound up with Jesus' commission to witness and the apostles' obedience to that command.[41] This is the hinge upon which the whole of the apostolic mission revolves. The narrative flow of Acts demonstrates how the apostles have construed this mandate and fulfilled it themselves.

Further to the fourfold stratification of Acts given above, Luke's introduction of conversion summary statements at strategic turning points in the narrative neatly divide Acts into six blocks, as shown below, again highlighting Luke's emphasis on conversion.

---

38 Italics mine to show Luke's emphases.

39 κηρύσσω and εὐαγγελίζομαι in Lucan vocabulary designate the pivotal element of Christian witness, namely, the act of preaching. See Conzelmann, *Theology*, pp. 218-25; Fitzmyer, *Luke*, 1.245-49.

40 Italics mine for emphasis.

41 "You shall be" (Acts 1:8) can be taken as an imperative. Cf. I. Howard Marshall, *The Acts of the Apostles*, (Sheffield: JSOT Press, 1992), 43.

	Description	Summary
1:2-6:60	The genesis of the church at Jerusalem and Peter's preachings.	The word of God continued to spread; the number of the disciples increased greatly in Jerusalem, and a great many...became obedient to the faith (6:7).
6:8-9:30	The spread of the church throughout Palestine; Stephen's address and the conversion/call of Saul.	...the church throughout Judea, Galilee, and Samaria had peace andwas built up...it increased in numbers (9:31).
9:32-12:23	The church expands to Antioch; the conversion of Cornelius; trouble from the Jews and Herod.	But the word of God continued to advance and gain adherents (12:24).
12:25-16:4	Advance from Syria to Asia . Minor	The churches were strengthened in the faith and increased in numbers daily (16:5).
16:6-19:19	Paul in Macedonia and Achaea	So the word of the Lord grew mightily and prevailed (19:20).
19:21-28:30	Paul arrives in Rome and the events leading to it.	proclaiming the kingdom of God and teaching about the Lord Jesus Christ with all boldness and without hindrance (28:31).

Luke starts his summary statements with the word of God (6:7) and ends them with Paul's proclamation and teaching in Rome (28:31), showing how the mandate to witness to the ends of the earth has been successfully implemented, though symbolically and provisionally. Thus, the structure of Acts points to the fact that conversion is indeed one of Luke's dominant themes and that in turn, this theme provides Luke's writing a thematic coherence. From here we proceed to discuss Luke's notion of divine providence to see whether it bolsters our argument.

Divine Providence

The concept of 'divine providence' is central to Luke's purpose in Acts, for this is the sole determinant of the ongoing mission of the church.[42] As D.L. Tiede suggests, no other New Testament author is concerned so much as Luke to testify to the accomplishment of God's will and plan.[43] Throughout Acts he shows Christian mission as emanating solely from ἡ βουλή τοῦ θεοῦ (2:23; 4:28; 5:38; 13:36; 20:27). He conveys the same idea by the use of the word δεῖ[44] or similar expressions such as μέλλω (17:31; 26:22,23), ἀναγκαῖος (13:46), ὁρίζω (2:23; 10:42; 17:26,31) and certain προ compounds.[45] These terms, occurring in the kerygmatic sections of the proclamations, both to the Jews and to the Gentiles, collectively stress the divine plan of salvation for Jews and Gentiles alike.

As shown already, Luke introduces a supernatural phenomenon in each stage of the advance of the Christian witness towards its final destination, in order to demonstrate that its progress and the resultant conversions are solely due to God's own initiative. This is evident particularly from the frequent occurrence of the hendiadys σημεῖα καὶ τέρατα in the conversion stories (2:22,43; 5:12; 6:8; 7:36; 14:3; 15:12).

Moreover, through predictions and oracular warnings that communicate the divine will, Luke provides his readers with a forward-looking outlook, suspense, and a sense of expectation. We might cite just one example here. In Acts 1:4-5, Jesus promises the baptism of the Spirit as the fulfilment of God's promise, which the readers come to know in Acts 2 as predicted by Joel (3:1-5 [LXX]). In Acts 2:1 Luke overtly builds the tension by introducing Pentecost as a supernatural event occurring with suddenness like a rush of a mighty wind (2:2). His πνοὴ βιαία stands for πνεῦμα ἅγιον. When the apostles are filled with the Spirit, the readers can now recall Jesus' promise in 1:5. On the basis of this, they can look forward to similar events in future. For example, while

---

42 For the theme of providential necessity in Luke-Acts, see John T. Squires, *Plan of God in Luke-Acts*, (SNTSMS 76; Cambridge: CUP, 1993), 228-77.

43 David L. Tiede, *Prophecy and History in Luke-Acts*, (Philadelphia: Fortress, 1980), 33.

44 Walter Grundmann ("δεῖ", *TDNT*, II:21-25, esp. 2:23) states: "The whole of God's will for Christ and for man is thus comprehended in the δεῖ as Luke conceives it". This term occurs frequently in Acts, but relevant to our purpose are Acts 3:21; 4:12; 5:29; 9:6,16; 14:22; 16:30, etc. See also Charles H. Cosgrove, "The Divine Δεῖ in Luke-Acts: Investigations into the Lucan Understanding of God's Providence", *NovT*, 26, (1984), 168-90.

45 πρόγνωσις (2:23); προκαταγγέλλω (3:18; 7:52); προχειρίζω (3:20; 22:14; 26:16); προορίζω (4:28) and προχειροτονέω (10:41).

reading 8:15-17, they understand the receiving of the Spirit by the Samaritans as both the sealing of their conversion and also as referring back to the Pentecost account, though there is no reference to speaking in tongues. On the basis of the 'Samaritan Pentecost', Luke's readers can also look forward to the 'Gentile Pentecost'—the coming of the Spirit on Cornelius' household (10:44f.), which again had been interpreted as the granting of repentance that leads to life (11:18). All these are in fulfilment of Jesus' prediction internally in 1:5 and externally by Joel (3:1-5 [LXX]).

Similarly, prophetic discernment give Luke's plot a decisive and strategically important turn towards Rome (19:21; 20:22-25, 28-30; 27:10). The narrative of Acts ends with the prophetic explanation of how the Gentile acceptance of God's salvation has come to pass (28:25-28; cf. Isa. 6:9-10). By means of these indications of divine intervention and control, Luke shows the movement of the Christian witness towards its final destination as divinely guided. Therefore, it would not be an exaggeration to conclude, along with Wilkenhauser, that behind the continuous progress of the Christian message Luke sees the wonderful operation of the power of the Spirit.[46]

In the same way as the supernatural phenomena, for Luke, Christian testimony too originates from God himself. Proclamation, for Luke, is a supernatural fact.[47] Van Unnik affirms this by pointing out that the purpose of Acts is to confirm the word for the world.[48] The following table illustrates the divine origin of the word in Acts.

Table of Mandates to Witness/Proclaim/Teach

	The Source/Human Agent	Content
1:8	Jesus to the Disciples	"you will be my witnesses"
5:20	Angel to the Apostles	"Go...tell the people the whole message about this life."

46 So A. Wilkenhauser, *The New Testament Introduction*, (ET; London: Nelson and Herder and Herder, 1958), 326. Conzelmann (*Acts of the Apostles,* [Trans. A.T. Kraabel, et al; Philadelphia: Fortress, 1987], 131-32) points out: "The idea of God's plan...underlies the whole structure of Luke's account."

47 Cf. H. Chadwick, *The Circle and the Ellipse*, (Oxford: Clarendon, 1959), 16.

48 W.C. van Unnik, "Confirmation", 58-59.

8:26,35	Angel to Philip	"...go...Philip proclaimed...the good news about Jesus.
9:15	The Lord to Ananias l about Sau	"...he is an instrument whom I have chosen to bring my name before Gentiles...."
10:22	Angel to Cornelius to send for Peter	"...to hear what you (Peter) have to say."
10:32-33	Angel to Cornelius	"...to listen to all that the Lord has commanded you (Peter) to say."
11:4	Angel to Cornelius	"...he (Peter) will give you a message by which you and your...household will be saved."
16:9-10	A man in a vision to Paul	"...come...help us...being convinced that God had called us to proclaim the good news to them."
18:9,11	The Lord to Paul	"Do not be afraid, but speak and do not be silent"...he stayed...teaching the word of God...."
22:15	Ananias to Paul	"...you will be his witness also in Rome..."
26:16 26:19-20	Jesus to Paul	"...to appoint you to serve and testify...I declared.
26:23	Moses and Prophets about	"...he would proclaim light to our people and Jesus to the Gentiles."
27:14	Angel to Paul	"...you must stand before the emperor..."

This table confirms that the divine origin of the word impels, empowers, and sustains Christian proclamation as an ongoing endeavour until it reaches its final destination. These divine mandates to proclaim disprove Fiorenza's claim, stated earlier, that the Christian missionaries were more miracle workers than anything else.[49] By contrast, they were first and foremost preachers of the word. This is why, as stated above, although both the supernatural phenomena and Christian proclamation originate from God's providence, Luke accords proclamation a functional lead over the miracles. Meanwhile, it is important to note that although there is not even one such mandate to perform miracles, God is still the dispenser of these two together to actualise conversions.

The success of the Christian mission is a result of the interplay between human and divine action.[50] The word grows under the divine aegis and through human witnessing. This is demonstrated primarily through the phenomenal growth that the coordination between the divine and human factors accomplishes. The following table of specific instances of and general references to it in Acts confirms this.

Table of conversion/Growth Statistics in Acts

2:41	Those who welcomed his message were baptized...about three thousand were added.
2:44	Day by day the Lord added to their number whose who were being saved.
4:4	Many of those who heard the word believed; and they numbered about five thousand.
5:14	More than ever believers were added to the Lord, great numbers of both men and women.
8:12,14	The Samaritans believed...were baptized and accepted the word of God.
8:38	The Ethiopian eunuch is baptised.
9:1-19;	Saul baptized; apostle to the Gentiles appointed.

49 Fiorenza, "Miracles, Mission", 12.
50 Cosgrove, "Divine Δει", 178, 181-83, 188.

22:1-16; 26:9-18	
9:31	The Church throughout Judea, Galilee, and Samaria...increased in numbers.
9:35	All the residents of Lydda and Sharon...turned to the Lord.
9:42	Many believed in the Lord.
10:1-11:18	The Spirit comes upon Cornelius' household; they are baptised.
11:21	A great number became believers and turned to the Lord.
12:24	The word of God continued to advance and gain adherents.
13:12	Sergius Paulus believes the teaching of the Lord.
13:48-50	Many...became believers.
14:1	A great number of both Jews and Greeks became believers.
14:21	Many in Derbe are made disciples.
16:5	The churches were strengthened in the faith and increased in numbers daily.
16:33-34	The Philippian jailer's household baptised; the jailer comes to believe in God.
17:12	Many Jews and Greeks believed.
17:32b, 34a	Some show interest, and some of them joined Paul and became believers.
18:6-8	Crispus believes with his household.
19:18	Many Jews and Greeks of Ephesus became believers.
19:20	The word of the Lord grew mightily and prevailed.
28:24	Some were convinced.

Besides these concrete examples, Luke also shows how the divine δεῖ can totally control an individual's life to accomplish the God-ordained task of proclaiming the word. The clearest example of this is the first account of Paul's conversion/call (9:1-19). The divine mandate for Paul is that he must *preach* to the Gentiles (9:15-16). From this point forward, Luke characterises Paul as being totally controlled by this divine will (22:1-21; 26:23). Even Paul's own self perception is that he has been divinely appointed to *testify* to the Gentiles of God's salvation (22:14,21; 26:17). Therefore, he declares, "*I was not disobedient to the heavenly vision*" (26:19).

The period following his conversion/call shows Saul/Paul as carrying out this divine commission. At Pisidian Antioch, along with Barnabas, he declares that "*it was necessary*" (ἦν ἀναγκαῖον) to preach to the Jews first and when rejected by the Jews they turn to the Gentiles (13:46), fulfilling, in Luke's scheme, Isa. 49:6: "*...That my salvation may reach to the end of the earth*" (Acts 13:47; cf. 1:8). This illustrates their understanding of the divine plan concerning the universal nature of God's offer of salvation. Paul himself is deeply convinced about it (19:21), which is further confirmed by the Lord (23:11) and his angel (27:24). In these ways, Luke portrays the Christian witnessing as initiated and totally controlled and guided by the divine decree.

Luke portrays that in the final analysis, the progression of the Christian witness is solely God's doing. It needed even persecution (8:1-3) and supernatural events such as the descent of the Spirit (2:1-13) and visions (10:1-16) to fructify this. We cannot say whether or not persecution is God-intended, but its outcome certainly shows that it did lead to proclaiming the word of God (8:14) and the Lord Jesus (11:21) just as much as the visions in the Cornelius story (10:1-11:18) did. These collectively suggest that God can and does make use of any means and situations to fulfil his divine will concerning mission. Having discussed Luke's notion of divine providence, we examine some of Luke's literary techniques that he employs in Acts to support our argument.

Luke's Literary Techniques

First of all, the *preface* of Acts (1:1-3), as a mark of historiographical writings[51], sets a pattern of combining miracles and teaching for the ensuing apostolic mission: "*what Jesus did and taught*" (1:1). This is not explicitly articulated, but demonstrated subsequently.

Secondly, as a historian Luke adopts the literary form of *speeches* in Acts, which is one of the determinants of conversions in Acts. Christopher Pelling emphasises that speeches are essential for historical writing,[52] and illustrates this from a much-quoted text from Thucydides:

> "First, concerning what they said…it was difficult, both for me in the case of the speeches I heard myself and for my various informants, to remember the precise things that they said; but I have put things so as to capture how each speaker would most have seemed to me to say what he should about the issues at hand, keeping as close as possible to the general sense of what was really said."[53]

---

[51] This is not to establish *historiography* as the genre of Acts. Its reference here is just to prove a point and to account for the presence of a preface and the speeches in Acts. Without debating the genre of the book of Acts, this investigation simply proceeds from the widely held scholarly view that Acts is a historical writing. See for instance, W.C. van Unnik, "Luke's Second Book and the Rules of Hellenistic Historiography", in J. Kremer (Ed.), *Les Actes des Apôtres: Traditions, rédaction, théologie*, (Gembloux: J. Duculot/Leuven: Leuven University Press, 1979), 37-60; G.E. Sterling, *Historiography and Self-Definition*, 311-89; L.C.A. Alexander, *The Preface to Luke's Gospel: Literary Convention and Social Context in Luke 1:1-4 and Acts 1:1*, (SNTSMS 78; Cambridge: CUP, 1993). There are also other genres such as *Biography* and *Romantic Novel* suggested for Acts. For Acts as a biography, see C.H. Talbert, *What is a Gospel? The Genre of the Canonical Gospels*, (Philadelphia: Fortress, 1977); idem, "Biographies of Philosophers and Rulers as Instruments of Religious Propaganda in Mediterranean Antiquity", in C.H. Talbert (Ed.), *New Perspectives*, 63-88; L.C.A. Alexander, "Acts and Ancient Intellectual Biography", in B.W. Winter and A.D. Clarke (Eds.), *The Book of Acts in its First Century Setting. I: Ancient Literary Setting*, (Grand Rapids: Eerdmans/Carlisle: Paternoster, 1993), 31-63; C.W. Votaw, "The Gospels and Contemporary Biographies", *AJT*, 19, (1915), 45-73, 217-49; P. L. Shuler, *A Genre for the Gospels: The Biographical Character of Matthew*, (Philadelphia: Fortress, 1982) and R.A. Richard Burridge, *What are the Gospels? A Comparison with Graeco-Roman Biography*, (SNTSMS 70; Cambridge: CUP, 1992). For Acts as a romantic novel, see S.P. and M.J. Schiering, "The Influence of the Ancient Romances on the Acts of the Apostles", *Classical Bulletin*, 54, (1978), 81-88; S.M. Praeder, "Luke-Acts and Ancient Novel", *SBLSP*, (Chico, CA: Scholars Press, 1981), 269-92.

[52] C. Pelling, *Literary Text and the Greek Historian*, (London/New York: Routledge, 2000), 115.

[53] Thucydides, *HPW*, I.22.2. Translation Pelling's (*Greek Historian*, 114).

Chapter 4 in the study will discuss the Thucydidean speeches and their literary functions in detail. Here they point out that speeches are a literary tool in the hands of a historian for his investigation.

Luke too attributes speeches to many of his leading characters. Speeches have come to play so crucial a role in his narratives that without them Acts would be, in Ryken's words, a torso consisting primarily of a miscellany of episodes and summaries.[54] Luke's missionary speeches are integral to his story—the story of the proclamation of the word of God.[55] This is amply evidenced by the fact that the speeches in Acts (including short statements) make up 25% of the narrative.[56] Amongst the speeches in Acts, of particular relevance to the present investigation are the missionary discourses. They are

a) Missionary sermons to the Jews 2:14-36, 38-39; 3:12-26; 4:8-12, 19-20; 5:29-32; 13:16-41

b) Missionary Sermon to a Gentile God-fearer 10:34-43

c) Missionary Sermons to Gentiles 14:14-17; 17:22-31

We shall discuss in detail the literary functions of the missionary speeches in chapter 4. The Table of Mandates to Witness/Proclaim/Teach has already demonstrated the way Luke attributes divine origin to proclamation/witnessing/teaching, investing the verbal articulation of Christian testimony with divine sanction and, thereby, according it a functional primacy over the miraculous. Luke's missionary speeches present what God has done, primarily in and through the person of Jesus and prepare the hearers for a response of repenting, believing and turning to God.

Closely connected to the speeches is the idea of *persuasion*, aimed at convincing the hearers, to appeal to their emotions, and to promote a particular attitude and action by responses such as empathy, admiration, shock, despair, or perplexity.[57] Of the three ways of persuasion *ethos*, *pathos* and *logos* in rhetoric,

---

54 Leland Ryken, *The New Testament in Literary Criticism*, (New York: Frederick Ungar Publishing Company, 1984), 54.

55 Paul Schubert, "The Final Cycle of Speeches in the Book of Acts", *JBL*, 87, (1968), 1-16, esp.16.

56 David E. Aune, *The New Testament in its Literary Environment*, (Cambridge: James Clarke, 1988), 124-25.

57 Pelling, *Greek Historian*, 1-2.

pathos is particularly relevant to our study. It is the emotions the listeners experience as the speaker manipulates their feelings.[58] In Aristotle's words, "...Persuasion is effected with reference to the hearers, when they are aroused to emotion (πάθος) by the speech...."[59]

Pathos is common to many of Luke's missionary speeches as well. Although, he does not make his persuasive intent explicit, his missionary speeches aim at persuading and creating a receptive disposition in the hearers and evoking a response such as repentance (e.g., 2:38). One way of arousing *pathos* is to introduce *tragic embellishments*, which make it easier for the narrative audiences to identify themselves with a character or characters that appeal to their emotions.[60]. By focusing on the sufferings of a character, Pelling suggests, Greek writers attributed to tragedy a sense of timeless relevance.[61]

In order to appeal to the emotions of his narrative audience, Luke presents Jesus as a tragic character in his missionary speeches in Acts. Although he was attested by God with deeds of power and signs, he is crucified and killed by the Jerusalem Jews and the lawless (2:22-23). He is the God-glorified servant, the author of life (3:13,15a), but now he is rejected and killed. God anointed him with the Holy Spirit and with power; he is the doer of good deeds and a healer (10:38-39a), yet he is hanged to death (10:39b). This has the desired impact on the narrative audience; it arouses a sense of guilt (2:37) and the result is the conversion of the 3000 (2:41) at one time and the 5000 (4:4) at another. Although such a response is not explicit in all the conversion accounts, it may not be an exaggeration to assume so. It can be expected that Luke's characterisation of Jesus as a 'tragic hero' invites the readers to identify with and participate in the Jesus story. In Jesus, they may find their own personal tragedies represented; they may feel for the miscarriage of justice; and eventually respond afresh to the invitation to relate to him at a closer level.

Moreover, the *epideictic rhetoric* of the missionary speeches in Acts praises virtues and censures vices. Cicero emphasises this as follows:

---

58 G.A. Kennedy, *New Testament Interpretation Through Rhetorical Criticism*, (Chapel Hill: University of North Carolina press, 1984), 15.

59 Aristotle, *The Art of Rhetoric*, II.1.2. (Tr. H.C. Lawson-Tancred; London/New York: Penguin Books, 1991).

60 Aristotle, *Poetics*, 1461. Cf. Alex Preminger, Leon Golden, at al (Eds.), *Classical Literary Criticism: Translations and Interpretations*, (New York: Frederick Ungar Publishing Co., 1974), 138.

61 Pelling, *Greek Historian*, 164.

> "...Who more passionately than the orator can encourage to virtuous conduct, or more zealously than he reclaim from vicious courses? Who can more austerely censure the wicked, or more gracefully praise men of worth?...Whose comfortable words can soothe grief more tenderly?... For men's...zeal for others' service is applauded."[62]

In Acts, Luke introduces epideictic rhetoric primarily by his characterisations. For instance, characters such as Peter, Paul, Philip and the believers are portrayed in such a way as to positively impact on the readers (e.g., 5:13). Meanwhile the unrepentant are blamed (cf. 13:46; 18:6; 28:28). Moreover, the retributive miracles show the denunciation of some characters and the punishment invoked on them (5:1-11; 8: 18-24; 12:19-24; 13:6-12). Thus, virtues are praised for the readers to emulate and vices are denounced, though implicitly.

Another literary feature we notice in Acts is the presence of *tensions and their resolution*. In Graeco-Roman literary convention such a device is required to treat a literary work as "*an organic whole*".[63] Aristotle compares complete tragic works to living bodies and organisms.[64] In Acts we notice tensions between Jews and Gentiles[65] (e.g., 6:8-8:3; 9:1-2; 10:1-11:18; 13:44-52, etc). Although the Apostolic Council (Acts 15), appears to have resolved these tensions conclusively, they become much more vehement later (e.g., 17:5-9; 18:5-6, 12-13; 21:10-11, 27-36, etc). To resolve them, Luke repeatedly refers to certain earlier conversion accounts in his narratives. For instance, he refers to the Cornelius episode in the Jerusalem Council (15:7-12a; cf. 10:1-11:18). The same occasion is also used by Luke to authenticate a Gentile mission on

---

62 Cicero, *De Oratore*, II.8.35, 207. (Trans. E.W. Sutton; LCL; London: William Heinemann/ Cambridge, Mass.: HUP, 1942).

63 Polybius, *The Histories*, I.3.3-4; 1.4.7. (LCL; Tr. W.R. Paton; London/Cambridge, Mass: Heinemann, 1922-27).

64 Aristotle, *Poetics*, 1451, 1459. Cf. Preminger, *Literary Criticism*, 115.

65 For the conflicts between Jews and Gentiles in Acts, see J.T. Sanders, "The Salvation of the Jews in Luke-Acts", in Talbert (Ed.), *Luke-Acts: New Perspectives from the Society of Biblical Literature Seminar*, (New York: Crossroad, 1984), 104-28; idem, *The Jews in Luke-Acts* (London: SCM/Philadelphia:Fortress1987); idem, "Who is a Jew and Who is a Gentile in the Acts of the Apostles", *NTS*, 37, (1991), 434-55; J.B. Tyson, "The Jewish Public in Luke-Acts", *NTS*, 30, (1984), 574-83; idem (Ed.), *Luke-Acts and the Jewish People: Eight Critical Perspectives*, (Minneapolis: Augsburg, 1988); D.L. Tiede, " 'Glory to Thy People, Israel': Luke-Acts and the Jews", in J. Neusner et al. (Eds.), *The Social World of Formative Christianity and Judaism: Essays in Tribute to H.C. Kee*, (Philadelphia: Fortress, 1988), 327-41.

the basis of Scriptural validation through James (15:13-19). Similarly, Luke punctuates his narrative sequence thrice with Paul's conversion accounts (chapters 9, 22 and 26) to highlight the divine involvement. This kind of multiple repetitions of tensions and their resolution not only strengthens Acts as one body, but also point out how effectively Luke employs this device to accomplish his evangelistic motif.

Further, the *reversal of roles* of the main characters in Acts is another literary device that contributes to our argument. For example, Paul changes from being a persecutor of persons belonging to the Way (9:2) to its most zealous preacher after his conversion/call. His experience is recounted three times (chapters 9,22,26) in order to highlight the reversal of roles. Similarly, Peter transforms from being a reluctant preacher of the Gentiles (10:9-20,28) to an ardent defender of Gentile conversion (11:1-18; 15:7-11). About role-reversals Aristotle writes,

> "Plots are divided into the simple and the complex...complex when its change...arises through ... reversal...these aspects of the plot must develop...from prior events....".[66]

The sudden metamorphosis in Paul and Peter, characterised by double visions, signify that these dramatic transformation and role-reversals are sudden and yet are solely according to God's plan.

Thus, a conflation of evidence, from the structure of the book of Acts as a whole, from Luke's concept of divine providence, and from some of the literary techniques that he employs in Acts, establishes that conversion is not just a fanciful idea that is imposed on Luke. Rather, most importantly, the book of Acts itself is a reservoir of evidence demonstrating that conversion is one of Luke's chief motifs. It is on these grounds that the present investigation has undertaken to study the theme of conversion in Acts, particularly the literary roles that the miraculous and the Christian proclamation play in its scheme.

All said, we do acknowledge that Luke's purpose is complex. No one purpose can perhaps be regarded as one definitive and all-encompassing, for the literature he writes is not a tract designed with only one purpose in mind. His readers may find Acts relevant to a range of issues involving a variety of people, places and times. What we argued so far in this chapter is that whenever the purpose of Acts is considered Luke's evangelistic concern needs to be heeded since its

---

[66] Aristotle, *Poetics*, 1452a12-1452b13. Cf. Preminger, *Literary Criticism*, 118.

presence is felt so prominently. If, then, we grant that conversion is indeed one of Luke's chief motifs in Acts, then there must be some reason for it.

By putting forth two literary tropes—the miraculous and proclamation together, Luke argues that when these work together in Christian witnessing, they form the most effective means of bringing people to God. The stories that combine these two crucial components demonstrate Luke's construction of an all-determining worldview that centres on God. In the past God has acted decisively in the person and mission of Jesus and now he continues to act so in the apostolic mission. Therefore, he is the author of all the conversions everywhere.

In the conversion stories, Luke juxtaposes three perspectives vis-à-vis mission: a) the Jewish reluctance to break geographical (implied by Acts 1:8) and ritual barriers (10:9-16; 11:2-3; 15:1); b) the Gentiles as 'outsiders' and c) the divine δεῖ that challenges all these assumptions. Thus, the conversion stories reassure Luke's readers that within God's providence, there is no room for 'exclusivism' or 'exclusion' of anyone in any sense. Everyone who believes is a full and equal member of the believing community irrespective of humanly constructed barriers. God, in Christ, has set a new criterion for this membership: "*Everyone who calls on the name of the Lord shall be saved*" (2:21; 4:12). In the final analysis, there is no Jew or non-Jew, but only disciples, believers and brothers. Luke demonstrates the feasibility and the credibility of this criterion in the conversion of the 3000 (2:41), 5000 (4:4), a multitude of Samaritans (8:12), households (10:44-48; 16:33; 18:8), and individuals (8:36-38). In these stories, he also shows the importance of human instrumentality and obedience in bringing to fruition God's grand worldwide plan of redemption. Christian witness cannot reach its final destination without the obedience of the followers of Jesus to the mandate to witness (1:8).

Thus, one dominant concern of Luke's is to show the movement of the Christian testimony towards the ends of earth by according a universal perspective to all of God's actions. Christian witnessing is God's will (11:21), Jesus' vision (1:8), and the Spirit's initiative (2:1-13), implemented by Jesus' followers.

Luke's starting point is God. The subject of his writing is God's dealings with Jesus and what he continues to do through his followers. The end of his writing is that all people everywhere should turn to God. The scope of this plan of God's is the ends of the earth (cf. 1:8). The most effective means to achieve this objective are the miracles and Christian proclamation, both of which claim a divine origin. The next two chapters examine their literary functions in the overall scheme of Christian witnessing.

3

THE MIRACULOUS IN ACTS

INTRODUCTION

The preceding chapter demonstrated that conversion is one of Luke's foremost concerns and that this concern is, in many cases, manifested through the reciprocal relationship between the miraculous and proclamation. The present chapter explores the literary role performed by the miraculous in the overall scheme of apostolic witnessing in Acts.

The frequent occurrences of τέρατα (2:43; 4:30; 5:12; 6:8; 14:3; 15:12) and σημεῖα (4:16,22; 8:6) and visions (10:3-6, 9-16) that characterise the missionary enterprise of the early church (cf. 2:19) confirm Luke's special interest in the miraculous P.J. Achtemeier affirms,

> "...Luke appears to have...more...reliance on...miracles....Acts confirms...the extent to which Luke understood the miraculous to play an important...role in the origins of the Christian church."[1]

The prominence that Luke accords the miraculous phenomena in Acts becomes much clearer in a tabular form.

---

[1] Achtemeier, "Lukan Perspsective", 560.

TABLE OF MIRACLES IN ACTS (TM)

		I AGENT(S)	II MIRACLE	III REACTION
Miracles Through Human Agency	3:1-10	Peter/John	Lame man healed	The healed man: αἰνῶν τὸν θεὸν (3:8); Crowds: ἐπλήσθησαν θάμβος καὶ ἐκστάσεως (3:10)
	5:1-12	Peter	The death of Ananias and Sapphira	ἐγένετο φόβος (5:11)
	9:10-19; 22:12-16	Ananias	Saul's sight restored	
	9:32-35	Peter	Aeneas made to walk	All the residents of Lydda and Sharon: ἐπέστρεψαν ἐπὶ τὸν θεὸν (9:35)
	9:36-42	Peter	Tabitha raised to life	ἐπίστευσαν...ἐπὶ τὸν κύριον (9:42)
	13:6-12	Paul	Elymas blinded	ἐκπλησσόμενος (13:12)
	14:8-18	Paul and Barnabas	Lame man healed	Misunderstanding (14:11); Hostility from Jews (14:19)
	16:16-24	Paul	Exorcism	Hostility and imprisonment (16:19-24)
	20:7:12	Paul	Eutychus raised to life	παρεκλήθησαν (20:12)
	28:7-10	Paul	Man with fever healed	Many honours conferred on Paul and others

		I AGENT(S)	II MIRACLE	III REACTION
Miracles Without Human Agency	2:3		The sound like the rush of a violent wind + Polyglot (2:3)	ἐξίσταντο…ἐθαύμαζον (2:7)
	5:17-21		Apostles released from prison	διηπόρουν (5:24)
	8:39		Philip transported	
	9:10-16		Vision to Ananias	
	10:3-6, 10-16		Visions to Cornelius and Peter	ἔμφοβος (10:4)
	12:1-19		Peter released from prison	χαρᾶ ς(12:14) and ἐξέστησαν(12:16)
	12:20-24		Herod struck dead	
	16:25-34		Earthquake	ἔντρομος (16:29) + Question: "What must I do to be saved?" (16:30)
	19:13-16		The sons of Sceva routed	φόβος (19:17a); ἐμεγαλύνετο τὸ ὄ νομα τοῦ κυριοῦ Ἰησοῦ (19:17b)
	28:1-6		Paul surviving after snakebite	Misunderstanding: Paul was a god (28:6)

TABLE OF MIRACLES IN ACTS (TM)

		I AGENT(S)	II MIRACLE	III REACTION
Summaries	2:43	Apostles	Signs and Wonders	φόβος
	5:12	Apostles	Signs and Wonders	High esteem [for the apostles](5:13); μᾶλλον δὲ προσετίθεντο πιστεύοντες τῷ κυρίῳ (5:14)
	5:16	Peter	Healing of the multitude	
	6:8	Stephen	Signs and Wonders	Hostility (6:9ff.)
	8:4-8	Philip	Signs, Exorcisms, Healings	Great joy (8:8)
	14:3	Paul and Barnabas	Signs and Wonders	Division (14:4)
	15:12	Paul and Barnabas	Signs and Wonders	
	28:9	Paul	The sick on Malta healed	Paul and his entourage conferred many honours (28:10).
Healing by Relics	5:15f.	Peter	Healings by Peter's shadow	
	19:11-12.	Paul	Healings by Paul's handkerchiefs or aprons	

The overwhelming presence of miracles and visions demonstrates Luke's deliberate portrayal of the early community as living in a climate infused with a sense of the supernatural, a climate corresponding to the popular interest in the miraculous in Luke's contemporary Graeco-Roman and Jewish society.[2] This is one reason why scholars study the miraculous in Acts against the Hellenistic and Hellenistic-Jewish backgrounds.[3] Luke's presentation of the miraculous in Acts is discussed later in the chapter, but first, in order to locate clearly what is distinctive in his treatment of the miraculous, the concept of the miraculous and its literary functions in the contemporary Hellenistic and Hellenistic-Jewish thought-world, is examined.

THE MIRACULOUS IN GRAECO-ROMAN UNDERSTANDING

This section looks at the various ways in which the different sections of Graeco-Roman society understood the miraculous and its functions. Since Graeco-Roman literature is not a homogeneous body, but diverse in its range, genre, perspective, and time, we do not attempt here to evolve a unified definition of the miraculous in Graeco-Roman society. Only some representative views are singled out in order to approximate Luke's own position within this complex network of ideas. Although our conclusions can only be provisional, yet this exploration can help elucidate Luke's distinctive position.

Definition of the Miraculous

Since the definition of the miraculous is contingent upon its explanation, we first look at some Graeco-Roman explanations of supernatural phenomena and, then, their definition. In the Graeco-Roman world three strands of thought interface with each other in a very subtle way: historians' perspectives, popular understanding, and philosophical views.

Livy's account of a lunar eclipse that took place during a battle between the Romans and the Macedonians (*History*, XLIV.37), exemplifies a historian's perspective on the 'miraculous'.[4] The Roman officers knew beforehand that a lunar eclipse was to occur the following night; therefore, they explained it to their soldiers lest they were terrified or consider it 'miraculous'. When the

---

[2] For a fuller treatment of this subject see D.L. Tiede, *Charismatic Figure as Miracle Worker*, (SBLDS 1; Missoula, MT: SBL, 1973).

[3] H.J. Cadbury deals with this particular aspect generally in *The Book of Acts in History*, (New York: Harper and Bros., 1955), 32-85.

[4] Cited in H. Remus, *Pagan-Christian Conflict over Miracle in the Second Century*, (Patristic Monograph Series 10; Cambridge, MA: The Philadelphia Patristic Foundation Ltd., 1983), 4.

eclipse occurred, the Romans knew it was a natural phenomenon, whereas the Macedonians were terrified, thinking that it was a portent from the gods, predicting their doom. Consequently there was mourning in their camp until the moon reappeared.

This incident illustrates the differences in understanding. For the Macedonians the eclipse was a doomsayer from the gods, whereas the Romans knew that in nature there is regularity and therefore, a natural phenomenon, i.e., the lunar eclipse, cannot be from the gods and therefore, miraculous. Two things become clear here: a) the notion of divine causation is the interpretative key to explain whether or not events are miraculous; b) rational approaches to the miraculous may divest an event of any 'miraculous' connotation by their causal explanations. Conversely, it means that when an event defies reason, it may be considered 'miraculous'.

Besides rational explanations, *medical explanations* may also make references to a deity superfluous and, thereby, divest events of any 'miraculous' notion.[5] Diodorus Siculus, for instance, reports that Asclepius claims to have raised a person from the dead. But according to Diodorus, it is actually due to Asclepius' medical knowledge,[6] whereas, Asclepius himself and his followers, could have considered this as a miraculous event. Similarly, *attaching pejorative labels* also denies divine causation to events.[7] For instance, Lucian portrays Alexander as a charlatan and therefore, Alexander's claims to divine ecstasy (*Alexander*, 12-13), epiphanies (7, 13-17), and oracles (19-22, 26, 28, 37, 53-54) are dubious (24, 28, 36, 59).[8] Again, for Alexander himself and his admirers, all his claims are not counterfeit, but genuine.

Summing up the historians' sentiments well, Cicero, the philosopher, explains that whatever happens in nature has a cause, however extraordinary it might appear. If something happens that would have happened any way, it is not miraculous.[9] Thus, one of the ways of explaining events is to assign them a cause.

---

5 See Remus, *Pagan-Christian Conflict*, 37-39.

6 Diodorus Siculus, *The Library of History*, IV.71.1, (LCL; Tr. C.H. Oldfather, et al; 12 Vols.; Cambridge, Mass.: HUP, 1933-68).

7 Cf. Remus, *Pagan-Christian Conflict*, 40-42.

8 Lucian, *Alexander the False Prophet*, (LCL; Tr. A. Harmon; Vol. IV; London: Heinemann, 1961).

9 Cf. Cicero, *De Divinatione*, II.28.60-61, (LCL; Tr. W.A. Falconer; London/Cambridge, Mass.: HUP, 1996).

Sometimes certain phenomena are considered wondrous, but they are neither causally explained nor attributed to the gods.[10] Herodotus reports that it was a most wondrous phenomenon when it rained in Thebes where it had never rained before and where it never rained since.[11] But he neither attributes this to a deity nor does he report that the Thebans did so.[12]

Sometimes, events may also be attributed to the gods. While attributing statues that sweat, weep, and bleed, to atmospheric moisture, Plutarch suggests that still the gods can use such phenomena to communicate to humans, for what is unreasonable for humans is possible for the deities (38.3-4).[13] When events are thus considered miraculous, they could lead to conversion. Ovid reports that Acoetes, a priest of Dionysius, became a follower of the god when an epiphany was revealed in a miraculous event.[14] Similarly, Apuleius reports that when Isis restored Lucius' human form miraculously, it led to his conversion to the Isis cult.[15]

The tendency to explain extraordinary occurrences causally, divesting them of any miraculous meaning can also be seen in the Graeco-Roman 'Miracle' vocabulary. The hendiadys σημεῖα καὶ τέρατα is singled out, because, as already pointed out, Luke employs these terms in Acts as part of his miracle vocabulary, which is discussed briefly later in the chapter. In Graeco-Roman literature, however, these terms could sometimes be employed even in non-miraculous sense. Some illustrations from Homer illustrate this better.

For Homer, τέρας is basically a sign, a token, especially of natural phenomena such as thunder, lightning, rainbows, or the flight of birds. However, when these are attributed to the gods, it was believed that the gods used them to presage the future. τέρας is basically a sign, but since it is attributed to Zeus, it is a portent sent by him; therefore, it is τέρας Διός. For instance, an eagle, flying high, carrying a snake, still alive and struggling, drops it among the

10 Cf. Remus, *Pagan-Christian Conflict*, 36-37.

11 Herodotus, *History*, III.10. (Tr. C. Hude; Oxford: Clarendon, 1927).

12 Attributing events to the gods is 'superstition'. See J. Ferguson, *The Religions of the Roman Empire*, (London: Thames and Hudson, 1970), 80-81; R. MacMullen, *Paganism in the Roman Empire*, (New Haven CT: YUP, 1981), 70,73.

13 Plutarch, 'Coriolanus' (38.1), *Lives*, (LCL; Tr. Bernadotte Perrin; London: Heinemann, 1916).

14 Cited in C.H. Talbert, *Reading Luke: A Literary and Theological Commentary on the Third Gospel*, (New York: Crossroad, 1982), 241.

15 Apuleius, *Metamorphoses*, X.11, (LCL; Ed. & Tr. Arthur Hanson; London/Cambridge, Mass.: HUP, 1989).

Trojans. They shudder when they see the snake in their midst, thinking that it was a portent from Zeus.[16]

Sometimes portents from the gods could convey divine displeasure. Odysseus, in his address in the court of the king of Achaeans, narrates an incident about a snake eating up a sparrow and all her nestlings. It was considered as a dreaded portent from Zeus himself, warning them of the delay in winning a war (*Il.*, II. 324ff.). Further, just as there is τέρας Διός, there is also τέρας ἀνθρώπων. For example, the breastplate that the son of Atreus gave to the Achaeans, had serpents, three on either side, like rainbows, it was referred to as τέρας ἀνθρώ – πων (*Il.*, XI.28). But here τέρας does not possess any 'miraculous' quality; it is merely a sign that the breastplate belonged to Atreus. Sometimes, even malformations could be called τέρας. Aristotle explains that τέρας in the animal world is a kind of malformation.[17] It is τέρας because it does not resemble any other animals, but reaches a point where it begins to appear as some strange species.

Thus, things that happen naturally belong to the ordinary course of events in nature and can, therefore, be explained without reference to the gods or without considering them miraculous. But when they are attributed to the deities, they become portents from the gods.

Similarly, the term σημεῖον also does not possess any inherent notion of the divine to the rationally inclined sections in Graeco-Roman society. It can simply mean an ensign or an identifying mark whereby something is known. For example, as the helmet of the horseman, Nestor of Gerenia, was passed around, nobody recognised it. But when Aias, who had marked it, sees it, he†"knew at a glance the mark..." (σῆμα, *Il.*, VII. 188). However, when referred to a god, the σημεῖον becomes a divine portent revealing a hidden quality. For instance, lightning and thunder are Zeus' signs of presaging the future.[18] Although there is nothing objectively miraculous in lightning and thunder, they become miraculous when attributed to Zeus. Thus, one way of treating events miraculous in Hellenistic thought is to attribute them to the gods.[19]

---

16 Homer, *Illiad*, XII.209. (LCL; Tr. A.T. Murray; London: Heinemann, 1925). See also *Ody.*, XVI.320 for another example.

17 Aristotle, *De Generatione Animalium*, 770 b.3cff. Cf. Richard McKeon, (Ed.), *The Basic Works of Aristotle*, (New York: Random House, 1941).

18 Homer, *Il.*, II.353. See also VIII.170-71; XIII.244.

19 R. Swinburne, (*The Concept of Miracle*, [London: Macmillan, 1970], 1) defines miracles in a modified form: they are extraordinary events, some of religious nature that are effected by a god.

The examples cited above demonstrate the coexistence of rational explanation of the miraculous and its popular acceptance in the Graeco-Roman society. Rationalisation argues that the 'miraculous' is in the eyes of the beholder, whereas popular opinion accepts the improbable as communication from the gods through usual/unusual happenings to communicate their intent. It is from this popular belief that we identify one main literary function of the occurrences deemed miraculous.

Demonstrative/Communicative

As stated above, when events are considered miraculous, they demonstrate the intervention of the gods to guide human affairs. Even Tacitus, who is generally sceptical of the supernatural[20], considers prodigies as communicative signs from the gods.[21]

Sometimes, the miraculous might evince divine approbation. Vespasian, for example, claims power by declaring that the Egyptian deities have conferred on him special benefactions.[22] Likewise, the Roman imperial power is a manifestation of divine providence.[23] While sailing the sea Odysseus comes across a strange landscape, which, he believes, conveys that the gods have concluded, "It is his (Odysseus') fate to escape from the great bonds of the woe which have come upon him."[24]

Besides demonstrating their approbation and providence through miraculous events, the gods and goddesses can also appear in dreams and visions to guide human affairs. Isis guides her devotees through her revelations.[25] When Brutus

---

20 Tacitus, *Annals*, VI.21-22,28, (Tr. D.C.A. Shotter; Warminster: Aris & Phillips, 1989).

21 Tacitus, *The Histories*, I.3, (LCL; Tr. C.H. Moore; London/Cambridge, Mass.: HUP, 1999).

22 Cf. Dio Cassius, *Roman History*, 61:35; 63:185,235, (LCL; Tr. Ernest Cary; 8 Vols.; London: Heinemann, 1914-27]).

23 Cicero, *Leg.*, I.21; II.15-16. Cf. R.M. Ogilvie, *The Romans and Their Gods in the Age of Augustus*, (London: Chatto & Windus, 1969), 10, 17; J.R. Fears, "The Cult of Jupiter and Roman Imperial Ideology", *ANRW*, I.17.1, (1981), 3-141, esp. 43; idem, "The Cult of Virtues and Roman Imperial Ideology", *ANRW*, I.17.2, (1981), 827-948, esp. 833, 837.

24 Homer, *Odyssey*, V.286ff. Cf. Raymond Adolph Prier, *Thauma Idesthai: The Phenomenology of Sight and Appearance in Archaic Greek*, (Tallahassee: Florida State University Press, 1989), 57.

25 Dio. Sic., *Lib. Hist.*, I.25.3,5. For such acts of benevolence by Asclepius, see H.C. Kee, *Miracle in the Early Christian World*, (New Haven: YUP, 1983), Ch.3: "Asklepios the Healer". See also A.H.M. Kessels, *Studies on the Dream in the Greek Literature*, (Utrecht: HES, 1978), 152; R.C.A. van Lieshout, *Greeks on Dreams*, (Utrecht: HES, 1980), 116-18.

him.[26] Sometimes, visions can also be given to commission people for a particular task. Apollonius changes his plan on the basis of a dream.[27] Likewise, Apollo, in a vision, instructs the Athenians to bring home the hero's bones.[28] This aspect of visions to commission people for a task is particularly relevant for our study. Luke also records in Acts visions, angelophanies, and heavenly voices to commission people for mission (e.g., the Cornelius story). We shall discuss this later in the chapter and also in chapter 6 of our study.

There are also examples of healing-visions in Graeco-Roman society. Isis appears in visions to heal her devotees.[29] A man with a paralysed hand comes to the sanctuary in Epidauros as a suppliant to the god. In his sleep, the suppliant sees a vision in which the god appears, springs on his paralysed hand and stretches out his fingers. The suppliant goes back home healed. Similarly, a blind woman comes to Epidauros as a suppliant to the god. In her sleep, she sees a vision in which the god was standing beside her, saying that he would restore her sight. Having said this, he pours medicine into her eye. When the day came she went away cured.[30] Although Acts does not record similar healing-visions, these cases illustrate the importance accorded to visions in Graeco-Roman popular religious experience.

Thus, the miraculous, whatever form it might take, evinces the presence of the gods, their intervention in human affairs, and the communication of their intent. This evokes certain reactions in people.

Reactions to the Miraculous

A strong and fearful act or the presence of something 'other' evokes *amazement*. In the *Odyssey* Telemachus says, "This is a great marvel that my eyes beheld. Certainly, the walls...glow...as if...god is within...."[31] Sometimes wonder can be mere stupefaction. Achilles is shocked (θάμβησεν) when Athena prevents him from killing Agamemnon (*Il.*, I.199). Likewise, wonder grips people when the gods appear in the flight of the birds,"people seized with wonder (θάμβησαν) at the birds when their eyes beheld them...and pondered...what

---

26 BDAG, 718.

27 Philostratus, *Life of Apollonius*, 4:34. Cf. BDAG, 718.

28 Robert Parker, *Athenian Religion. A History*, (Oxford: Clarendon, 1995), 169.

29 Dio.Sic., *Lib. Hist.*, I.25.3,5.

30 Cited in Graham Shipley, *The Greek World after Alexander, 323-30 B.C.*, (London/New York: Routledge, 2000), 164.

31 Homer, *Ody.*, XIX, 36-40.

was to come to pass" (*Ody*.II.155-56). In these cases, clearly the spectators make something wondrous out of an appearance and react in fear or amazement.

On the other hand, sometimes, one can react to a 'miracle' by expressing a sense of confidence in the likelihood of its occurrence. Lucian of Samosata records an incident where Cleodemus, one of his characters, confesses, "I myself...thought it in no way possible that they could happen; but when first I saw the foreign stranger fly...I believed (ἐπίστευσα)."[32] Here believing is made possible by a tangible evidence. Similarly, while offering other explanations to an unusual event, Plutarch explains that what is impossible for humans, is possible for the gods.[33]

Some of the references seen above point out that while fear and wonder is a common reaction, when events are deemed miraculous they are mainly oriented towards the extraordinariness of the occurrences and not at the gods themselves. Where a form of believing is involved, it rests on confidence that the gods can perform miracles.

In contrast to the above views, Graeco-Roman philosophical approaches evince a totally different perspective on the miraculous. Without necessarily rejecting *a priori* the possibility of miraculous happenings, they consider them as secondary since, in their view, morality and wisdom make a person divine, and not necessarily teratological displays.[34]

Talking of Socrates, Plato remarks that since he loved wisdom and kept company with the divine, he is himself divine.[35] Besides Socrates' wisdom, his death also demonstrates his divinity. His whole life was a pursuit after good, but his trial brings his unceasing search for the good to an abrupt end, yet he faced his death with complete equanimity.[36] His trial scene demonstrates that his assumption of poverty to serve the god (*Apol.* 23C) and to defend wisdom at the risk of his own life (*Apol.* 28E), elevate him above the mortals.

---

32 Lucian, *Philopseudes*, 13. (Tr. A.M. Harmon; London: William Heinemann/New York: G.P. Putnam's Sons, 1921).

33 Plutarch, 'Coriolanus', *Lives*, 38.

34 Arthur W.H. Adkins, *Merit and Responsibility: A Study in Greek Values*, (Oxford: Clarendon, 1960), 31, 60. See also Werner W. Jaeger, *Paideia: The Ideals of Greek Culture*, (Oxford: Basil Blackwell, 1939-45), 1.

35 Plato, *Republic* VII. 500, (Tr. C-D. Benjamin Jowett; London: Encyclopedia Britannica, Inc., 1952).

36 This is one of the most compelling passions in all literature. Cf. M. Hadas and M. Smith, *Heroes and Gods: Spiritual Biographies in Antiquity*, (New York: Harper & Row, 1963), 55.

Similarly, Diogenes Laertius too calls good men "images of the gods" and distinguishes the divine philosophers from those who look for divine presence in miracle-working powers.[37] Hercules is also considered divine on the basis of his virtues. His sacrificial death alone can make him divine.[38]

These examples illustrate the tendency in Graeco-Roman philosophical circles to treat the miraculous as inferior or subordinate to morality and wisdom. Wisdom, communication of divine truth, and a virtuous life make one divine to the exclusion of miracle-working powers. In this sense, the miraculous is either subordinate to morality or irrelevant.

Summary

The illustrations from Graeco-Roman literature are not exhaustive. The representative examples presented above show the wide-ranging views concerning the miraculous interfacing with each other. Historical approaches explain events causally by and large, but they do not rule out the possibility that they may be considered miraculous by a vast majority of people. Thus, in popular understanding, *a miracle is an occurrence attributed to the gods, which can communicate their intent, providence, and judgement.* Meanwhile, at the philosophical level, the image of the ideal wise man, his virtues, and moral excellence provide a control by which the supernatural elements can be subordinated to morality/wisdom or deemed irrelevant. It is, therefore, moral excellence that reveals divine presence and not necessarily miraculous phenomena.

In the following section we explore the function of the miraculous in the OT and in Hellenistic-Jewish writings. The insights gained here can also help us understand Luke's position in the overall thought world and his distinctive contribution.

---

37 Diogenes Laertius, (*Lives of Eminent Philosophers*, VI. 51, [LCL; Tr. R.D. Hicks; London/ Cambridge, Mass.: HUP, 2000]. For more examples see John C. Lentz, *Luke's Portrait of Paul*, (Cambridge: CUP, 1993), 68ff.

38 Seneca, *Hercules*, 794-96, 1700-25; (Tr. David R. Slavitt; Baltimore: John Hopkins University Press, 1995). See also Philostratus, *Life of Apollonius of Tyana*, I.19; II.29,37,40, etc., (Tr. F.C. Conybeare; London: HUP/Cambridge, Mass.: William Heinemann, 1912-1950).

THE MIRACULOUS IN THE OLD TESTAMENT

Demonstrative

Miraculous events in the OT basically demonstrate divine providence. When Abimelech attempts to take Sarah as his wife (Gen.20:12), he is issued a death warning. Abraham prays for him and God heals Abimelech, his barren wives, and others (Gen. 20:17-18). This demonstrates God's healing power. Besides being a healer, God is also a communicator (Gen. 28:11-26; 37:5-11; Cf. 1 Kgs., 3:4-15).[39] Through divinatory mediums such as Urim and Thummim (Ex. 28:30; Num. 27:21; Deut. 33:8; 1 Sam. 14:41-42) and Ephod (1 Sam. 23:9-12; 30:7-8) and through dreams and visions[40] he makes his will known to his people.

Miracles also manifest God's power, his care for his people (Num. 16:30; Josh. 10:10ff), and his intervention in their affairs (Gen. 24:12ff.; Ex. 14:21f.; 1 Sam. 14:23,45). Although all miraculous events exhibit God's guidance and communication of his will, the greatest of them all is the Exodus from Egypt.[41] This is God's great work (Ex. 14:31a), a manifestation of his power, salvation, love (Ex. 13:14; 15:2-3,15), and a proof that he alone is the Lord (Ex. 15:11). The hendiadys "σημεῖα καὶ τέρατα (e.g., Deut. 4:34) vis-à-vis the Exodus reveals God's actions on behalf of his people[42] and proves his power (Ex. 7:5,17; 8:6,18; 9:14,16,29; 12:12).

Moreover, the Elijah-Elisha cycles also demonstrate God's power. Elijah heals the widow's son (1 Kgs. 17) and Elisha restores the Shunamite woman's son to life (2 Kgs 4) and cures Naaman's leprosy (2 Kgs. 5). After his cure, Naaman confesses, "*Now I know that there is no God in all the earth except in Israel*" (2 Kgs. 5:15). Further, the vindication of Daniel and his companions also demonstrates God's intervention in the affairs of his people. He delivers them from the fiery furnace and from the lion's den (Dan. 3:1-25; 6:27). After the miraculous deliverance of Daniel's companions from the furnace,

---

[39] See D.E. Aune, *Prophecy in Early Christianity and the Ancient Mediterranean World*, (Grand Rapids: Eerdmans, 1983), 82-3; J. Blenkinsopp, "Prophecy and Priesthood in Josephus", *JJS*, 25, (1974), 253-4.

[40] See also A. Oepke, "ὄναρ", *TWNT*, V.220-30, esp. 228-31.

[41] See J.P. Ross, "Some Notes on Miracle in the Old Testament" in C.F.D. Moule, (Ed.), *Miracles: Cambridge Studies in Their Philosophy and History*, (London: Mowbray, 1965), 43-60; B. Lindars, "Elijah, Elisha and the Gospel Miracles", C.F.D. Moule, (Ed.), *Miracles*, 61-79.

[42] Ex. 3:20; 4:30; 7:30; Deut. 4:34; 7:19; 26:8; 29:3; 34:11; Neh. 9:10; Pss. 78:43; 105:27; 107:24; Isa. 8:18; Jer. 32:20-21; Joel 2:30.

Nebuchadnezzar confesses that the God of the Hebrews is "*God Most High*" (3:26) and praises Yahweh (3:28-29). Similarly, after Daniel's deliverance from the lion's den, king Darius understands this deliverance as a "*sign and wonder*" (6:29) and passes a decree that everyone in his dominion should "*fear before the God of Daniel; For He is the living God...He delivers and rescues, and he works signs and wonders...*" (6:27-28).

Besides this, the OT also records accounts of Theophany. For instance, Elijah's confrontation with the priests of Baal on mount Carmel and the coming of fire from heaven at his invocation reveals God's presence in what transpires (1 Kgs. 18). At its sight, the prophets of Baal and the spectators "*fell on their faces and ...said, 'The LORD, He is God...*" (v.39). A similar Theophany is recorded in 1 Kgs. 19:11ff where Yahweh appears and speaks to Elijah at Horeb, preceded by wind and fire and re-commissions him to go and anoint Elisha as his successor. Luke also records a Theophany in Acts (wind and fire, 2:2-3), which is particularly important for our study. We shall discuss this in detail in chapter 5.

Further, the OT often records visions and divine appearances, particularly to bless and to commission. The LORD appears to Abraham in a vision and blesses him (Gen. 15:1; 18:1). Similarly, he appears to Jacob at Bethel in a dream (Gen. 28:10-15), and to Moses in the burning bush to commission him to bring the Israelites out of Egypt (Ex. 3:2; cf. Acts 7:30). The OT also records instances where people hear just the heavenly voice. When Hagar was fleeing from Abraham and Sarah and when her son was about to die of thirst, she hears the reassuring voice from heaven (Gen. 21:17).

Sometimes, such dreams and visions are followed by an interpretation. Pharaoh's dream about the cows and grain was followed by Joseph's interpretation (Gen. 41). Similarly, Nebuchadnezzar's dream was followed by Daniel's interpretation (Dan. 2:3-45; 4:1-7) and the writing on Belshazzar's wall (5:2-28). These examples show that sometimes dreams and visions may not be self-explanatory. They are made intelligible and meaningful only through an interpretation. This has direct relevance to our study since Luke also records a Theophany (Acts 2) and visions, and heavenly voices in for instance, the Cornelius story (e.g., Acts 10:3-6; 9-16), which necessitate an interpretation. We shall discuss this in more detail later in this chapter and in chapters 5 and 6.

Importantly, however, this positive portrayal of the miraculous in the OT comes with a caveat. In the OT Miracles are valuable only insofar as they point to Yahweh, particularly because, even those who oppose him can perform similar acts (Ex. 7:11,22; 8:7; Deut. 13:1ff.). The Egyptian magicians too repeat a few of the same plagues that Moses and Aaron performed at Yahweh's behest (Ex. 7:3, 11-12a, 22; 8:3), although from the third plague, they find that they are no match for Yahweh (8:14ff). Thus, miracles cannot be final or sole proofs of Yahweh's intervention. Secondly, where faith in Yahweh is absent, miracles are useless. Pharaoh does not believe the divine origin of Moses' miracles (Ex. 7:13,22-23; 11:10, etc.).

Confirmative/Authenticative

The Graeco-Roman philosophical debate as to what authenticates people as divine—teratological powers or morality—has no parallel in the OT. Miracles in the OT authenticate the miracle workers not as divine, but as God-sent, as mediums of divine revelation, and as messengers of God (Ex. 4:1-9; Num. 12:1-2; 17:1-8; 21:5-9.) by confirming and attributing prophetic character to their word.

In the narratives about Moses in the book of Exodus and Deuteronomy, this particular aspect is shown by terms such as σημεῖον (Ex. 4:8), τέρας (Ex. 4:21; 15:11), and σημεῖα καὶ τέρατα.[43] These signs are meant to persuade the Israelites that they are special displays of God's power; they attest the divine presence and confirm that God had spoken to Moses; therefore, Moses' words are actually God's words. Therefore, Pharaoh must also listen to Moses, failing which God will act in judgement (Ex. 7:4). Here miracles perform a confirmatory function—to complement, illustrate, and confirm the words of God's messengers. Further, that miracles authenticate the prophets as the men of God is seen particularly in the Elijah-Elisha cycle.[44] When Elijah raised the widow's son, she confesses, "*Now I know that you are a man of God, and that the word of the Lord in your mouth is truth*" (1 Kgs. 17:24).

Reactions to the Miraculous

When miracles demonstrate God's power and providence and confirm the words of the prophets, they evoke a response of *worship*. This is sometimes expressed by the idea of 'falling on one's face', particularly, in contexts of epiphanies or

---

[43] Ex. 7: 3,9; 11: 9,10; Deut. 4:34; 6:22; 7: 19; 11: 3; 13: 2,3; 26: 8,28,46; 29: 3; 34: 11.

[44] 1 Kgs. 17: 17-24; 18: 36-39; 2 Kgs. 1: 10,12; 20: 8-11.

angelophanies.[45] As shown earlier, in 1Kgs. (18:39) people fall on their faces and confessed that the Lord is God on Mt. Carmel when they saw the fire coming from heaven and consuming the sacrifice.

Besides attitudes of worship, the miraculous can also arouse *fear and amazement*. A great fear fell on Abraham after his vision (Gen. 15:2); Jacob was afraid after his vision (Gen. 28:17). Trembling, pangs, and dismay come over the inhabitants of Philistia over God's mighty acts (Ex. 15:14-6). Likewise, David fears God after he strikes Uzziah for touching the ark (2 Sam. 6:9). In Jonah 1:16, the sailors greatly fear God after the sudden calming of the sea after Jonah had been thrown into the sea. In 2 Maccabees (12:22), terror and fear comes upon the enemy at the manifestation of God; Esdras (2 Esd. 2.43) trembles after a revelatory dream. In 3 Maccabees (2:23) God's punishment of Ptolemy arouses fear. Thus, even in reactions of wonder, there is a recognition that God is at work; this further affirms his centrality and providence.

As the examples above illustrate, the OT presents the miraculous from a thoroughgoing Theocentric perspective. A miracle in the OT is, then, *a happening in the human realm that manifests God's providence, his power, and involvement in human affairs and that leads to worshipping God*. The OT, thus, affirms divine centrality in the miraculous both in terms of their functions and human responses.

The following section discusses the way the Hellenistic-Jewish writings present the miraculous with a view to finding out Luke's relation to his contemporary thought-world.

THE MIRACULOUS IN HELLENISTIC-JEWISH WRITINGS

This section briefly examines Philo's and Josephus' presentation of the miraculous, beginning with Philo.[46] We will first discuss some of his writings in which Philo tends to rationalise and subordinate the miraculous to virtues/ wisdom.

---

[45] Gen. 17:3; Lev. 9:24; Num. 14:5; 16:4,22,45; 20:6; Josh. 5:14; Judg. 13:20; 3 Kgs. 18:39; 2 Chron. 6:13; 7:3; 20:18; Tob. 12:16; Ezek. 1:28; 9:8; 11:13; Dan. 8:17.

[46] For more information on Philo's interpretative patterns, see Folker Siegert, "Early Jewish Interpretations in a Hellenistic Style" in Magne Sæbø, (Ed.), *Hebrew Bible/Old Testament: The History of Its Interpretation*, (Göttingen: Vandenhoeck & Ruprecht, 1996), 162-89.

Philo

Subordination of the Miraculous to Virtues

For Philo, all the patriarchs epitomise virtues: Enos is the hoper; Enoch migrates from vice to virtue; and Noah was "perfect in his generation" (cf. Gen. 6:9); and all of them yearn for virtues (*Abr.* II-IX.[7-48]; *Praem.* II-IV.[13-24]).[47] Philo portrays Moses in similar light as a wise man and as a man of moral excellence (*Virt.* XXXIII.177).

Moses marries virtue rather than a woman because Zipporah is "virtue...a just comprehension of the divine and blessed virtues..." (*Cher.* XII.41). He is divine in terms of the unity between his body and soul (*Mos.* II.LI.[288]). Therefore, God has favoured and advanced him beyond human nature and stationed him beside himself (*Sac.* III.8; *Virt.* XII.77-79; Cf. Deut. 5:31).

As a perfect 'man of God' (*Mut.* III.24-25 cf. Deut. 33:1) Moses, has the divine mind and, therefore, he can intercede for the transgressors (*Mut.* XXII.129). Because of his wisdom, he is prized by God (*Sac.* III.8); he is God's friend (*Mos.* I.XXVIII.[156-58]). As the best legislator, he possesses all the virtues fully and completely (*Mos.* II.II.[8]). As a priest, his life is characterised by piety (*Mos.* II.XIII.[66]) and he possesses foreknowledge (*Mos.* II.XXXV.[190]; cf. II.XLVIII.[269]). He is an inspired prophet, but his prophecies do not automatically produce results; they merely anticipate God to bring them to pass.[48] Thus, Moses' role as a prophet and his deeds rest upon his virtues (*Praem.* IX.53) and upon God's confirmation. All along, the noetic argument is consistent: Moses is attributed a kind of divine status because of his identity as a virtuous man and not because of his ability, if any, to perform miracles. In this sense, miracles are secondary to virtues and wisdom. This recalls the Graeco-Roman philosophical tendency, seen above, to consider morality and wisdom as authenticating a person as divine rather than his miracle-working powers.

The dominance of virtues over miracles, exemplified particularly in Philo's characterisation of Moses, explains why he either rationalises or allegorises some miracle accounts. The burning bush symbolises those who were wronged and the flaming fire, those who committed the wrong (*Mos.* I.XII.[67]); the

---

47 All the references are from C.D. Yonge (Tr.) *The Works of Philo*, (Peabody, MA: Hendrickson Publishers, 1997).

48 *Mos.* II.XLVI.(253), II.XLVII.(262), II.XLVIII.(263-269), II.L.(284).

bitter spring may have been sweetened by a tree with a previously unknown natural quality (*Mos.* I.XXXIII.[185]); the rock yielding water may have held a hidden source of spring (*Mos.* I.XXXVIII.[211]); and the rod cast down is the serpent pleasure, but picked up is schooling in virtue (*Leg. All.* II.XXII.[90-93]). When Aaron's rod swallows the rods of the Egyptians, it symbolises the devouring of all the arguments of the sophists (*Mig.* XV.[85]).

Philo does not deny the reality of miracles, but treats them as tools to interpret philosophically the lives of moral exemplars, a concept paralleling the Graeco-Roman practice in philosophical circles. However, miracles are real for him only insofar as they demonstrate divine-centrality. This leads to the consideration of the literary function of the miraculous in Philo.

Demonstrative

A random survey of some of Philo's texts shows that for him the miraculous demonstrates the divine majesty and centrality. They exemplify the fact that everything is possible for God, including things that are impossible for humans (*Abr.* XX.112, XXXI.175). The order in creation displays God's miraculous powers (*Mos.* I.XXXVIII.[212]; II.XLVIII.[267]). His miraculous activities prove that he is the master of the whole world and, therefore, physical elements can naturally assume qualities and functions not usually theirs. The air producing manna is but one example.[49] God demonstrates his will by proofs of signs and wonders (*Mos.* I.XVI.[95]) which only underscore his reliability (*Mos.* I.XIV.[82]), presence (*Mos.* II.XXX.[154]) and how different his ways are from human ways (*Mos.* II.XXXII.[173]).

For Philo, then, *a miracle is an event that manifests God's majesty, centrality, power, and will.* Philo strikes a fine balance between rationalisation and Theological orientation. He presents the miraculous as historically credible and as affirming Theocentricity. However, he does not mention any audience-reaction to it, perhaps because of his rationalising tendencies.

Josephus

Since some of Josephus' texts demonstrate an apologetic interest in presenting the miraculous, we discuss it first. Next we look at Josephus' characterisation of Moses, which sheds further light on his general outlook to the supernatural. A brief discussion of the function of the miraculous in Josephus will follow.

---

[49] *Mos.* I.XXXVI.(201-202); II.XXXIX.(216); II.XXX.(154).

Josephus and his Apologetic Interests

Although Josephus is interested in the miraculous, as MacRae puts it,

> "As a Jew, Josephus does not balk at accepting the miraculous whenever he encounters it because what he sees in it are God's πρόνοια and δύναμις. But as a Hellenist, he does not hesitate to offer a pseudo-scientific or pseudo-philosophical explanation."[50]

Josephus aims at combating anti-Jewish polemics, particularly those by Apion, by positively portraying Moses' leadership. He defends Moses against the charges that he was evil and that he mobilised the Jews to attack Egypt and did not show goodwill to anyone, that he ill-treated people, plundered them, and burnt the temples.[51] By contrast, Josephus depicts Moses as the noblest instructor in virtue who trained his people in gentleness and humanity and prevented them from doing exactly what Apion had accused them of having done (*Apion*, II.30.[211-13]). Also Moses is such an illustrious lawgiver that his laws are universal (*Apion*, II.17 [167]; II.40.[284]); even the "Egyptians acknowledge him to have been a...divine person..." (*Apion*, I.31.]279]).

Josephus' apologetic interests are also evident in the way he edits some of the OT accounts. We may cite just one example here. The OT records the first confrontation between Moses-Aaron and Pharaoh in Ex. 7:10-12 as follows: "*...Moses and Aaron...went to Pharaoh and did as the LORD had commanded; Aaron threw down his staff before Pharaoh and his officials, and it became a snake. Then Pharaoh summoned the wise men and the sorcerers; and they also the magicians of Egypt, did the same by their secret arts. Each one threw down his staff, and they became snakes; but Aaron's staff swallowed up theirs.*" Josephus redacts this incident in such a way that highlights Yahweh's supremacy, power, providence, and Moses' superiority as follows: "And...he (Pharaoh) had...commanded the priests to let him see the same wonderful sights....But Moses...said, "O King...what I do is so much superior to what these do by magic arts and tricks...divine power exceeds the power of man...what I do is...by the providence and power of God. And when he had said this, he cast his rod down upon the ground, and commanded it to turn itself into a serpent. It obeyed him, and went all round, and devoured the rods of the Egyptians...It

---

50 George MacRae, "Miracles in the Antiquities of Josephus", in C.F.D. Moule (Ed.), *Miracles*, 127-47, esp. 142. See also H.R. Moehring, "Rationalization of Miracles in the Writings of Flavius Josephus", *SE*, 6, (1973), 373-86; Steve Mason and Robert A. Kraft, "Josephus on Canon and Scripture" in Magne Sæbø, (Ed.), *Hebrew Bible*, 217-35.

51 Josephus, *Against Apion*, I.26.237-250, I.34.304-310

then returned to its own form..." (*Antiq*. II.13.3.[286-87]). Here Josephus portrays the Egyptian magicians as creating a kind of optic illusion to make their rods look like serpents. Moreover, to add greater credibility to the story, Josephus presents Moses as turning his rod into the serpent, whereas in the OT it is Aaron who does it. Thus, in order to accomplish his literary aims, Josephus so edits the Biblical account that eventually there is a huge discrepancy between the OT and his own account of the same.

Further, in Josephus' characterisation of Moses, we also notice a tendency to subordinate the miraculous powers to morality, paralleling Graeco-Roman philosophers and Philo.

Josephus' Characterisation of Moses

For Josephus Moses is a sage, a lawgiver, a miracle worker, a prophet, a military genius and most of all, a divine man (*Antiq*. III.7.7.[180)—a paradigm of virtues (*Apion*, II.16.[153]). His leadership, not his miracles, demonstrates his piety and virtue; it is a means of providing lasting welfare for the Israelites (*Apion*, II.17.[159]). This was possible, because God was his counsellor (*Apion*, II.17.169) who made his prophecies reliable (*Apion*, II.40.[286]). The ultimate demonstration of Moses' virtuous life is the timeless relevance of his laws (*Apion*, II.39.[279]); actually they are God's laws (*Antiq*. III.6.3.[85-87]) that display his majesty, (*Antiq*. III.6.3.[85]). As such, they prove Moses' semi-divine status (*Antiq*. III.7.7.[179-80]). Therefore, he was the noblest of the Hebrews in terms of intellect and contempt of toils (*Antiq*. II.10.6.[229]). His miracles[52] demonstrate that he was God-sent; that he did everything solely according to God's commands; that God was intervening on Israel's behalf; and that he always takes his side with God (*Antiq*. III.13.1.[298]). Ultimately, it is Moses' virtue, not miracles, that ensures God's continued protection (*Antiq*. III.4.1.[69]). In Josephus, even where Moses' miracles are highlighted, it is not Moses, as miracle worker who occupies the centre-stage, but God. [53].

Thus, in Josephus Moses the epitome of virtue is highlighted more than Moses the miracle worker, illustrating Josephus' tendency to subordinate the teratological powers to virtues and wisdom—a tendency paralleling Graeco-Roman philosophical and Philo's approaches to the miraculous. For Josephus, miracles are important but only next to virtues and wisdom. However, despite his subordinating tendency, he does show the miraculous as pointing to the supremacy of God.

---

52 *Antiq*. II.12.3.(272-74); II.12.4.(276); cf. Ex. 4:2-9.

53 Cf. MacRae, "Antiquities", 42.

Demonstrative

In his portrayal of Moses' miracles, Josephus has already pointed out their divine providence.[54] Miracles, in Josephus, are a demonstration of God's work (*Antiq*. II.16.4.[345-46]); they are invitations to rely on his providence (*Antiq*. II.13.1.[280]; *War*, VI.6.4.[310]). His acts in history emphasise that only he can save (*Antiq*. II. 16.1.[334-37]). The notion present in different miraculous events is "God watches over the common welfare of all" (*Antiq*. II.9.3.[215]; *War*, VI.5.4.[310]). Thus, for Josephus, *a miracle is an act of God's providence and salvation*.

Reactions to the Miraculous

The demonstration of God's centrality, his acts, and his providence in miraculous ways arouses *astonishment* (*Antiq*. II.13.1.[279-80]), horror, and disquiet (*War*, I.9.3.[188]). Pharaoh, for example, is amazed and becomes restless after his dreams (*Antiq*. II.5.5.[82]). Josephus himself marvels at God's dealings with Esther (*Antiq*. XI.6.11.[268]). Similarly, Petronius of Syria is amazed at God's providence over the Jews (*Antiq*. XVIII.8.6.[286]). God's intervention can also arouse *consternation*. The Syrians are dismayed at the divine act in the story of Elisha (*Antiq*. IX.4.4.[58]). Thus, in Josephus even human reactions to the miraculous are a realisation of God's centrality. However, it is not clear whether these reactions mean anything more than this.

Moreover, in Moses' confrontation with Pharaoh, Josephus illustrates that miracles should ideally lead to believing in Yahweh, but they are ultimately ineffective to instil such a response.[55] Moses tells Pharaoh that the miracles God had shown him are intended to inspire faith in his commands and that unbelief thwarts God's purposes (*Antiq*. II.13.2.[283]), but Pharaoh discredits Moses' signs as deceptive and rejects their divine origin (*Antiq*. II.13.3.[284-85]). Moses tries to make Pharaoh understand that he is not dealing with another magician, but with God himself (*Antiq*. II.13.3.[286]). It was neither Moses, nor his staff that are the agents of the plagues; they happened at God's behest (*Antiq*. II.14.1.[294]; II.14.2.[296]; II.14.4.[304-306]). But Pharaoh totally refuses to believe (*Antiq*. II.14.3.[302]). This ultimate powerlessness of miracles to induce faith in Yahweh could, perhaps, be one reason why Josephus subordinates them to virtues, as seen earlier.

---

54 *Antiq*. II.12.3.(272-74); II.12.4.(276); III.13.1.(298).

55 See Sir. 48:12-15.

Thus, in Josephus, miracles do originate from God and demonstrate his centrality and the way he intervenes in the lives of his people; however, they are secondary to virtues/wisdom since ultimately they cannot induce faith.

Summary

In the Graeco-Roman world three significant strands of thought concerning the miraculous coexist: causal explanations (represented by historians), acceptance of the miraculous as divine mediums (popular position), and its subordination to virtues/wisdom (represented by philosophers). By contrast, the miraculous in the OT is solely God's act that always demonstrates his power and providence. Philo and Josephus, on the other hand, while not rejecting *a priori* the possibility of miraculous happenings, focus more on virtues and wisdom than on external teratological displays. In sum, we notice the miraculous playing a dual role. First, it adds a divine perspective to the external world and events and, secondly, it plays a secondary or subordinate position to virtues and wisdom. In the following section we explore Luke's perspective on the miraculous in Acts against this background.

THE MIRACULOUS IN ACTS

The Table of Miracles in Acts given early in this chapter shows the presence of the miraculous throughout Acts, occurring through both divine and human agency.[56] This, as H.C. Kee observes, is evidence that Luke wants to demonstrate to his readers that at every significant point in the progression of the apostolic witness towards its final destination, God is at work.[57] On this basis, we may form two propositions: a) Luke's concern is primarily to show God in action and b) miracles are important to him only insofar as they serve this purpose.

---

[56] Writings on the miracles in Luke's writings abound: H. van der Loos, *The Miracles of Jesus*, (NovTSup.; Leiden: Brill, 1965); C.F.D. Moule (Ed.), *Miracles*; C. Brown, *Miracles and the Critical Mind*, (Grand Rapids: Eerdmans/Exeter: Paternoster, 1984); H.C. Kee, *Medicine, Miracle and Magic in New Testament Times*, (Cambridge: CUP, 1986). See also G.W.H. Lampe, "Miracles and Early Christian Apologetic" in Moule (Ed.), *Miracles*, 205-18; idem, "Miracles in the Acts of the Apostles", in Moule, (Ed.), *Miracles*, 65-78; Gail Smith, "Jewish Christian and Pagan Views of Miracle Under the Flavian Emperors", *SBLSP* 20, (1981), 341-48; H. Remus, "Does Terminology Distinguish Early Christian from Pagan Miracles?", *JBL*, 101, (1982), 531-51; J. A. Hardon, "The Miracle Narratives in the Acts of the Apostles", *CBQ*, 16, (1954), 303-18; F. Neirynck, "The Miracle Stories in the Acts of the Apostles, An Introduction", in Kremer, *Les Actes*, 169-213 and P.J. Achtemeier, "Lukan Perspective", passim.

[57] Kee, *Miracle in the Early Christian World*, 220; Cf. J. A. Hardon, "Miracle Narratives", 311.

The Table of Miracles shows how frequently Luke introduces healing miracles, visions, angelophanies, and Theophany in the apostolic mission. Peter's Pentecost discourse, for instance, prophetically anticipates future miracles and signs (2:17-19).[58] It begins with Luke's citation of Joel (3:3 [LXX]), which performs two functions here. First, it establishes continuity between the present and the past—between Luke's narrative and an OT prophecy. Joel had prophesied that on the last day God would perform τέρατα and σημεῖα. By citing this prophecy at Pentecost (2:17-21), Luke implies that the descent of the Spirit is one such τέρας and σημεῖον that God himself is performing as prophesied by Joel earlier. The continuity-motif here establishes at the outset God as the sole cause of the miraculous. Secondly, Joel's prophecy creates an internal Prophecy-Fulfilment scheme, anticipating what Luke summarily states—wonders and signs were being performed by the apostles in 2:43.[59] This summary statement is also prophetic, in that, hereafter miraculous elements such as healing, visions, Theophany, and angelophanies will be an inevitable part of the apostolic mission.

As the Table of Miracles (Row 1, Column I) shows, the first missionary activity of the apostles, following Pentecost, begins with a series of miracles by Peter (3:1-10; 9:32-42). Besides him, except for James, the brother of Jesus, many other important characters also perform miracles. Stephen's mission is characterised by powerful acts (6:8); Philip's Samaritan mission is full of signs and wonders (8:4-7,13); and Paul's mission is also characterised by miracle working (13:4-12; 14:8-10; 16:16-18; 19:13-20; 20:7-12; 28:1-6, 7-8). Even Barnabas (along with Paul) performs miracles (14:3; 15:12). The apostles heal (3:1-10; 9:10-19 [22:12-16]; 9:32-35; 14:8-18; 28:7-10), exorcise (16:6-24), and raise people from death (9:36-42; 20:7-12).

Although all these Lucan characters perform miracles, it is God who really performs them all; the apostles perform miracles only in Jesus' name and with the same God-given power that Jesus had (2:22; 3:12ff.; 4:7ff.; 6:8; 16:17; 19:11). Stephen's signs and wonders are attributed to the power (δύναμις) he possessed (6:8). It is the same power that all the disciples share (1:8; 2:33). They are the human agents through whom God performs his acts as a token of his intervention and guidance. Besides these miracles performed by human agents, as the Table of Miracles in Acts (Row II) shows, there are also

---

[58] So J. Jervell, *The Unknown Paul: Essays on Luke-Acts and Early Christian History*, (Minneapolis: Augsburg, 1984), 81.

[59] The term σημεῖα is not used in Joel 3:3 (LXX), but in Acts 2:43. Perhaps Luke alters the quotation in anticipation of the statement in Acts 2:43.

miraculous events that occur directly through divine agency (e.g., Pentecost [2:1-13], angelophany [10:3-6], and visions [10:9-16]).

True, God is the sole author of the miraculous and sometimes the human characters are his instruments, but what is a 'miracle' according to Luke? The following is a brief study of Luke's 'miracle' vocabulary in Acts and the literary roles the miraculous plays in order to arrive at its provisional definition.

The Miracle Language

A brief study of some of Luke's terms such as δύναμις, σημεῖον, τέρας, and ἔκστασις/ὅραμα/ὀπτασία which he employs as his miracle vocabulary in Acts, can help towards finding his core thought about the miraculous.

We have alluded above to Luke's frequent use of σημεῖα καὶ τέρατα. The term σημεῖον occurs quite extensively in Acts. Σημεῖον, which simply means a sign or a distinguishing mark as shown earlier, signifies, for Luke, an event that demonstrates God's intervention; it is a miracle and a portent from God (2:19,22,43; 4:16,22,30; 5:12; 6:8; 7:36; 8:6,13; 14:3; 15:12). Pentecost, for instance, is one σημεῖον that God has performed (2:19,22; 4:30; 5:12). In the same way, the miraculous is also the means by which God testifies to the word of his grace (14:3).

The related term that Luke uses in Acts is τέρας (2:19,22,43; 4:30; 5:12; 6:8; 7:36; 14:3; 15:12). While in Graeco-Roman understanding this can be any phenomenon that astounds, for Luke this is solely an act of God. It is a sign from heaven (2:19) and a demonstration of God's acts through Jesus (2:22) and his apostles (4:30; 7:36; 14:3; 15:12). As the Hellenistic popular thought holds that an ordinary event, when attributed to the gods, becomes miraculous, and also as the divine centrality held in the OT, Philo and Josephus demonstrate, Luke also sees God's hand behind the miraculous happenings. However, unlike the Graeco-Roman rational approaches to the miraculous, for Luke, its interpretation is not in the eyes of the observer, but how God reveals himself in the realm of the natural.

The other term that Luke employs in the context of the miraculous in Acts is δύναμις (1:8; 2:22; 3:12; 4:7,33; 6:8; 8:13; 10:38; 19:11). It is the potential, the power, the strength, or the ability to do something. This is the power of the Spirit given to the apostles for the express purpose of witnessing (1:8; 4:33; 6:8). Also this is the power that works wonders too. For example, the Sanhedrin asked Peter and John, after the healing of the paralytic (3:1-10), "*By what power* (δυνάμει)...*did you do this?*" (4:7). This is the same power with which God endowed Jesus to perform miracles (10:38).

Besides the 'power' to perform miracles, δύναμις can also denote the 'miracle' itself (2:22; 8:13; 19:11). It was at work in the healings that Jesus performed (2:22; 10:38), which was imparted to the disciples also to exorcise and cure diseases (6:8; 8:13; 19:11). For Luke, God is powerful and therefore, such acts are demonstrations of his power. In fact, no powerful act ever takes place, or can take place outside God's jurisdiction in Acts. Since the δύναμεις are basically his deeds, one cannot buy the power to perform (8:18-20) or counterfeit them (19:13-16).

When describing vision-scenes, Luke introduces terms such as ἔκστασις, ὅ ραμα, and ὀπτασία as part of his miracle vocabulary. But he does not employ them consistently. Sometimes he speaks of visions in terms of a heavenly voice. For instance, the angel of the Lord speaks to Philip and guides him to the Ethiopian Eunuch (8:26). Such a miraculous occurrence, coupled with a short proclamation (8:35) results in the Eunuch's baptism (8:38). Sometimes, Luke explains people's visions in angelophanic terms. An angel appears to Cornelius and instructs him to send for Peter, who would proclaim to him the message of salvation (10:3-6, 11:14).

On other occasions, Luke couples heavenly voice with light from heaven as part of his description of the vision-scene, as happened in Paul's conversion/ call experience (9:3-7; cf. 22:5ff.). Importantly, recollecting this experience, Paul later claims that Jesus appeared to him while he was in ἔκστασις and commissioned him to go to the Gentiles (22:17). In his second autobiographical reconstruction of the same experience, Paul refers to this as ὀπτασία (26:14), which is a transcendental experience given by God either to reveal himself or something else hidden hitherto.[60] Perhaps Luke implies here that Paul never realised that his conversion had such far-reaching consequences, which would not have become clear but for the vision. Similarly, Peter also experiences ἔκστασις which prepares him to meet Cornelius (10:9ff.) and plays an important role in the eventual conversion of Cornelius' household.

ὅραμα is another term that Luke employs to explain people's vision experiences. It is a vision, something that can actually be seen in contrast to imagination.[61] For instance, in a ὅραμα, a man invites Paul to come to Macedonia and preach

[60] BDAG, 717.

[61] Ibid., 718.

the word (16:9). Luke explains Paul's mission in Corinth also as a result of a ὅραμα (18:9). It might be that Luke here refers to real experiences as visions.

As is clear from the above cases, Luke's visions denote God's presence and the communication of his message. More importantly, it is also evident in all the examples shown above that through visions God orchestrates and prepares the human characters for a breakthrough in their mission towards the ends of the earth (cf. 1:8). This reinforces our earlier observation that Luke situates the early church in the climate of the supernatural.

Through this study we have gained an insight into Luke's perspective about the way the miraculous should be understood in Acts, particularly in relation to Christian witnessing. It is first and foremost God's providential act. Most importantly, all of God's acts, whatever form they might take, occur most frequently in the context of conversion. How then, does the miraculous function in Acts? To this we now turn.

Functions of the Miraculous in Acts

Demonstrative

As seen earlier, differing totally from Graeco-Roman rationalising tendencies, but coinciding with the OT, there is a thoroughgoing Theocentricity to Luke's notion of the miraculous. As shown above, all of Luke's miraculous accounts inevitably converge at the point of God's activity, particularly in the progress of the apostles' witness, demonstrating that the miraculous does not and cannot happen apart from God's own initiative. This is Luke's pattern throughout Acts.

In Luke's miracle language we have already had glimpses of how miraculous occurrences in Acts demonstrate God's providence, his presence, the communication of his will, and the way he guides his followers in their mission. Further, in his Pentecost speech, Peter declares to the narrative audience that the descent of the Spirit was not simply an attention-catcher, but the actual fulfilment of God's own promise, prophesied through the prophet (2:14-21). It is also a demonstration that God had raised Jesus from the dead (2:24) and exalted him as the Lord and Messiah (2:36). Moreover, the deeds of power and the wonders and signs that Jesus performed are portrayed as God's own acts to attest Jesus (2:22). Luke would expect this to arouse in his readers a sense of anticipation to look forward to other similar demonstrations of God's providence, particularly in the advance of the Christian witness. Therefore, while reading Peter's reaffirmation at Cornelius' house that Jesus performed miracles because "*God was with him*" (10:38), they will immediately associate it retrospectively with Peter's Pentecost speech and understand the way Luke portrays Jesus not only as the primary referent of God and his works, but also realise that both the person and work of Jesus are demonstrations of God's providence and power.

Not only do Jesus' miracles demonstrate God's activity, but the miracles performed by his followers also perform the same function of demonstrating God's providence. In the healing account of the paralytic (3:1-10), Peter announces that the healing he had performed was a demonstration that God was glorifying Jesus (v.13). As for Luke, this primacy of God is the foremost reason for the advance of the Christian witness. He demonstrates the divine origin of the word by confirming it through signs and wonders (14:3). This takes us to the consideration of the confirmative role of the miraculous in Acts.

Confirmative

Just as the miraculous in the OT confirms the proclamation of God's messengers, so too in Luke's scheme do miracles confirm proclamation.[62] They do not authenticate the miracle workers as divine, but as men of God. The apostles do not act on their own, but as God's legates (2:22; 3:8,16; 14:3,15; Cf. 1 Kgs. 17:24; 18:36b; 2 Kgs. 1:10,12); they are God-sent (4:31). The divine confirmation of the word through the miraculous is sometimes seen in the way certain obstacles to Christian witnessing are removed by invoking divine punishment. Herod had been a hindrance to the apostles and their proclamation. He "*laid violent hands upon some who belonged to the church. He had James...killed with the sword...he proceeded to arrest Peter also...When he had seized him, he put him in prison...intending to bring him out to the people after the Passover*" (12:1-5). But later "*an angel of the Lord struck him down, and he was eaten by worms and died.*" As a result, "*The Word of God continued to advance and gain adherents*" (12:23-24).[63]

Moreover, when miracles confirm the divine origin of the word, it makes proclamation more powerful and persuasive (2:37,47; 11:14). For instance, in

---

[62] Conversely, proclamation interprets the miracles. This will be elaborated in Ch. 4. See also Neil Richardson, *The Panorama of Luke: An Introduction to the Gospel of Luke and the Acts of the Apostles*, (London: Epworth, 1982), 52.

[63] Other examples are Acts 9:1-18,20,22; 13:1-13; 19:11-20.

the context of persecution, the apostles pray for power to preach God's word boldly (παρρησία). The second outpouring of the Spirit upon the apostles confirms the granting of boldness and the power to proclaim the word (4:31); the accompanying signs and wonders are its evidence (4:23-31). Here Luke shows his readers that from this moment onward, the apostolic mission would be marked primarily by bold proclamation; signs and wonders that God performs would make this possible by confirming the word. Later, following the debacle that Barnabas and Paul experienced in Lystra, Luke records their preaching ministry at Iconium (14:3). Despite the opposition from the Jewish Christians, Paul and Barnabas continue preaching the word: "*So... the Lord...testified to the word...by granting signs and wonders*" (14:3). This perhaps represents what is implicit in all other references to signs and wonders. Thus, the miraculous as a manifestation of God's power, seals apostolic proclamation as God's word. When miracles play such roles, they evoke certain reactions of wonder.

Reactions to the Supernatural in Acts

Reactions of Wonder

"Reactions of wonder", collectively express astonishment fear, terror and amazement.[64] As the Table of Miracles (Column III) shows, in Acts, reactions of wonder are expressed by terms such as θαυμάζω (2:7; 3:12; 7:31), φόβος/φοβέομαι (2:43; 5:5,11; 10:4; 19:17), ἐξίστανω/ἐξίστημι (2:7; 8:9,11,13; 12:16), θάμβος (3:10-11), ἔκστασις (3:10), διαπορέω (2:12; 5:24), ἔντρομος (16:27), and ἐκπλήσσομαι. (13:12). These terms occur in situations of healing, exorcism, deliverance miracles, and angelophanies. Sometimes amazement leads the narrative audiences to follow or give undivided attention to a person (e.g., to Simon Magus [8:9,11]). But in all the references to the reactions stated above, amazement remains just as a state of awe. It does not make a qualitative difference in the way the narrative the audience perceives and relates to the miraculous occurrence.

In most cases, the miraculous functions only as an awe-inspirer. A sense of awe falls upon people (2:43; 5:5,11) following the apostles' signs and wonders and the death of Ananias and Sapphira. Importantly, in the aftermath of the signs and wonders performed by the apostles, the audience was so awe-struck that no one even dared to join them (5:12). Here Luke's readers might notice

---

64 Gerard Theissen, *The Miracle Stories of Early Christian Tradition*, (Trans. Francis McDonah; Ed.: John Riches; Edinburgh: T&T Clark, 1983), 69-71.

that he is beginning to show the limitations of the miraculous, particularly in terms of the kind of reactions they provoke.

Besides reactions of wonder, the crowd may also applaud or praise in response to a miraculous occurrence. T. Klausner calls this an 'acclamation'[65], directed either towards a miracle or towards the miracle worker (14:11ff.; 16:30; 28:16). Acclamation of glorifying God (δοξάζων τὸν θεόν) occurs only once in Acts. In 3:1-10, following his healing, the healed man entered the temple *praising God* (v.8). In such an acclamatory response, the individual involved may realise God's own presence, and providence. In this sense it is functionally equivalent to believing or turning to God (cf. 9:35,42). However, this does not evoke a corresponding positive response in the spectators. Seeing this (v.9) the crowd is only "*filled with wonder and amazement at what had happened to him*" (v.10). Here again, we notice the inadequacy of miracles to evoke a much more favourable response in people.

Besides such acclamations of wonder, Luke also records certain titular acclamations conferred on a miracle-worker, namely ἡ δύναμις τοῦ θεοῦ (8:10), Δίος, ʼ Ερμης (14:12), and θεὸς (28:6). While, as the readers may notice, in the case of Simon Magus (8:10), Barnabas and Paul (14:12; 28:6), the narrative audiences are mistaken, this suggests the plausibility that conferring titles on different individuals was a very common practice in Luke's time and therefore, such titular acclamations may not carry any deeper significance.

It is obvious, then, that in Luke' scheme in Acts, *reactions of wonder* do not ensure a right perception of God and his work. Apparently, similar to Graeco-Roman evidence that unusual events may arouse fear and amazement, but may not contain any divine-element, Luke too thinks that similar reactions may not necessarily recognise God. Further, he highlights the insufficiency of the *reactions* of wonder by juxtaposing them against *responses* that direct people to God. This takes us to the consideration of the response of 'believing' through miracles.

The Miraculous as Leading to Believing and Turning to God

As seen earlier, in Graeco-Roman writings an anticipation of miracles could arouse confidence in the likelihood of a miracle or a realisation that a miracle had taken place. In his presentation of the encounter between Moses-Aaron

---

[65] Klausner cited in Theissen, *Miracle Stories*, 71.

and Pharaoh, Josephus showed that miracles should ideally lead to recognising God behind the miraculous, but they are ultimately ineffective to evoke such a response. By contrast, Luke occasionally presents miracles as being capable of arousing responses such as believing and turning to God (TM: Column III).

In Acts 3:1-10, the crippled man does not demonstrate 'faith' before his cure, but as a result of his healing, Peter sees in him faith (πίστις, 3:16) in Jesus' name. Similarly, the healing of Aeneas and the restoration of Dorcas' life results in many turning to (9:36) and believing in the Lord (9:42). In the Sergius Paulus episode Luke illustrates this further. The invoking of temporary blindness on Elymas by Paul (13:10f.) clearly aids the Proconsul's coming to believe, though in the context, the focus is on Paul's teaching (13:12). Likewise, the earthquake and its aftermath in Philippi pave the way for Paul's short exhortation to believe on the Lord, leading to the jailer's conversion, i.e., he had come to *believe* in God (16:34b). Thus, miracles do, can, and therefore, should evoke positive responses in people.

Luke makes clear in Acts that for him, a miracle is not merely an event attributed to God as the last option, as the Graeco-Roman historical approaches do. It is God's act, always. *It is an objective demonstration of God's power, providence, a mode of confirming Christian proclamation and a possible means of leading people to God.*

So far, we have shown that miracles do function independently of anything else to demonstrate God's providence and power, to confirm the word, and occasionally to evoke faith. However, many miracle narratives in Acts contain an internal tension. If miracles are fully capable of leading people to God, why, then, does Luke not set it as a pattern in all the conversion accounts? His reasons for this are as follows:

Miracles and Counter-Effects

We have already shown above that miracles most often provoke reactions of wonder such as θάμβος and φόβος. Further, just as Josephus showed the inadequacy of the miraculous to convince Pharaoh to believe in Yahweh, Luke also presents the miraculous as being unable to evoke a positive response always. For example, Peter and John heal a crippled man (3:1-10) and the disciples heal many others (5:12-16). They escape miraculously from prison (5:17-19). But all these arouse only fear (5:11) because of which none of the rest dared to join the disciples' company (5:13). Stephen performs powerful deeds (6:8); yet he is arrested and stoned to death (7:12,54-60), leading to a much more fierce and full-scale Sanhedrin-sponsored persecution (8:1-3). In Lystra, even after healing the paralytic, Paul is stoned till people believed he was dead (14:8-19). Similarly, his exorcism in Philippi leads to public flagellation and subsequent imprisonment (16:19ff). All these show that miracles that can and, therefore, should always lead people to God are ultimately ineffective to accomplish this. There is opposition, rejection, persecution, and even martyrdom regardless of miracles.

Luke's presentation of the miraculous in Acts so far has been both positive and negative. Positively, it shows God in action, his providence, power, the communication of his will, and his guidance to the Christian mission. We also saw that miracles can sometimes lead people to believing in and turn to the Lord, yet not every miraculous occurrence leads to conversion. Besides this limitation, they also lead to persecution, opposition and even martyrdom. What are we to conclude from such a picture of the miraculous in Acts?

Conclusion

As seen above, miracles do have their own identity and function, but can only occasionally lead people to God. What is Luke's reason for this? His portrayal of Jesus' and the apostles' ministry in Acts suggests something about his perspective and the role he envisages for the miraculous in his entire scheme.

Luke's Presentation of Jesus' Mission

In Acts 1:1 Luke refers to the task he had undertaken to do in his earlier work, i.e., to record "*all that Jesus did and taught from the beginning....*" This verse identifies two distinct aspects of Jesus' mission: doing and teaching.

In the first apostolic proclamation Peter reminds the Pentecost audience, "*Jesus...a man attested...by God with deeds of power, wonders, and signs that God did through him...*" (2:22). Later, in Cornelius' house, he emphasises that Jesus "*went about doing good...for God was with him*" (10:38). Nevertheless, beyond summarily stating that God had attested him with δύναμεις, σημεῖα καὶ τέρατα, Luke does not elaborate Jesus' miracles. However, for him, it adequately summarises the miracle-working aspect of Jesus' mission. Jesus' miracles were God's way of attesting him to his people and demonstrating his presence with him. Having shown Jesus as a miracle-worker, Luke presents Jesus also as a preacher/teacher.

In his prologue Luke juxtaposes Jesus' miracle working with his teaching (1:1). Although Luke does not elaborate the content of Jesus' teaching anywhere in

Acts, in Peter's address at Cornelius' place we get an idea of what it could have been: "*...the message* (τὸν λόγον) *he sent to the people of Israel, preaching* (εὐαγγελιζόμενος) *peace by* (διὰ) *Jesus Christ...That message spread throughout Judea, beginning in Galilee....*" (10:37a). Here Luke declares that the content of Jesus' teaching was the message of peace. Retrospectively, this is the message that Luke refers to in his preface when he talks about what Jesus taught (διδάσκειν, 1:1).

Thus, at the outset, Luke presents Jesus' ministry not as characterised by either the 'doing' or the 'teaching', but by an integration of 'both miracle-working and teaching'. Although brief, by making paradigmatic this balance between the miraculous and proclamation in Jesus' own mission, Luke sets it up as a norm for the subsequent apostolic mission. Here we gain an idea of the role Luke envisions for the miraculous—it has to function in reciprocal relationship with teaching/proclamation.

By demonstrating the balance between 'doing and teaching' in Jesus' own mission, Luke makes it an indispensable means of Christian witnessing. In Calvin's words, it is "a holy knot, which may not be dissolved."[66] By showing Jesus both as a miracle worker and as a teacher/preacher, Luke does not present an "either miracle or proclamation" situation, but a "both miracle and proclamation" balance for the ensuing apostolic mission. But does the apostolic mission itself reflect this integration?

Luke's Presentation of the Apostles' Mission

Apostles as Miracle Workers

Since the Table of Miracles (Row 1 Column 1) has adequately shown Luke's portrait of the apostles as miracle workers, we will not repeat the details here. In addition, where Luke cannot specifically record the miracles that the apostles performed, he summarily states, "*...many wonders and signs were being done by the apostles*" (2:43; cf. 5:12, etc.). Further, Luke's phrases such as "*what God had done*" through the apostles (14:27; 15:4; 21:19), διὰ τῶν ἀποστό λων (2:43) and διὰ τῶν χειρῶν τῶν ἀποστόλων (5:12) portrays the apostles as miracle workers[67], also indicating Luke's penchant to fill the apostles' mission with wonders and signs that are prophetically envisioned in 2:43. After

---

[66] Cited in C.K. Barrett, *Acts*, 1.66.

[67] Cf. J. Jervell, *Unknown Paul*, 83.

presenting the apostles as miracle workers, Luke presents them also as preachers of the word.

Apostles as Preachers of the Word

In the Table of Mandates to Witness/Proclaim/Teach, we have already shown Luke's portrayal of the disciples principally as preachers of the word. Furthermore, as shown earlier, Acts 1:8 programmatises the witnessing aspect of the apostles' mission: "*...be my witnesses...to the ends of the earth.*" The same emphasis, running through Acts as an undercurrent, is further corroborated by the following references.

5:42 Every day...they *did not cease to teach and proclaim* Jesus as the Messiah.
8:4 Those who were scattered *went from place to place, proclaiming the word.*
8:40 Philip...*proclaimed the good news to all the towns until...Caesarea.*
14:7 They *continued proclaiming the good news.*
15:35 Paul and Barnabas...*taught and proclaimed the word of the Lord.*
28:31 Paul: welcomed all...*proclaiming the kingdom of God and teaching about the Lord Jesus Christ...*

Thus, the proclamation motif that starts from the early chapters of Acts culminates in 28:31 providing a coherent structure to Luke's record of the advance of Christian witnessing towards the ends of the earth (1:8). Moreover, Luke's growth statements, interspersed throughout Acts, also portray the apostles as preachers of the word, as shown below:

6:7 "The word of God continued to spread; the number of the disciples increased... and a great many ...became obedient to the faith."
12:24 "The word of God continued to advance and gain adherents."
19:20 "The word of the Lord grew mightily and prevailed."
28:31 "proclaiming...and teaching...without hindrance."

These growth statements demonstrate the way the mandate to witness has been successfully carried out. With the arrival of Christian witness in Rome, Dibelius affirms, the promise of 1:8 is fulfilled.[68] By showing that the growth of the 'word' best expresses the fulfilment of the apostolic witnessing prophesied in

---

[68] M. Dibelius, *Studies*, 134.

1:8, Luke demonstrates that the followers of Jesus are principally preachers and only secondarily miracle workers. This contrasts with Fiorenza's claim referred to earlier that the apostles were first and foremost miracle workers.[69]

Having shown the apostles as miracle workers and as the preachers of the word, Luke portrays the apostolic mission also as the continuation of Jesus' own mission that effectively demonstrates the complementarity between miracles and proclamation.

The Complementarity between Miracles and Proclamation in the Apostolic Mission

Luke elaborately depicts the miracle-working and proclamation combination in the apostolic missionary enterprise in Acts. Although it has been shown earlier, we may repeat it here for reasons of emphasis.

	Miraculous Phenomenon		*Proclamation*
2:1-4	The appearance of tongues of fire and polyglot (=Descent of the Spirit)	2:14-36	Peter's Address to the Jerusalem Jews
3:1-10	Crippled Beggar Healed	3:12-26	Peter's Address in Solomon's Portico
8:6b-7, 13b	Philip's Signs and Wonders In Samaria	8:5a, 12a	Philip proclaims the Kingdom of God and the name of Jesus Christ
8:26,39	The angelic message to Philip; miraculous transportation	8:35	Philip proclaims to the Ethiopian Eunuch the good news about Jesus
10:3-6, 9-16,46	Angelophany; Visions to Peter; polyglot	10:34-43	Peter addresses Cornelius' Household
14:8-10	Paul heals a crippled man in Lystra	14:15-17	Barnabas and Paul's address to the Lystrans

69 Fiorenza, "Miracles, Mission", 12.

16:25-26 Earthquake	16:31-32	The Philippian jailer asked to believe on the Lord Jesus; the word of the Lord spoken

Chapters 5 and 6 in the book will demonstrate in detail from 2:1-41 and 10:1-11:18; 15:7-21 the balance and the complementarity that Luke seeks to establish between supernatural phenomena and proclamation as an effective means of Christian witnessing in Acts. Here, from the table above, we may illustrate in Philip's mission the efficacy of the miracle working and proclamation combination in Christian mission.

Philip's mission as one among the scattered, following Stephen's martyrdom, may be broadly termed "*proclaiming the word*" (8:4). First, he went to Samaria and proclaimed the Messiah, the kingdom of God and the name of Jesus (8:5,12) and the crowds *listened* to him with rapt attention (προσεῖχον: 8:6), and *saw* the signs that he did, perhaps to confirm the message proclaimed (vv.5-6). Haenchen holds that Philip performed miracles in order to establish "the superiority of the Christian miracles over the magical practices current in the area."[70] But the reality in Acts is different.

Philip in Samaria is God's messenger just as Moses was to Pharaoh; his miracles authenticate him as one and confirm his message just as they did Moses' message (cf. Ex. 7:8-12). We have already shown from the OT and from Acts that the miraculous performs three functions in the context of Christian witnessing: a) demonstrates God's providence and power; b) authenticates the messengers as God's envoys; and c) confirms the word proclaimed.

Although Luke does not explicitly articulate it, he demonstrates the effectiveness of the balance between the visual and aural phenomena in Philip's mission. While listening to Philip's words (ἐν τῷ ἀκούειν) the Samaritans witness Philip's miracles (βλέπειν τὰ σημεῖα ἃ ἐπόει: 8:6). This complementarity between listening and seeing (ἀκούειν...καὶ βλέπειν: 8:6) leads them to believe in Philip's proclamation (8:12). As shown earlier, when πιστεύειν occurs with the dative, it denotes the object of one's belief. Therefore, in the context, the focus is not on Philip the messenger, but on his message.

---

[70] Haenchen, *The Acts of the Apostles: A Commentary*, (ET; Oxford: Basil Blackwell, 1971), 308.

It is true that Luke employs προσεῖχον (8:10) to describe also the Samaritans' attraction to Simon Magus' mighty works. However, significantly, Simon's magical works (8:11) only entertain the audience, but do not lead anyone to believing or baptism (8:11b).[71] Even Simon's own believing and his baptism are purely due to his attraction to Philip's miracles (8:13). Luke does not link Simon's response to hearing the word at all. This not only confirms the superficiality of Simon's response as evidenced by the later developments in the narrative, but also our position that while miracles may evoke a semblance of faith, they cannot guarantee its depth, seriousness and continuance.

Philip's mission to the Ethiopian Eunuch (8:26-40) also illustrates Luke's predilection to pair the miraculous and proclamation. In a supernatural act, the Spirit gives Philip the exact geographical details so that he may meet the Eunuch (8:26). Later the Spirit guides Philip to go and join him (8:29). Thus, there is divine initiative, communication, and direction in Philip's mission to the Ethiopian Eunuch. This miraculous element is complemented by Philip's obedience (8:27a, 30) and proclamation to the Eunuch (εὐαγγελίσατο αὐτῷ) of the good news about Jesus (8:35), leading to the Ethiopian's baptism (8:38). Later in the same episode, the Spirit miraculously transports Philip to Azotus leading to the proclamation of the good news (εὐηγγελίζετο) to all the towns until he reaches Caesarea (8:39a, 40). These are but two examples, from Philip's mission, of Luke's demonstration of the complementarity between the miraculous and proclamation in Christian mission.

So far we have looked at some of Luke's evidence concerning the balance he establishes between the miraculous and proclamation in witnessing, both in the mission of Jesus and in the apostolic mission. In what follows we investigate Luke's narratives about Paul and his characterisation of Paul's mission.

The Miracle and Proclamation Balance in the Narratives about Paul

Since the Table of Miracles (Row 1, Column 1) shows some of Paul's miracles, we need not repeat them here. We now know Paul as a miracle worker. However, most significantly, Luke's narratives, particularly about Paul's sufferings, and Paul's own autobiographical reconstructions of his life do not mention his miracles at all. Why?

---

[71] In Acts we do not find any miracle performed simply for entertainment, unlike the *Acts of Peter* where Peter contests with Simon Magus to perform miracles simply to entertain. Cf. Montague R. James (Tr.), *The Apocryphal New Testament*, (Oxford: Clarendon, 1972), 9-15.

In all the call/conversion accounts of Paul (9:15-16; 22:15, 18-21; 26:16-18.), we find only Paul's proclamation, sufferings and persecutions (9:15; 22:15; 22:18; 26:19ff). The absence of miracles is also pronouncedly felt in his farewell speech in Ephesus (20:17-35). In the final recounting of his whole life (20:18-21), Paul recollects his sufferings (20:18), his proclamation and teaching (20:20) and the content of his proclamation—conversion and faith in the Lord Jesus Christ (20:21), but makes no reference to his miracle working at all.

Moreover, in Acts, it is Paul, the suffering missionary, and not Paul, the miracle worker, who gains primary reference. His miracle working powers abandon him totally in his sufferings. There are assassination attempts on Paul's life (9:29; 23:12ff.), torture, stoning, and persecution (14:5-6, 19-20; 16:16ff.; 20:17-38; 23:12ff.), but Paul does not stage a 'miraculous' escape. Only in exceptional cases such as an attempt on his life (14:19-20), a shipwreck (27:41-44), and snakebite (28:2ff.) is Paul spared. In Philippi, even after the earthquake, the chains falling off their hands and the prison doors flinging open (16:26-40; cf. 5:17ff.), Paul and Silas remain in prison until they are released (16:35ff.), not miraculously, but for political reasons (16:37ff.). Paul flees for life, but is not rescued (9:23f.,25; 13:50f.; 14:5-6,19,20; 22:18, etc.). In general, Paul is not spared any suffering. Luke underscores this further by applying the term πάθω only to Paul in Acts (1:3; 3:18; 9:16; 17:3.). This brief survey is evidence that miracles are not really necessary for Luke's portrait of Paul.

Further, John C. Lentz convincingly argues that what is important for Luke's depiction of Paul is not Paul's miracles, but his virtues such as φρόνησις, σωφροσύνη, ἀνδρεία and δικαιοσύνη.[72] This points back to the subordination of the miraculous to morality by the philosophically oriented in Graeco-Roman society, and in Philo and Josephus. What role, then, does Luke accord Paul's miracles?

The function that Luke envisions for Paul's miracles becomes clear when studied in conjunction with Paul's mission of proclamation. A few examples may be cited here. In the Sergius Paulus episode (13:4-12) the temporary blindness invoked on Elymas removes the obstacle to the proclamation of God's word (τὸν λόγον τοῦ θεοῦ: 13:7f.). When the hindrance is overcome, Sergius Paulus believes the teaching about the Lord (ἐπίστευσεν...ἐπὶ τῇ διδαχῇ

---

[72] Lentz, *Luke's Portrait*, Ch. 4: "Paul the Man of Virtue". See also W. E. Phipps, *Paul Against Supernaturalism: The Growth of the Miraculous in Christianity*, (New York: Philosophical Library, 1987), passim.

τοῦ κυρίου: 13:12). The overpowering divine power that belongs to the preaching is manifested through the miracle.

The miracle and proclamation combination is also presented cogently by other sayings regarding miracles. In the summary statement (14:3; cf. 4:25-31) against the resistance of the unbelieving Jews, God himself bears witness to his word by performing signs and wonders through Paul and Barnabas.

Besides situations where there is an explicit connection between the miraculous and proclamation, there are also instances where Luke juxtaposes miraculous events with proclamation, but without logical sequence. In 14:8-10, the healing of the lame man is recorded together with Paul and Barnabas' preaching (14:7). Although, this episode does not clearly illustrate the logical connection between the healing and proclamation, it does demonstrate Luke's predilection to pair them to show the importance of their unity.

Here the healing, by itself, leads to a misunderstanding, necessitating a preaching aimed at rectifying mistaken notions and highlighting divine providence and universal concern (14:11-18). This event further strengthens our stand that when removed from proclamation, miracles can mislead. Here again, the functional priority that Luke accords to proclamation over miracle working is obvious. We have already shown above the inadequacy of the supernatural phenomena to lead people to God always on their own. By contrast, earlier we demonstrated the phenomenal results accomplished when the miraculous functions in tandem with proclamation in Christian witnessing. In light of this, it will not be an exaggeration to claim that even in the Lystra-Derbe episode the presence of the miraculous and proclamation could have produced an overwhelming response from the Lystrans if not for the negative role of persuasion by the Jews (14:19).

Similarly, Paul's exorcism in Philippi (16:16-18) implicitly illustrates the connection between the word and the miracle. Here the exorcism leads to persecution and imprisonment from which there emerges a miraculous situation that leads to a proclamatory possibility and eventually to the conversion of the Philippian jailer's household (16:25-34). Likewise in 19:13-20, the routing of the sons of Sceva only serves the growth of God's word (19:20). Even the raising of Eutychus (20:7-12) shows the juxtaposition of the word and miracle (20:7). In Luke's narratives about Paul, there may or may not be a logical connection between the miraculous and proclamation, but they strongly demonstrate Luke's concern that they function together in his mission accounts in Acts. That is why even where they do not appear to follow each other logically he shows them together.

In sum, we may suggest that for Luke, Paul's miracles play *an integral and yet functionally dependent role* in his preaching and teaching. Miracles are necessary only insofar as they legitimate his proclamation[73], and prove the irresistibility of God's word.[74] In view of the inherent limitations in the miraculous seen earlier, Luke grants it a place of permanent effectiveness and sustained importance vis-à-vis conversion by placing it in a complementary relationship with proclamation.

So far we have shown that the question of divine causation, generally considered irrelevant by the historical approaches, and the subordination of the miraculous to virtues by the philosophically oriented in the Graeco-Roman world, demonstrate where Luke's distinctiveness lies. Whilst Luke adopts much of the Theocentric perspective of the OT and the Hellenistic-Jewish writings, he parts company with both Philo and Josephus in their tendency to subordinate miracles to morality.

Although Luke occasionally presents the supernatural as playing a faith-evoking role on its own, he fails to sustain such a perspective throughout Acts for two reasons, first, because of the lack of inherent ability of the miraculous always to lead people to God; secondly, because of the continued persecution of Christian preachers even in the face of miracle working. For Luke, integrating the miraculous into the Christian proclamation is the antidote to this problem. The miraculous can attain its full potential of leading people to God and assume permanent effectiveness if it functions in a reciprocal relationship with Christian proclamation. In this respect, it is both functionally dependent and at the same time crucial to demonstrate God's providence and power and confirm the divine origin of the word.

Thus, a collation of evidence proves that instead of subordinating miracles, Luke integrates them into Christian proclamation and teaching. This balance is uniquely Lucan. The miraculous and the word share together a reality that evolves out of their complementary and symbiotic functions. Luke sees no dichotomy or an "either-or" situation; rather he operates with a "both-and" principle—a reciprocity between the miraculous and the proclamation, which he demonstrates first, from Jesus' ministry and secondly, from the apostolic mission in Acts.

---

73 Also Jervell, *Unknown Paul*, 90.

74 So M.M. Adams, "The Role of Miracles in the Structure of Luke-Acts" in E. Stump & T.P. Flint, *Hermeneia and Athena: Biblical Exegesis and Philosophical Theology*, (Notre Dame, IN: University of Notre Dame, 1993), 235-72, esp. 247-52.

4

THE MISSION DISCOURSES IN ACTS

INTRODUCTION

We have thus far argued that for Luke the complementarity between the miraculous and Christian proclamation is the formula that governs Christian witnessing in Acts and which, in light of the growth statistics in Acts, has been a generally successful one. The previous chapter explored the miraculous and its literary functions in Acts. This chapter studies the literary functions of the other component of the Christian mission in Acts—the missionary speeches.

At the outset in Acts, Luke expresses the kind of mission he envisions for the apostles—witnessing to the ends of the earth, and invests it with the highest authority—divine sanction and imperative (1:8). The Table of Mandates to witness/teach/proclaim given earlier also shows the utmost importance that Luke assigns to it. Christian proclamation in Acts is not a spontaneous act of the apostles; it originates from God's own providence and advances under his own auspices.

Moreover, Luke's frequent use of terms such as εὐαγγελίζειν (5:12; 8:4,12,25,35,40; 10:36; 11:20; 13:32; 14:7,15,21; 15:35; 16:10; 17:18), κηρύσσειν (8:5; 9:20; 10:37,42; 15:21; 19:13; 20:25; 28:31.), and μαρτύρειν (6:3; 10:22,43; 13:22; 14:3; 15:8; 16:2; 22:5; 22:12; 23:11; 26:5.) in Acts also shows the supreme importance he accords to the act of proclamation. This further reiterates the position we have taken earlier that Luke accords Christian proclamation a position of functional primacy over the miraculous in Christian mission. For Luke, the apostolic mission proceeds from the word and hinges upon its proclamation. By situating miraculous events mostly in the context of preaching Luke demonstrates not only their close literary kinship but also the functional priority that Christian proclamation naturally assumes.

This chapter analyses the literary functions of the missionary discourses in Acts, particularly in light of the functions of the speeches in Graeco-Roman historiography, the OT and Josephus. This is to situate Luke's (missionary) speeches within their literary landscape in order to draw certain insights that can help understand better the literary roles that Luke's missionary speeches play in Acts.

The examples discussed under each function are not exhaustive. Only some representative illustrations are presented to highlight the different functions of the speeches, assuming that perhaps speeches elsewhere also function in much the same way. Therefore, the conclusions are generalised only in a qualified sense. They are neither dogmatic nor universal but are mere helps to understand Luke's missionary speeches and their literary roles.

As regards the description of speeches, the study proceeds from William C. West's description that speeches consist of reports, direct or indirect speeches of what was said in any particular instance and a summary statement that a discussion took place and that a decision was reached.[1]

SPEECHES IN GRAECO-ROMAN HISTORIOGRAPHY

Although for the ancients history consisted of actions and speeches, the latter are the most striking feature of writing history.[2] Most ancient historians include speeches of some sort, ranging from full-scale discourses and debates to reports, conversations, letters, messages, and other forms of verbal expression.[3] These were introduced to make history more readable, to expound the issues of the times[4], to dramatise, and to help the readers understand the events,[5] to provide an insight into the total situation, into the meaning of the historical moment concerned, and into the general ideas that are introduced to explain the situation.[6] These functions of the speeches establish beyond doubt their crucial importance to historians.

---

1 W.C. West, "The Speeches in Thucydides: A Description and Listing," in Philip A. Stadter, (Ed.), *The Speeches in Thucydides: A Collection of Original Studies with a Bibliography*, (Chapel Hill: University of North Carolina, 1973), 3-15, esp. 4.

2 D. E. Aune, *Literary Environment*, 91.

3 For Luke's speeches in relation to Graeco-Roman historiography, see Dibelius, "The Speeches in Acts and Ancient Historiography" in *Studies*, 138-55; F.F. Bruce, "The Acts of the Apostles: Historical Record or Theological Reconstruction", *ANRW*, II.25.3, (1985), 256-603.

4 Aune, *Literary Environment*, 91.

5 George A. Kennedy in his introduction to Philip A. Stadter, (Ed.), *Speeches*, xi.

6 Dibelius, *Studies*, 139-40.

Considering Thucydides as the major exponent of speech-composition and, therefore, as the appropriate representative of ancient Graeco-Roman historiography, this chapter first studies some of his speeches in the *History of the Peloponnesian War* (*HPW*) to locate their literary functions.

Stadter estimates that in *HPW* there are about 137 speeches including direct and indirect speeches, letters, dialogues, debates, and personal remarks.[7] In his preface, Thucydides claims to give a reliable account of what the original speakers needed to say to accomplish their objectives in a given situation.[8]

Sometimes speeches in the *HPW* are employed not simply to express a personal opinion, but to persuade the narrative audience for a particular course of action deemed right in the given situation.[9] Let us consider the following examples. The first one is the debate over Mytilene (III.36-49).

In the episode, Lesbos, a large island, with Mytilene as its chief city, was one of the few independent allies left and the revolt was a deadly threat to Athens. The Lesbians had depended on Spartan help, which never came. The revolt was crushed, and the Lesbians surrendered. How were they to be treated? It was for the Assembly in Athens to decide. Whatever decision results from this debate would decide not only the fate of Mytilene, but also the future relation between Athens and other states in the region.

Given this situation, Cleon, the first speaker, argues as follows: "...a democracy is incapable of governing others...leadership depends on superior strength and not on any goodwill...Let them (Mytilenians)...have the punishment which their crime deserves...Let there be no hope...held out to the Mytilenians...to forgive them...To feel pity, to be carried away by...decency...are entirely against the interests of an imperial power...As for compassion...not in the case of...our enemies...these...must be punished...pay them back in their own coin...do not grow soft just at this present moment...punish them as they deserve, and make an example of them to your other allies, plainly showing that revolt will be punished by death." (III.36-40).[10]

---

7 Stadter (Ed.), *Speeches*, 7-15.

8 Cf. *HPW*, 1.22.2

9 S. Hornblower, *Thucydides*, (London: Duckworth, 1987), 163-4. See also A.J. Woodman, *Rhetoric in Classical Historiography*, (London/Sydney: Croom Helm/ Portland: Areopagitica Press, 1988), 28ff.

10 Translations are from Rex Warner, *Thucydides. History of the Peloponnesian War*, (London: Penguin Books, 1972).

Responding to Cleon, Diodotus, the other speaker, argues: "...Haste and anger are...the two greatest obstacles to wise counsel—haste...usually goes with folly, anger...the question is not so much whether they are guilty as whether we are making the right decision for ourselves...our discussion concerns the future rather than the present...death penalty will (not) be useful to us in the future as a means for deterring other cities from revolt...the question is how Mytilene can be most useful to Athens...in human societies the death penalty has been laid down for many offences...Yet...individuals are by nature disposed to do wrong, and there is no law that will prevent it...We...should be employing moderation in our punishments...in future secure for ourselves the full use of those cities which bring us important contributions. And we should recognize that the proper basis of our security is in good administration rather than in the fear of legal penalties...the right way to deal with free people is...to take...care of them...to prevent them even contemplating the idea of revolt...those who make wise decisions are more formidable to their enemies than those who rush madly into strong action" (III.41-48).

It is not difficult to predict the audience-response to these proposals. The motion of Diodotus carried the day (III.49.2). Although it is not certain whether historically Athens continued to exercise restraint, even long since the debate, for the moment, Diodotus' speech persuades Athens to spare Mytilene. Since they have already sent the first ship with full instructions to put all the men at Mytilene to death and to sell women and children into slavery, at once they sent another warship with all speed, that they might not find Mytilene already destroyed.

In the Mytilenean debate, Thucydides presents two totally antithetical speeches before the readers, one arguing for war, and the other for peace. Cleon's speech is clever and persuasive, but since it encourages violence and the savagery of warfare, the readers might disagree with Cleon. On the other hand, Diodotus is assigned a speech that is appropriate to the occasion with long-term goals in view. He does not resort to emotionalism, but disclaims appeals to pity; and does not draw pictures of rows of bodies lying on the seashore, weeping widows and orphans being driven into captivity (contra, Josephus, *War*, II.16.4 [345-401; II.16.5 [402]). Diodotus argues his case solely on the grounds of expediency and of common sense. The occasion calls for reason and not for emotion.

The Mytilenian debate and the resultant Athenian response are not merely a record of what a particular people did in particular circumstances, but they present the readers with an analysis of human behaviour in the form of description of people's overall response to different situations. Thucydides shows Athens as impulsive, Cleon as vindictive and warmongering, and Diodotus as exhibiting political acumen and far-sightedness.

Readers might also notice here two different ways of handling speeches. Words in the mouth of a wrong person, but with rhetorical skills, can cause strife, war and destruction. By contrast, words, when handled rightly, can lead to proper decisions, and the right course of action, or at least to diplomacy. But why did Cleon and Diodotus take totally opposite positions? What were their motives behind their respective speeches? Thucydides does not resolve this mystery.

The Corinthians' speech to the Spartans (I.68-71) also demonstrates how a persuasive speech can force the hearers to an action that is sometimes even contrary to their own nature. Twice before the present Corinthians' speech, Athens had defeated Sparta in war. Now, the Corinthians convene the Lacedaemonian congress hoping to conscript Sparta against Athens, declaring that Athens had violated the previous peace pact. The success of the Corinthians' speech would initiate a new phase in war between Athens and Peloponnese as a whole. To achieve their end, the Corinthians adopt a contrast-scheme:

> "The Athenians are addicted to innovation...swiftness...in conception and execution; you have a genius for keeping what you have got, accompanied by a total want of invention, and when forced to act you never go far enough. Again, they are adventurous...daring...sanguine...your wont is to attempt less than is justified by your power, to mistrust even what is sanctioned by your judgment...there is promptitude on their side against procrastination on yours...they are swift to follow up a success, and slow to recoil from a reverse...." (I.70.1).[11]

Here the purpose of the positive portrayal of Athens and the negative characterisation of Sparta by the Corinthians is to convince Sparta that Athens is so great a power that nothing short of the qualities of the Athenians themselves can match their power. The contrastive force in the Corinthians' speech persuades Sparta to vote for war (I.88). The readers might notice here that the speech brings out the sharp contrast in the qualities of different characters and also indicates what qualities make one successful. Also, in the list of the qualities of Athens that made them successful, the readers might notice that

---

[11] Citation from Marc Cogan, *The Human Thing: The Speeches and Principles of Thucydides' History*, (Chicago/London: University of Chicago Press, 1981).

speeches can be employed to put before the hearers certain ideals and qualities that they can rise to and to imitate.

The result of the speeches discussed above clearly suggests that speeches can be an orator's powerful weapon *to influence* the listeners *and to convince* them about the rectitude of a particular course of action in a given situation. Such a persuasive force of speeches is particularly relevant to the missionary speeches in Acts where the preachers present before their audiences what they think is the right decision and right course of action when responding to Christian testimony. We shall discuss this later in the chapter.

A related function of the Thucydidean speeches is to impact on the listeners for a particular action by putting forth certain confirmative patterns of qualities, ideals, and behaviour. We alluded to this immediately above. The Corinthians' speech discussed above (I.70.1), while persuading its listeners to adopt a particular course of action, sets the qualities of the Athenians as something that the Spartans should appropriate themselves. The Corinthians praise the Athenians for their innovative thinking, swiftness in planning and executing, courage, risk-taking, optimism, illustriousness, and industriousness in warfare. At the same time, this implicitly censures the Spartans for not being like the Athenians. Although not explicit here, the Corinthians' speech suggests that speeches may perform an *epideictic function*—to praise and to blame with the hope that it would also motivate the listeners to aspire for what is praiseworthy in the speech.[12]

In the Corinthians' speech (I.68-71), the readers might also notice the way the speech motivates the hearers for particular decision and course of action by appealing to their emotions. The Corinthians' speech adroitly exploits Sparta's fear of Athens induced by the past defeats and aggravates it by frightening them that if they do not agree for war with Athens, then political freedom is beyond reach. Predictably, the eventual Spartan decision for war with Athens stems from their fear (I.88).[13] What might catch the attention of the readers of the Corinthians' speech is the way a shrewd speaker can effectively manipulate and exploit the hearers' emotions for his/her own ends. This also suggests the need

---

[12] Thucydides also shows that the epideictic function of speeches can become ineffective, particularly if it is self-praise. See *HPW*, I.73-78. For a detailed analysis of this speech see A.E. Raubitschek, "The Speech of the Athenians at Sparta", in Stadter, (Ed.), *Speeches*, 32-48.

[13] The evocative function of the speeches can also be illustrated from the Melian Dialogue (*HPW*, V.85-113).

for the speaker to be sensitive to the audience-situation and their emotional make up.[14]

Summary

The Thucydidean speeches discussed above suggest certain possibilities for speeches in any context. First, speeches, when introduced in the course of ordinary events, serve to highlight the importance of the moment and the active participation of the characters in the movement of these events. Secondly, speeches also betray the mindset of the speakers, influenced particularly by behind-the-scenes factors, in order for the readers to reconstruct a total situation from what is spoken. In this sense, the readers are at an advantageous position over the narrative audience. For instance, since Athens had defeated Sparta twice before, it would never expect Sparta to join any enemy coalition. Therefore, it might come as a surprise to Athens when it learns that Sparta has joined the enemy camp. Here, the readers have an edge over the narrative audience, i.e., the Athenians, for they do not know what has transpired. But the readers know about the Corinthians' speech (I.68-71) and the role it played in persuading Spartans to decide for war. Thus, the author constructs his plots, shaped by speeches, in such a way as to provide a privileged knowledge to his readers to understand what happens in the present moment, what has led to it and how events are likely to unfold in future, etc. Thirdly, speeches can be powerful weapons to impact on the audience to decide for a particular action by praising certain virtues and censuring some other qualities and by appealing to emotions.

Speeches, in general, demand a response from the hearers by setting before them certain imitable patterns of behaviour. However, this may not be the case always. Sometimes, they present only evaluative situations. In Thucydides' political speeches the readers may not necessarily find any emulative patterns, but only evaluative. They may evaluate the response of the narrative audience to the speeches and pass a judgement whether or not, under the circumstances, the speeches have led to right decision and right choice. Thus, through the speeches, the author may place before the readers either emulative patterns of choice, decisions, and behaviour or evaluative patterns. The relevance of these conclusions for Luke's missionary discourses will become clear later in the chapter.

---

[14] See Henry R. Immerwahr, "Pathology of Power and the Speeches in Thucydides" in Stadter, (Ed.), *Speeches*, 16-31, esp. 31.

The Thucydidean model of speeches and their functions within Hellenistic historiography do not compare with the speeches in the OT. The former are political in nature, with no one particular theme unifying them all together, whereas the latter are religious in nature, and, therefore, its speeches, if any, would be totally different in their content and functions from Thucydidean speeches. The following section looks at some of the speeches from some books of the OT in order to identify their literary functions.

SPEECHES IN THE OLD TESTAMENT

Luke's speeches in general may fall within the Graeco-Roman historiographical conventions, but his obvious use of the OT in direct quotations, probable allusions and implicit references, the contents, and the Septuagintal tone of the language of the (missionary) speeches in Acts, indicate a definite affinity between them. Therefore, it will be instructive to study the OT speeches.

One problem that we encounter in the OT is a lack of speeches in historical passages. Instead, most often it records prayers such as Solomon's prayer of dedication (1Kgs. 8:22-53), and Ezra's prayer (Neh. 9:6-37), which function to recount Israel's history and interpret it for the audience present. Despite this paucity of speeches, Marion L. Soards, citing Martin Noth[15], identifies at least four speeches in the OT, namely the speeches by Moses (Deut. 1:6-30:20); Joshua (Josh. 23), the unnamed prophet (Judg. 6:8-10), and Samuel (I Sam. 12:25).[16]

These few speeches in the OT highlight themes such as the authority of the Lord, his commandments, and warning against disobeying them.[17] Noth observes that in these speeches, there is a "tendency towards a systematic theological interpretation of history."[18] According to him, the theme of divine retribution contained in the speeches of the Deuteronomistic History unifies the different periods of Israel's history. We proceed from this premise.

The first of these speeches by Moses (Deut. 1:6-30:20) functions as a reminder. It first recounts the historical events (1:6-3:29) and then proclaims the Deuteronomic law (4:1-30:20), and finally it recollects God's dealings with his

---

[15] M. Noth, *The Deuteronomistic History*, (JSOTSup. 15; Sheffield: JSOT Press, 1981).

[16] Cf. M.L. Soards, *The Speeches in Acts: Their Content, Context, and Concerns*, (Louisville: Westminster/John Knox, 1994), 144.

[17] Cf. G. A. Kennedy, *Classical Rhetoric in Its Christian and Secular Tradition from Ancient to Modern Times*, (London: Croom Helm, 1980), 140.

[18] M. Noth, *Deuteronomistic History*, 30.

people, their disobedience towards God, and their refusal to respond to Moses' entreaty (cf. Num. 13-14) and, therefore, the ensuing punishment. This retrospective summary of the events of the Mosaic period concludes with the proclamation of the law.

Joshua's speech in Josh. 23 follows much the same course and performs the same function as Moses' speech. Coming at the end of the era of the occupation of the land, it recounts the great events now at an end and warns the people of the gods and cults of the lands occupied, and concludes with a warning about divine retribution in the case of disobedience to him (cf. Deut. 4:25-28, esp. v.26).

The third speech (Judg. 6:8-10) by an unidentified prophet similarly warns against apostasy that issued in external affliction (v.1). The prophet points out that the Israelites cannot expect God's saving activities while continuing to disobey him (vv.6b-10). Finally, Samuel's valedictory address (1Sam. 12) reminds the audiences of what God has done, i.e., the Exodus. He emphasises that despite their ungodly demand for a king, the audience can still choose between obeying God and disobedience and thus, between preservation and total annihilation.

Noth concludes that through these speeches the

> "Deuteronomist...intended it to teach the true meaning of the history of Israel...that God was recognisably at work in this history, continuously meeting the accelerating moral decline with warnings and punishments and, finally, when these proved fruitless, with total annihilation."[19]

Thus, from the few speeches in the OT and from their function, the readers notice that speeches can be employed to summarise the history of past events and draw lessons for the present and future by Theologically explaining past occurrences. By constructing a consistent or unified picture of God and his acts in the realm of his people, speeches encourage hearers to learn lessons from the past so that their lives might be marked by new beginnings, particularly in relation to God.

Therefore, speeches can be instrumental in imparting a particular worldview and certain values appropriate to that worldview by evoking a definite response that is deemed appropriate in light of that worldview. In addition, they provide the readers with a hermeneutical key to interpret events theologically, both present and future, in light of God's purposes.

---

[19] Ibid., 89.

However, the readers might also notice in the speeches above the one-way communication—communication through speeches, but with no corresponding direct audience-response. None of the main speeches, identified by Soards and others persuade the hearers to act. By contrast Joshua's speech in ch. 24 recounts Israel's past history (vv.2-13) and exhorts people to serve God faithfully by putting away the gods that their ancestors served (vv.14-15,19-20, 23). This affects the audience in the desired way. They repeatedly respond saying "*Far be it from us that we should forsake the LORD to serve the other gods*" (vv.16-18,21,24). This is perhaps the only OT example of a favourable audience-response to a speech.

The unifying function of the speeches in the OT on the basis of one central concept of God's dealings with his people and the encouragement for the hearers to learn lessons from the past, sets a literary precedent for the missionary speeches in Acts. This will become clear when discussing the literary functions of the missionary speeches in Acts later in the chapter. The following section examines some of Josephus' speeches and their literary functions and draw some insights that might further clarify the literary roles that Luke's missionary speeches play in Acts.

SPEECHES IN JOSEPHUS

Following his contemporary Graeco-Roman historiographical conventions, Josephus freely introduces speeches into his narratives, even speeches by non-Jews in praise of Yahweh.[20] Josephus' *Jewish War* alone contains nearly 59 direct speeches, 45 incomplete or virtually complete sections; the remainder are brief sayings or dialogues within the paragraph.[21] We shall study here only some representative speeches from *War* to identify their literary functions that might serve as points of comparison for the study of Luke's missionary speeches in Acts.

In Josephus' speeches persuasion plays a prominent role. In fact, the term πείθω occurs very widely in his writings.[22] We shall study two speeches from

---

[20] For instance, Josephus, *War*, VI.1.5.(39-41). Also *Antiq*. I.13.3.(228-31); II.6.8.(140-58; cf. Gen. 44:18-34), etc.

[21] Colin J. Hemer, *The Book of Acts in the Setting of Hellenistic History*, (Tübingen: Mohr, 1989), 417.

[22] There are about 497 references to πειθώ in Josephus' writings (*War*, 134 + *Antiquities*, 306 + *Life*, 39 + *Against Apion*, 18).Cf. K.H. Rengstorf, (Ed.), *A Complete Concordance to Flavius Josephus*, (Leiden: Brill, 1979), 366-70.

Jewish War where the persuasive intent is very clear.[23] The first of them is Agrippa's speech to the Jews.

Agrippa's speech to the Jews (II.16.4.[345-401]) is made at a time of suffering and of hatred towards the Roman procurator Florus, who had abused his authority, persecuted his subjects, and had caused widespread destruction in Jerusalem. Subsequently, the Jews pressure Agrippa to send an emissary to Nero in order to depose him. In his speech, Agrippa tells the Jews that this could be construed as rebellion against Nero. Therefore, if they want to prove to the Emperor that they are not rebellious, they must rebuild the gates and pay taxes. He argues that their accusations against Florus do not justify war. Moreover, if the other nations, much stronger than the Jews, could not resist Rome, how can Jews, as a small state, resist the military might of the Roman Empire?

To bolster his political arguments, Agrippa presents some religious arguments to dissuade the Jews from war. The Jews must submit to Rome because there is no help from God himself. He has taken the side of Rome and has abandoned the Jews. Moreover, the Jewish religion itself teaches to hope in God rather than take up arms; failing this would further distance God from them. The impending danger of the Jews is everywhere; their defeat is sure. Therefore, the only escape from the imminent utter destruction is to give up war. The finale of Agrippa's speech is the emotional touch he adds to his speech by asking the Jews to have pity on their children, their wives, their city, and their temple.

The immediate response of the Jews to Agrippa's speech and his final emotional appeal[24] was very positive. People go back and rebuild the cloisters of the temple and pay taxes (II.17.1 [405]). Thus, Agrippa is able to avert the imminent war (II.16.5.[406]).[25] Here, the *persuasive* intent and *function* of Agrippa's speech and its positive outcome is very clear. This recollects the persuasive function of the Thucydidean speeches, particularly, the one by Diodotus, which similarly tried to persuade the narrative audience to abstain from war (*HPW*, III.36-49). Agrippa's speech also alerts the readers to the consequences of war had the Jews continued to rebel. Obviously, they will approve that, under the circumstances, the Jews have listened to Agrippa and rightly decided against war with Rome.

Agrippa's speech also provides the readers with the privileged knowledge that the immediate narrative audience lacks. The Jews may never know why

---

[23] See Josephus' own speech in *War*, V.9.3-4 (362-419) for a similar persuasive function.

[24] Even Agrippa and his sister wept at the end of the speech (*War*, II.16.5.[402]).

[25] In the long run, however, the Jewish warmongers did take the Jews to war (*War*, 16.5.[408ff.]).

Agrippa had been so keen on averting this war with Rome. But the readers might suspect that Agrippa had vested interests behind his speech. In order to gain some personal favours from Nero, later Agrippa could have informed the Caesar about the Jewish intention to send a delegation to depose Florus, and that he had dissuaded them by praising Rome's might in his speech. Thus, through the speeches, the readers gain an insider's view of events behind the curtain and can make some intelligent assumptions about things not explicit in the narrative.

Eleazar's speech at the fortress of Masada (*War*, II.8.6. [323-36]) also demonstrates the power of a persuasive speech, but negatively. He makes this speech when the whole region of Judea was under the Roman rule except for the fortress of Masada, occupied by those who did not submit to Rome (VII.8.1. [252ff]). Therefore, the Roman governor Flavius Silva lay siege to the fort (305ff.).

In his speech Eleazar argues that since God is on the side of Rome (VII.8.5. [318-19]), the only solution is mass suicide; the Romans will show no pity. Eleazar reasons that Jews could serve no one else, except God; now he gives them the opportunity to die freely (VII.8.6.[323-26]); the end of the Jewish race is God's will (VII.8.6.[327-32]). Therefore, they should die with honour rather than submit to Rome (VII.8.6.[333-36]).

When Eleazer's call for mass suicide fails to appeal to his audience, he argues on philosophical grounds. The soul is immortal (VII.8.7.[340]); God has sentenced the Jews to destruction (VII.8.7.[358-59]); they were born to die (VII.8.7.[381]). They should die together before seeing their women outraged and their sons and daughters killed (VII.8.7.[382-88]). At the end of Eleazer's speech the audiences have been so fully persuaded that they

> "made haste to do the work, as full of an unconquerable ardor of mind, and moved with a demoniacal fury...endeavoring to be before another...thinking that this eagerness would be a demonstration of their courage and good conduct; so great was the zeal they were in to slay their wives and children, and themselves also!" (VII.9.1.[389]).

Finally, except for an old woman and five children, nearly nine hundred and sixty people were massacred *en masse* (VII.9.1.[399-400]). In Eleazar's speech, the power of persuasion, though negative, is very clear, yet readers may be able to assess Eleazer's theology and the mob psychology. Reading Eleazer's speech, particularly in light of their prior knowledge of the way God had dealt with the Jews in the OT, they would know that he had been dealing with them in providence; they may also recollect all his salvific deeds, particularly the

Exodus. Now that Eleazer paints a picture of complete dereliction by God, the readers would know that he is misrepresenting the truth of God's providence.

Eleazer's speech also explains to the readers why the people at Masada committed mass suicide, and obviously they will not approve of it. This challenges the readers, particularly with oratorical skills to use them responsibly. It also gives an interpretation of the Roman victory, which the readers might accept or reject, particularly in light of the devastating consequences of war. Thus, the speech gives certain insights to the readers in whose light they may understand the story better.

Closely related to the persuasive function of the speeches is the '*aetiological*' function that inspires people to act by giving them a reason or a cause.[26] Pere Varneda illustrates this from Herod's speech (*War*, I.19.4.[373-79])[27] to the demoralised troops who suffered unexpected setbacks (I.19.2.[368]) such as defeats in war, earthquake, foreign invasion and the resultant massacre (I.19.3.[369-70]). To stir the troops to action, Herod awakens their patriotic spirit as a reason to fight (I.19.4.[376]). The Arabs have massacred their ambassadors and have broken all the pacts (I.19.4.[378]). Therefore, it is time that they now go out into battle in order to avenge their ambassadors (I.19.4.[379]).

The response to Herod's speech is overwhelming: "When Herod had encouraged them by this speech...he saw with what alacrity they went" (I.19.5.[380]). Herod's speech is specifically aimed to give the troops a reason to act and vanquish the Arab army. Later on, Josephus records the total destruction which the army had caused among the Arabs (I.19.6.[382b-85]).

The speeches from Josephus' *Jewish War* are akin to Thucydides' political speeches that we studied above. The thematic coherence of the OT speeches, missing in Thucydides, is also missing in Josephus. Josephus' speeches mainly suggest that speeches can be a rhetorical tool in the hands of an orator to persuade the audiences to opt for a particular course of action or decision deemed right according to the orator in a given situation. As is true of the Graeco-Roman (Thucydidean) speeches, Josephus' speeches also suggest a two-way process for a speech—a dialectic between communication and audience response.

---

26 Pere V.I. Varneda, *The Historical Method of Flavius Josephus*, (Leiden: Brill, 1986), 102.

27 See also Titus' speech to his army (*War*, III.10.2.[472-84]) for the same function.

Conclusion

Since the examples from Thucydides, the OT, and Josephus are limited, our conclusions are also limited and, therefore, only generalised in a limited sense. Yet, based on our brief study of these speeches, we can draw certain insights.

First, the different speeches we studied above, both political (Thucydides and Josephus) and religious (OT) in nature, demonstrate that they are crucial to understanding events, either in the present or in the past by furnishing readers with certain insights. Speeches also inform them about what is not obvious in the simple progression of the narrative and provide an alternative picture so that they may assess the information documented and based on the different perspectives given to the issue, gain an objective understanding of the story.

For instance, while reading a political debate in Thucydides, the readers, perhaps Athenian, impressed first, by the power of persuasive speech, might become critical of Athens' megalomania, particularly given the destructive power of war and the political instability it causes. They might decide that situations of armed confrontation could be avoided through political negotiations. In that respect, they might appreciate Diodotus' insight that a political crisis can be resolved and, therefore, in future can be averted, by sympathy, cooperation, and peace. They might see the pacifism here as the best solution in situations of conflict.

Further, the different choices presented to the narrative audiences demand a two-way communication process—the communication of a particular point-of-view and a corresponding audience response.[28] A mere listening to the speech is not, in and of itself, adequate. Persuasion should lead to appropriate action in the situation. These are some principles, in whose light Luke's readers might want to read his missionary speeches in Acts.

MISSIONARY DISCOURSES IN ACTS

As pointed out earlier, scholars study Luke's speeches against Graeco-Roman historiographical traditions.[29] Earlier, while not ruling out the possibility of other genres such as biography or romance for Acts, we also simply acknowledged that the book of Acts, as a historiographical writing, records

---

[28] Cf. William S. Kurz, "Hellenistic Rhetoric in the Christological Proof of Luke-Acts", *CBQ*, 42, (1980), 171-95, esp. 175.

[29] Cf. H.J. Cadbury, "The Greek and Jewish Traditions of Writing History" in *Beginnings*, II.7-29; see also idem "The Speeches in Acts", *Beginnings*, V.402-27, esp. 402.

speeches. Since there is no consensus among scholars about what constitutes a speech, there is no unanimity among them about the number of speeches in Acts. However, for the purpose of this investigation, we have already accepted William West's view that speeches consist of reports, direct or indirect speeches or what was said in any particular instance, and a summary statement that a discussion took place and a decision was taken.[30] Therefore, combining both longer and shorter ones, some scholars identify nearly thirty-six speeches[31] and some others suggest about 25 speeches in Acts.[32] The number of speeches in Acts may be disputed, but undoubtedly the missionary speeches demonstrate the exceptional premium that Luke places on the verbal articulation and the proclamation of the 'Christian faith'. Although Luke records missionary discourses to Jews (2:14-36, 38-39; 3:12-26; 4:8-12, 19-20; 5:29-32; 10:34-43; 13:16-41)[33], to the Gentiles (10:34-43; 14:14-17; 17:22-31), and defence speeches (7: 2-53; 22:1-212; 24:10-21; 26:1-23,25-27,29), our interest here is in the missionary discourses, particularly those occurring together with miraculous phenomena.

The study of speeches in Luke's literary contemporaries has provided not only a literary *topos*, but also more importantly, certain pointers as to the roles one could expect the speeches to perform. If Acts is a historiographical writing, one may expect Luke's speeches also to deepen the readers' interpretation by explaining the narrative audience and by providing the readers with hermeneutical tools for the future to understand and interpret events.[34] This does not deny the fact that at times his missionary speeches might go beyond the immediate situation in their interpretation of an event and introduce elements not obvious on the surface. This is particularly true in Acts where the miraculous phenomena mostly necessitate an interpretation.

As stated above, the scope of this section is limited to those missionary sermons that function together with miracles,[35] which, as acknowledged earlier, include

---

30 West, "Speeches in Thucydides", 4.

31 Soards, *Speeches in Acts*, 21-22. Joseph A Fitzmyer (*The Acts of the Apostles: A New Translation with Introduction and Commentary*, [AB; New York/London/Toronto/Sydney/ Auckland: Doubleday, 1997], 104) gives a list of 28 speeches.

32 Stanley E. Porter, *The Paul of Acts*, (WUNT 115; Tübingen: Mohr, 1999), 127.

33 G.E. Sterling (*Historiography and Self-Definition*, 372, n.301) erroneously classifies Peter's speech at Cornelius house (Acts 10:34-43) as a sermon to the Jews.

34 Cf. A. Stadter (Ed.), *Speeches in Thucydides*, xi; Aune, *Literary Environment*, 91.

35 These addresses may be considered missionary because they repeat not only what God has done (raising Jesus from the dead), but also they end with a proclamation of Jesus' exaltation and the saving power of his name. Most of these addresses also contain an invitation to respond to the proclamation (E.g., 2:38a; 3:19; 10:43 (?); 14:15 and 16:31) and an actual audience response (e.g., 2:38a; 4:4a; 8:12,14; 8:36-38b; 10:44-48; 16:33b-34).

one or two-line comments and Luke's summary statements.[36] Luke's smooth transition from formal addresses to summary statements shows how adeptly he adopts in his own narrative the medium of speeches.[37]

Before discussing the different literary functions of the missionary discourses in Acts, we may make some general observations on the Missionary Discourses. Cadbury suggests that the extended discourses (Discourses to the Jewish Audience: Acts 2:17-36; 3:12-26; and Discourses to the Gentiles: Acts 10:34-43) elaborate the shorter ones by supplying them with the information they lack because "they share with each other some elements...that go beyond mere style and vocabulary into the subject matter itself."[38] This is an important suggestion for the present study, for it helps the readers towards a sequential reading and consistency-building that Iser suggests.[39]

Moreover, the longer missionary speeches (2:14-36; 3:12-26; 10:34-43) tie together thematically. There are some common elements in these texts namely, *the kerygma* (a short narrative of what God has done in the person of Jesus + the culpability of the Jews + Divine-contrast scheme; *Prophecy-Fulfilment* (10:43); and *exhortation to repent and believe*). These details are missing in the shorter speeches, dialogues, and summary statements (8:5,12,35; 14:15-17; 16:31-32). Therefore, in all likelihood, Luke designs the longer speeches as 'control texts' or 'boundary texts' since they contain details that are missing in the shorter ones. By reading them together, the readers may be able to construct a total perspective by supplying from one speech the information that the other speech lacks.

The three common elements identified above in the longer speeches may often blend with each other, but they do not always occur in straightforward sequence. Each element is developed differently in each occasion. For instance, in Peter's discourse at Cornelius' house the theme of Prophecy-Fulfilment (10:43a) is not developed by supporting Scripture quotations, as in the other sermons (e.g., 2:25ff.). On the other hand, the details about Jesus' ministry that Peter develops at Cornelius' place (10:37-38) are not referred to either before or after. Although

---

36 Acts 8:4-5,12; 8:35 and 16:31-32. West ("Speeches in Thucydides", p.4) suggests that the summary statements or reports may be accepted as speeches. Also we have taken the position from the beginning that Luke's summaries are treated in the study as implying the whole speech.

37 H.J. Cadbury, "The Speeches in Acts", in *Beginnings*, V. 402-27, esp. 404.

38 Cadbury, "Speeches in Acts", V.407.

39 Iser, *Act of Reading*, 119, 148-50.

the reasons for this gap are not explicit, we may assume that in the first instance, too many scriptural quotations from the Hebrew Scriptures may not make much sense to a Gentile audience (Cornelius).[40] Likewise, in the other two instances, since the audience are the Jews, Luke seems to have simply taken for granted their knowledge of the events having transpired in relation to Jesus. Sometimes, in the context of a Gentile audience, there is no quotation from the Scriptures and the speakers replace the Jesus-Kerygma by a Theological kerygma (e.g., 14:15-17), with one exception. Unlike Paul and Barnabas in Lystra, Paul and Silas give a short Jesus-kerygma in Philippi, a totally Gentile city (16:31-32; cf. 8:35). This shows that Luke generally, but not always, endeavours to make the speeches appropriate to his audiences.

Sometimes the contents of the longer missionary speeches do not repeat themselves exactly in every instance. Even when Luke makes a similar point, for instance, the guilt of the Jews in crucifying Jesus (2:23; 3:13-15; cf. 13:27-29), he alludes to different aspects of the Jesus story in order to make the same point. This may be to avoid repetition. By looking at different themes elaborated by each speech, readers may be able to tie them together to construct a holistic perspective. Such variations are more for reasons of interest and edification of the readers than contextual.[41] We proceed now to discuss the literary functions of the missionary discourses in Acts.

LITERARY FUNCTIONS OF THE MISSIONARY DISCOURSES

Luke employs missionary discourses in order to communicate his point-of-view, to construct a unified Theo-Christocentric worldview, to interpret (the miraculous, the Scriptures, and historical events), and to persuade the hearers to a particular course of action. These may be grouped together under different functions namely, constructive, interpretative, and persuasive, each of which is discussed below.

Constructive: Theo-Christocentric Worldview

Earlier we observed that narrative criticism expects that in order to understand and appreciate fully what the implied author says, it is absolutely necessary for the reader to enter into the author's worldview and read his writings in that light.

---

40 Scriptural quotations are missing in Paul's and Barnabas' speech at Lystra as well (Acts 14:15-17).

41 Richard. Bauckham, "Kerygmatic Summaries in the Speeches of Acts", in Ben Witherington, (Ed.), *History, Literature, and Society in the Book of Acts*, (Cambridge: CUP, 1996), 185-217, esp. 186.

Therefore, we have shown that Luke constructs a Theocentric worldview for himself and also expects his readers to share the same before they journey through the conversion stories. All these come to light when we look at the contents of the apostolic testimony.

In his missionary speeches, Luke constructs a coherent Theocentric worldview by showing consistently who God is, his dealings with Jesus, and what he continues to do through the apostles. This resembles the way the few speeches in the OT collectively construct a unified picture of God and his acts.[42] That Luke's missionary speeches also play the same sort of role becomes clear when we look at the emphases that the missionary speeches place on God and his works in Acts. Before illustrating this from the narrative framework of Acts, it may be helpful to illustrate Luke's portrait of God in the missionary speeches and locate his operative worldview with an analytical layout of the Missionary Speeches.

God's plan	2:23				
God attested Jesus	2:22	3:20		10:38	
God raised Jesus	2:24,32	3:15,26		10:41-41	
God exalted Jesus as Lord and Messiah	2:33,36	3:13	8:5	10:42	
God fulfils his promises, (prophesied by the prophets)	2:16-21,29	3:18,20, 24-25		10:43a	
God, the object of turning/believing	2:38	3:19		14:15a	16:34
The kingdom of God			8:12		
God offers forgiveness of sins in Jesus' name	2:38			10:43b	
God is impartial				10:34-35	
His message of peace				10:36-37	
God, the Creator					14:15b
Creation attests to God					14:17a
God is beneficent					14:17b

Here Luke constructs for his readers a thoroughgoing Theocentric worldview within which they could view conversions solely as an act of God. It is God's

[42] Cf. Kennedy, *Classical Rhetoric*, 140.

will and providence that regulates everything, especially the progression of Christian witnessing to the ends of the earth (1:8).[43]

Secondly, as shown above, people turn to God only as a result of God's acts. Luke expresses this through terms such as the ἡ βουλή τοῦ θεοῦ (2:23), δεῖ (3:21; 16:30)[44], and ὁρίζω (2:23; 10:42) in order to demonstrate that God intervenes in human affairs to accomplish his will for universal salvation, to initiate new relationships, and to guide into the future.[45] Although God is not an overt character in the conversion narratives, his presence is ubiquitous. We may illustrate this from two conversion accounts—the Cornelius story (10:1-11:18) and Paul's and Barnabas' experience in Lystra (14:8-17).

Although it was God's plan and mandate that Christian witness should reach the ends of the earth (1:8), the early chapters of Acts show that the disciples were at first confined to Jerusalem. Although the descent of the Spirit (2:1-13) was to empower them to embark on a worldwide mission of witnessing (cf. 1:8), nothing seems to be happening in that direction. It took factors such as persecution to force the disciples out of Jerusalem (8:1-4). In preparation for the centrifugal movement of Christian witnessing, God had to use visions in order to transform human the (i.e., Jewish Christian) thinking to accomplish the conversion of Gentiles.

In the Cornelius story (10:1-11:18; 15:7-21), God testifies to Gentile conversion through visions; he uses them to bring Cornelius and his household into the community of his people. While recounting his earlier experience before the Jerusalem plenary session, Peter's sole point of reference was the way ***God*** had led both him and Cornelius through visions, the message of salvation that was preached, and the descent of the Spirit on Cornelius' household (11:1-17). At its conclusion, the narrative audience says, "***God** has given even to the Gentiles the repentance that leads to life*" (11:18)." The conversion of Cornelius' household was first and foremost God's doing. Later, in the Jerusalem Council Peter again lists what God had been doing: "*...**God** made a choice...that...the Gentiles would hear the message of good news and become believers. And **God**...testified...by giving...the Holy Spirit...cleansing their hearts by faith...made no distinction...*"

---

43 H. Conzelmann, (*Theology*, 131-32): "The idea of God's plan...underlies the whole structure of Luke's account."; Also Tannehill, *Narrative Unity*, 1.xiii, 1,2.

44 For a detailed study on this see Cosgrove, "Divine ΔΕΙ", *NovT*, 26, (1984), 168-90; S.S. Smalley, "The Christology in Acts Again" in B. Lindars and S.S. Smalley, (Eds.), *Christ, Spirit in the New Testament: Essays in Honour of C.F. D. Moule*, (Cambridge: CUP, 1973), 79-93, esp. 88-92.

45 Cadbury, *Making of Luke-Acts*, 303.

(15:7-9). James, in his speech, reaffirms this: "...***God***...*looked favourably on the Gentiles, to take from among them a people for his name*" (15:14). The outpouring of the Spirit by God—the second supernatural phenomenon in the Cornelius story—(10:44-47; cf. 2:1-14) implies all these things. But this truth would have remained hidden to the narrative audience had not Peter's speech constructed such a consistent picture of God and his acts. Even here, the readers have an advantage over the immediate audience. Since they have the whole text and all the missionary speeches before them, they can see the way Luke constructs a coherent picture of God and his acts, whereas, the narrative audience gains insight into what happens only as much as the preacher informs them.

Likewise, in their speech at Lystra (14:15-17), following the healing of a paralytic, Paul and Barnabas proclaim God as the Creator and his concern for all the nations, seen particularly in his divine beneficence and patience. The Lystrans may have reduced God to idols, but when they turn to the living God, they will realise that he had always been there as the source of their sustenance and succour. Creation and all that they receive from God attest to his existence and his universal goodness. Significantly, the Lystrans are asked to abandon their worthless idols and turn to this living God (14:15).

Interestingly, Peter does not paint such a picture of God in his missionary speech at Cornelius' house. Conversely, in Lystra, Paul and Barnabas do not portray God as Peter does in Caesarea. Such a difference may be a literary technique, but it is possible for the readers to see that Luke is trying to adapt himself to the audience's needs and also to construct, through his missionary speeches, a consistent and thematically coherent picture of God. This coherence is made possible, not by repeating the same details everywhere, but by explaining different details in different texts and expecting the readers to put them together to construct a unified picture.

While constructing a coherent, unified Theocentric worldview, Luke invariably introduces, what may be called, the Jesus-Kerygma, which is an integral part of the way missionary speeches construct a consistent picture of God. Luke's intention here seems to be to add Christological specifics to his general presentation of God. We briefly develop this below.

Constructive: Kerygmatic

Invariably, all the missionary discourses (barring 14:15-17) contain some Christological specifics, both explicitly and implicitly, that point to God and his acts. Luke focuses on Jesus so much that Marion Soards observes, "The activities of the early church are an extension of what God did in Jesus Christ."[46] For Luke, Jesus is the prism through which humans can see God fully. A review of Luke's characterisation of Jesus will help locate the importance he accords to him in his overall Theocentric worldview.

Jesus attested by God	2:22b						
Worked Miracles	2:22c			10:38b			
Crucified	2:23	3:15		10:39b	13:27-29		17:3a
Raised from dead	2:24,31-2	3:13a		10:40	13:30-31		17:3b,31b
Exalted	2:23a						
Received the Spirit	2:33b,34b						
Lord and Messiah	2:36b		8:5		11:20		17:3c
Glorified by God		3:13					
Saviour						13:23	
Forgiveness of sins/ Freedom from sin through him				10:43		13:38, 39	
Anointed by God				10:38,42			
Preacher of peace				10:35			
Judge	2:35			10:42			17:31a
Object of conversion	2:21	4:12	9:35, 42		16:31		

The aspects of Luke's Christology becomes clear in three ways: a) they witness to the fact of Jesus' public ministry (Acts 1,2, and 10); b) to character, i.e., the holiness and righteousness of the life of Jesus (e.g., 3:14) and the positive works of healing and benevolence that flow from it (e.g., 10:38), and c) the Christian faith—a testimony to lead Jews and Gentiles to faith in Jesus, the Lord (cf. 10:36-43).

As shown here, for Luke, the roles that Jesus assumes and the deeds he performs are appropriate to his exalted status as the Lord and Messiah (2:36). Joel's prophecy (3:1-5 [LXX]) crystallises Israel's hope of salvation on the Day of the LORD and records that this should be preceded by signs and wonders. Pentecost, as a sign and fulfilment of what Joel had prophesied (2:16ff.), signifies the exaltation of Jesus as the Lord and Messiah (2:36). Therefore, everyone who calls on him shall be saved (2:21; cf. 16:31). For Luke, this is the

---

[46] Soards, *Speeches*, 188.

only way to salvation (4:12), which, in Luke's scheme, is available to everyone, to Jews and to πάντα τὰ ἔθνη as well. See, for instance,

2:21 πᾶς ὃς ἐὰν ἐπικαλέσεται τὸ ὄνομα Κυρίου σωθήσεται
10:43 πάντα τὸν πιστεύοντα εἰς αὐτόν
15:11 διὰ τοῦ χάριτος τοῦ Κυρίου Ἰησοῦ πιστεύομεν σωθῆναι
16:31 πίστευσον ἐπὶ τὸν κύριον Ἰησοῦν καὶ σωθήσῃ σὺ καὶ ὁ οἶκός σου

The references above show that salvation is freely available to anyone who believes. That πᾶς ὁ πίστευων includes Gentiles also is clear by the appearance of the same phrase in Peter's speech at Cornelius' place (10:43), where it refers to the inclusion of the Gentiles in the blessings of salvation.

The Missionary Discourses to the Jews show that for Luke salvation consists in the forgiveness of sins. In Acts 2, Luke promises "*forgiveness of sins*" (2:38) to those who undergo a repentance-baptism. The same idea runs through in Peter's Temple Speech and in his speech at Cornelius' house (e.g., 3:19; 10:43.). In some places, "Forgiveness" appears in apposition with or as a synecdoche for salvation (4:10-12//10:43; 10:43//11:14; 5:31).[47] Thus, forgiveness of sins, for Luke, is the content of salvation in Acts.[48]

Moreover, in the texts where we find a connection between salvation and forgiveness of sins in Acts, there Luke's focus is on the Saviour himself—everyone who believes in *Jesus* receives forgiveness of sins through his name (10:43) and shall be saved (16:31). The blessing of the forgiveness of sins is the reception of the Spirit. Peter promises the Pentecost audience that those who respond to the proclamation by repenting and by being baptised will receive the "*gift of the Holy Spirit*" (2:38). In the other conversion accounts, for example, in the Cornelius story, Luke simply demonstrates this (e.g., 10:43-44).

Thus, Luke very intricately interweaves his picture of God with his portrait of Jesus. Through all these things, Luke wants his readers to know that Jesus is the only way of understanding God. What he has done in and through the person of Jesus is the best way of knowing his dealings in the human realm. Therefore,

---

47 See B.H. Throckmorton, Σῴζειν, σωτηρία in Luke-Acts", *SE*, 6, (1973), 515-26, esp. 518.

48 So also J. Jervell, *Theology of the Acts of the Apostles*, (Cambridge: CUP, 1996), 99. See J.A. Fitzmyer, (*Luke*, 1:224) for his generalised definition of salvation. In this regard, Jervell, (*Theology*, 99, n. 186) contends that "forgiveness" in the LXX means the release from debt and release from captivity and that the association of "forgiveness" with sin is from Jewish religion, where "debt" is used in the sense of sin.

everyone who calls on Jesus or believes in him receives repentance and forgiveness of sins.

In the end, Luke's own presentation of God and Christ, suggests that one of his concerns is "to...proclaim the message of salvation...."[49] His concept of divine concentricity in the conversion accounts adds momentum to the progression of the conversion stories, summarises, and unifies the emphases embedded in different missionary discourses and helps the readers towards constructing a total picture.[50]

Moreover, from Thucydides and Josephus we learned that speeches provide the readers with an insider's view of events and new insights not obvious on the surface. From Luke's missionary speeches too, his readers gain a privileged knowledge denied to the immediate narrative audience. As stated above, since Luke's readers have all of his missionary speeches, they can build a consistent and coherent picture about God and Jesus from what Luke says in his missionary speeches. Luke's various narrative audiences do not have this access. What they hear is what the preachers say at a given moment. When Peter emphasises that Jesus was not an ordinary person, but God's chosen one, only Luke's readers, at least those knowing Luke's Gospel, realise that Peter was speaking with the authority of an original disciple, and, therefore, what he says about Jesus is true to the original account. Even when the narrative audience hears Peter speak, they do not know this.

Interpretative

Not only do the speeches help the readers to build a coherent Theocentric-Christocentric perspective, but they also illuminate, expound or interpret events in the present.[51] The interpretative role of the missionary speeches is even more relevant to the texts where a supernatural event precedes the missionary discourses. In such instances Luke introduces a statement of ignorance from the audiences and a statement of interpretation of the event by the preachers as follows:

the crowd...was bewildered...All were amazed and perplexed, saying "what does this mean?" (2:6,12).	Peter "...this is what was spoken through the prophet Joel...to one, another (2:14,16).

49 Cf. Dibelius, *Studies*, 166.

50 Cf. Iser, *Act of Reading*, 119.

51 Talking of the task of historians, Dibelius, (*Studies*, 138) comments: "The historians' art begins where he...endeavours to illuminate, and...interpret the meaning of the events."

They were filled with wonder and amazement at what had happened ...all the people...utterly astonished (3:10b,11).	Peter...why do you wonder at this... God...has glorified his servant Jesus ...(3:12,13a).
The crowds saw what Paul had done, they shouted..."The gods have come ...in human form!" (14:11).	Barnabas and Paul...why are you doing this?...we bring good news that you should turn from these worthless things to the living God..." (14:15).

This particular element conveys the fact that since supernatural phenomena are not self-explanatory, they need an interpretation. Therefore, the speakers make use of the situation to interpret miraculous events Theologically and/or Christologically. In the process, they might say much more than the immediate situation or the event might warrant. However, this exposition, for Luke, is not just an explanation of the miraculous phenomenon, but missionary since it comes with its own demands, expecting an appropriate audience-response. These observations can be made much clearer in light of one literary technique that Luke employs in some of his missionary speeches.

Through his "Prophecy-Fulfilment" motif Luke provides his readers with an interpretative key to understand that what happens in the present is actually the fulfilment of what had been prophesied in the past. Luke's logic behind this motif is that the deeper meaning hidden in the present occurrence can be understood and interpreted better in light of the ancient prophecy.[52] In this way, the Prophecy-Fulfilment motif establishes continuity with the past and functions as a hermeneutical tool to interpret the present events.[53]

Within the Prophecy-Fulfilment framework, the preachers in Acts turn to the OT prophets in order to comprehend and interpret the meaning of God's work and his plan and purposes for the present. Peter sums this up in 10:43, "*All the prophets testify about him that everyone who believes in him receives forgiveness of sins through his name.*" Taking recourse to prophecy, Luke

---

[52] Cf. Cadbury, *Making of Luke-Acts*, 303-05. Paul Schubert, "Structure and Significance of Luke 24" in W. Eltester (Ed.), *Neutestamentaliche Studien fur Rudolf Bulltmann*, (Berlin: Alfred Topelmann, 1954), 165-86, esp. 176. See also Robert J. Karris, "Missionary Communities: A New Paradigm for the Study of Luke-Acts", *CBQ*, 41, (1979), 80-97, esp. 94.

[53] Talbert emphasises "continuity" as an important aspect of Luke's purpose in "Promise and Fulfilment in Lucan Theology", in C.H. Talbert, (Ed.), *Luke-Acts: New Perspectives from the SBL*, (New York: Crossroad, 1984), 91-103.

declares "that the attested events of the life, death and resurrection of Jesus Christ are guaranteed...by the long foretold...prophecies which unfold in history the 'will' and 'plan' of God" (cf. 2:23).[54] We may illustrate this from the Pentecost episode (2:1-36).

In Acts 2:17-21, Peter quotes Joel 3:1-5 (LXX) to interpret the events of Pentecost, which explains the coming of the Spirit in the present and expresses a divine plan that will unfold progressively. Thus, Joel's prophecy performs a dual function in its context: i) it explains that what happens in the present is the fulfilment of what the prophet had foretold; ii) it interprets the events for the readers by giving them hints for the future about the way God works. This is vividly seen in the subsequent narratives.

Peter's reference to God's promise to pour out the Spirit on "*all flesh*" (2:17) creates an internal Prophecy-Fulfilment scheme that anticipates the descent of the Spirit on the Samaritans (8:15-17) and on the Gentiles (10:44-46). Moreover, the final words of the Joel quotation ("*Everyone who calls on the name of the Lord will be saved*" [2:21]), anticipates the realisation of this promise, in the following narrative, through repeated references to the powerful name of the Lord and to salvation through his name (2:38,40; 3:6,16; 4:12). This is how Peter's citation of Joel's prophecy interprets the present and provides hints in advance for interpreting subsequent developments in the narrative.

Further, in 2:25-32 and 36, Luke associates the present reality of Jesus' resurrection with Ps. 16:8-11 and construes it as prefiguring Christ. The argument in 2:31 is that resurrection ("*nor did his flesh experience corruption*") was prophesied for the Messiah. The logic is, "*This Jesus God raised up*" with its proof, "*and of that all of us are witnesses*" (2:32). The conclusion is that God has made Jesus the Lord and Messiah (2:36). After citing Ps. 16:8-11, the source

54 Cf. Schubert, "The Structure and Significance" 173-77. For a detailed discussion of this see Darrell Bock, "Scripture and the Realisation of God's Promises", in I. Howard Marshall & David Peterson (Eds.), *Witness to the Gospel: The Theology of Acts*, (Grand Rapids/ Cambridge, UK: Eerdmans, 1998), 41-62, esp. 49-61. For a descriptive study on Prophecy-Fulfilment motif in Luke's writings, see idem, *Proclamation from Prophecy and Pattern: Lucan Old Testament Theology*, (JSNTSup. 12; Sheffield: JSOT Press, 1987); idem, "The Use of the Old Testament in Luke-Acts" in D.J. Lull (Ed.), *SBLSP 1990*, (Atlanta: Scholars, 1990), 494-511; D. Peterson, "The Motif of Fulfilment and the Purpose of Luke-Acts" in Bruce Winter & Andrew D. Clarke, *The Book of Acts in Its First Century Setting*: Vol. I. *The Book of Acts in Its Ancient Literary Setting*, (Grand Rapids: Eerdmans/Carlisle: Paternoster, 1993), 83-104, esp. 86-100.

of the prophecy, Luke sets up a contrast. David died but has not been raised. His tomb is still there (2:29). This, in Greek rhetoric, is a sign of the continued dead state of the person.[55] Thus, David cannot be the one foretold in Ps. 16:10 ("*For you do not give me up to Sheol, or let your faithful one see the pit*"). Moreover, the apostolic witness proves beyond doubt the refutation of David's claim (2:32). Luke argues that David's psalm is a prophecy foretelling the resurrection of the Messiah. It is about one of David's descendants to whom God's promise of the throne is applied (Acts 2:30=2 Sam. 7:12-13=Ps. 89:4-5; 132:11). The prophecy from the Psalm, in Luke's view, is about Jesus' resurrection. Peter's speech explains that Jesus' resurrection has dual attestation: David's prophetic vision[56] and the descent of the Spirit. Together they irrefutably prove the resurrection of Jesus.

The same interpretative function of the Prophecy-Fulfilment motif is also seen in Peter's Temple speech. When interpreting the healing of the paralytic, Peter relates it to Jesus' present glorified state (3:13) by alluding to Isaiah 52:13. Apparently, Luke's purpose here is to show that Jesus' present glorified state is the fulfilment of what had been foreseen in Isaiah. The healing of the paralytic is its evidence.

Luke also demonstrates the interpretative function of the missionary speeches in the Cornelius story (10:1-11:18). In the Jerusalem plenary session, Peter refers to the coming of the Spirit on the Gentiles as he did in the beginning (11:15; cf. 10:44-47). This alludes to the beginning of the realisation of that promise in Acts 2, which, in turn, echoes the explanation of Joel 3:1-5 (LXX) and the infusion of the Spirit. By such inter-textual connections, Luke provides a hermeneutical tool for his readers to understand the OT explanation by echo to support the issue of Gentile conversion in Acts. In Luke's scheme, this is the proper Scriptural interpretation of events.

Through interpretative methods such as Prophecy-Fulfilment scheme, Luke explains the miraculous events and the prophecies and demonstrates for his readers that God does not act capriciously, but fulfils all his promises; he is a promise-keeping God. If he said, "*Everyone who calls on the name of the Lord shall be saved*" (2:21), it will be so.

---

55 William S. Kurz, "Hellenistic Rhetoric", 184. However, for Luke, the empty tomb is not the proof of Jesus' resurrection either. It is the apostolic witness that proves Jesus' resurrection.

56 Cf. J.A. Fitzmyer, "David, 'Being therefore a prophet'...Acts 2:30", *CBQ*, 34, (1972), 332-39.

Exhortative/Persuasive

It was shown earlier that both in Thucydides and Josephus, persuasion plays a dominant role, demonstrating the power of persuasion, particularly in political situations. Thucydides' political debates examine two sides of the same issue, what policies should govern inter-state affairs, and what decision should be taken—either war or peace. In Eleazer's speech, Josephus demonstrates the negative effect of a persuasive speech—to persuade his audience that suicide is preferable to accepting defeat from the Romans or surrendering. The impact of speeches on the hearers may differ from case to case, but the persuasive intent of the speeches and its effect on the hearers is unmistakable. Pelling sums up that persuasion in oratory includes such responses as

> "Approval or disapproval of an individual...or...a more complex mode of empathy, admiration, shock, despair, or perplexity...Persuasion...to act."[57]

However, one notable difference between Thucydides/Josephus and Luke is that whereas the speeches in Thucydides/Josephus are geared towards political action of some sort, Luke's missionary discourses are designed to persuade the audience to a spiritual action—repentance and turning to God. This function becomes clearer particularly in light of the speakers' focus on the audiences' guilt.

In his Pentecost address (2:16-36) Peter repeatedly refers to the rejection of Jesus by the Jerusalem Jews. He further accentuates the crime of the Jewish audience by showing the contrast between God's dealings with Jesus (resurrection and exaltation of Jesus as the Lord and Messiah) and the Jewish treatment of Jesus (crucifixion). Earlier in the Corinthians' speech to the Spartans (*HPW*, I.68-71), Thucydides demonstrated how a persuasive speech exploits the fear of the hearers to accomplish its purposes. In the Pentecost episode Peter awakens a sense of guilt in his audience to achieve the intent of the Jesus-kerygma.

He builds up the speech to a climax with a view to producing the effect referred to in the following verse. The listeners are "*cut to their heart*" (2:37). They interrupt Peter and ask for a remedy, which heightens the significance of the moment by dramatising it and by demonstrating the eventual outcome of the speech in terms of what follows (cf. 2:37; 4:1; 10:44).[58] In this sense, Lucan

---

[57] Pelling, *Greek Historian*, 1.

[58] Aune, *Literary Environment*, 127.

speeches, particularly the missionary speeches, are quite different from some of the speeches in the OT, which are not interactive.[59] In Acts 2:37 the audience-interruption leads to Peter's exhortation to repentance and the offer of forgiveness of sins. Peter's address has been persuasive enough to invite the audience to repentance for a specific crime, and his words have the desired effect.

Peter's Temple sermon (3:12-26) complements what he has already adequately highlighted in his Pentecost address. Here he develops the audience's guilt, using details of Luke's passion story (3:13-15; cf. Lk. 23:13-25), emphasising particularly the Jewish responsibility for Jesus' death by a double use of the emphatic pronoun ὑμεῖς. What effect does this speech have on the audience?

Whereas, Peter's Pentecost speech highlights the Jewish rejection and crucifixion of Jesus, the Temple address puts forward certain blessings to persuade the audience to action. The exhortation to repentance (3:19), followed immediately by a list of motivations for repentance in 3:19-21, places before the audience an "either-or" situation. Their own decision and choice will make possible i) the promise of the forgiveness of sins, stated figuratively as "the wiping out of sins" (ἐξαλειφθῆναι)[60]; ii) seasons of refreshment. The meaning of this expression is uncertain. Fitzmyer thinks of this as "times when they will be able to repent and convert before the end."[61] Despite its uncertainty, the expression brings different aspects of the "times of refreshment"—the coming of the Messiah and times of restoration of what God had announced through the prophets (3:20-21). Peter exhorts his Jewish audience to repent in order that God may send the Messiah, who will fulfil God's promises to Israel. However, this depends entirely on their repentance. Their refusal to repent will result in their being excluded from God's people (3:23). Here we are reminded of Samuel's speech where he exhorts his audiences to choose to obey God and thus, be preserved or face total annihilation (1 Sam. 12).

The exhortative function of the speeches can also be seen in Philip's Samaritan mission (8:4-25), particularly in the dialogical section of the narrative. While confronting Simon, Peter asks him "*Repent...of this wickedness...if possible, the intent of your heart may be forgiven you.*" (8:22). Peter commands (μετανόησον: aorist imperative) Simon to repent for thinking that he could buy God's gift with money and for the fact that his heart was not right with God

---

59 The only exception seems to be Josh. 24:16.

60 Cf. Soards, *Speeches*, 42.

61 Fitzmyer, *Acts*, 288.

(8:21). Moreover, he is "*in the gall of bitterness and the chains of wickedness*" (8:23). Therefore, Simon should repent.

In his address to Cornelius, while concluding, Peter refers to the "*forgiveness of sins through Jesus' name*" (10:43). It may be that by referring to sin here, Luke wants to point out the need for forgiveness of sins; conversely, forgiveness presupposes sins, which, in turn, strongly emphasises the need for repentance. Earlier, in the second part of his Pentecost address, Peter associates forgiveness of sins and the gift of the Holy Spirit with repentance (2:37). Thus, we may assume that in the Cornelius episode too the reference to the "forgiveness of sins" and the descent of the Spirit carry with them the idea of repentance.[62] The same implicit exhortation to repentance can also be seen in the speech of Barnabas and Paul at Lystra (14:15-17). They urge the Lystrans to "turn" away from the worthless things (14:15). The earlier occurrence of "to turn" along with "repentance" in Peter's Temple address (3:19) leads to this assumption.

Here Luke shows his readers that repentance, believing and turning to God are responses that a mere attraction to the miraculous event cannot evoke, but they are possible when the interpretation of the event and the Scriptures, the techniques of persuasion function together. Moreover, Peter's invitation to his hearers to repent may also function as a point of comparison for Luke's readers. Since they are already believers, they might compare their earlier response to such an invitation with the response of the narrative audience in the present story. Thus, Peter's invitation in the narrative functions as a reminder of and as an invitation to reassess and reaffirm their earlier experience. This is expected to further realign them with God. If any of Luke's readers are missionary minded, here Luke also gives them an evangelistic pattern that they could apply in their own contexts—preach God, his dealings with Jesus, and what he offers to humans if they repent, believe, and turn to him, i.e., forgiveness of sins and the Spirit. When they do this, God can achieve the same kind of results that follow Peter's Pentecost and Temple speeches—the conversion of the 3000 (2:41) and the 5000 (4:4).

CONCLUSION

Luke's missionary discourses are akin to the Hellenistic historiographical conventions in their form, but in their content, they reflect the thoroughgoing Theocentric perspective of the few speeches in the OT. Luke's missionary speeches demonstrate that the witness motif he establishes in the early chapters

[62] Haenchen (*Acts*, 351) too suggests that 10:42-43 is a summons to repentance.

of Acts has the preaching of the word at its heart.[63] Therefore, he highlights matters of salvific import in his missionary sermons, particularly by showing who God is and the forgiveness of sins he offers to everyone who repents, believes in Jesus, and turns to him. Luke's message in his missionary discourses is this: *God has revealed himself fully and normatively in Jesus by exalting him as the Lord and Messiah. Therefore, the only way to be saved or be forgiven of sins is to believe in him or to call on his name or to turn to him.* As for Luke, this is the message that should constitute the Christian witness that must reach the ends of the earth (1:8).

Moreover, the missionary speeches are employed to illuminate, interpret, and expound events. They make events more intelligible and understandable. As the readers progress through the missionary speeches, they may be able to trace Luke's line of argument and see how the speeches and the narratives are mutually illuminative allowing readers to gain insight into Luke's worldview and thus may be able to interpret events from his point-of-view.

Luke's missionary speeches also exhibit high sensitivity to the Jew-Gentile composition of the early church and the different dynamics at work there. Luke masterfully inserts a Jesus-kerygma for his Jewish audiences (Acts 2 & 3) and a Theological kerygma for his Gentile audience (Acts 14). Sometimes he deftly adds Christological specifics to his Theological kerygma by showing that God's plan of salvation has attained its finality in Jesus (e.g., Acts. 2, 3; Cf. 4:12). Thus, Luke exhibits his flexibility and sensitivity to the audiences' needs in order to instil an unwavering conviction (πίστις) in the listeners to believe in and turn to God.[64]

Summary of Part I

We have argued so far that conversion is one of Luke's dominant themes in Acts (ch. 2) by producing evidence from the book of Acts and that, for Luke, the complementarity between the miraculous and proclamation is the formula behind the apostolic mission in Acts. We showed that the presence of the

---

[63] Paul Schubert ("Final Cycle of Speeches", 16) suggests, "The speeches of Luke are an essential part of the story itself, the story of the proclamation of the word of God." See also U. Wilckens cited in Richard F. Zehnle, *Peter's Pentecost Discourse: Tradition and Lukan Reinterpretation in Peter's Speeches of Acts 2 and 3*, (SBLMS 15; Nashville, NY: Abingdon, 1971), 15; J.C. O'Neill *The Theology of Acts in Historical Setting*, [(London: SPCK, 1961), 124-27.

[64] So also Kurz, "Hellenistic Rhetoric", 177.

miraculous in many conversion accounts makes a proclamatory situation possible for the preachers to expound and interpret events. Moving beyond their simple explanation, they also introduce elements about who God is and what he has done, particularly through Jesus whom he has exalted as the Lord and Messiah. This Christological focus embedded in the missionary speeches, in Luke's scheme, naturally leads to extending an invitation to repent, to believe in, and turn to God in order to obtain forgiveness of sins.

Within this larger framework, chapter 3 studied some of the literary functions that the miraculous plays, particularly in the context of conversion. Luke presents the miraculous as demonstrating God's providence and thereby, confirming the divine origin of the word. We also pointed out that although occasionally miracles are able to turn people to God on their own, in Luke's scheme, they cannot do so always. Their limitations are also evident in the counter-effects they produce in terms of opposition, persecution, and even martyrdom. In this way, Luke assigns them a place of permanent effectiveness by *integrating* them into the mission discourses and setting them in a complementary relationship with the missionary speeches. This was then followed by a discussion of the literary functions of the mission speeches in conversion texts in chapter 4.

Missionary speeches utilise the miraculous as a starting point, not only to explain the event, but also to present a unified Theo-Christocentric worldview and eventually challenge the hearers to repent and turn to God. We have repeatedly shown that as a result of Christian witnessing through a combination of the miraculous and proclamation, people turned to God *en masse*, as households, and as individuals.

From here, we proceed to Part II of this study, where, by means of two detailed case studies—Pentecost (2:1-43) and Cornelius' conversion (10:1-11:18)—we shall demonstrate in detail the complementarity that Luke wishes to establish between the miraculous and proclamation and the way they function effectively as an integrated whole in the apostolic mission in Acts to make it successful.

5

THE MIRACULOUS AND PROCLAMATION IN THE PENTECOST STORY

INTRODUCTION

The preceding chapters have shown that conversion is one of Luke's dominant motifs in Acts and that according to him, the complementarity between the miraculous and proclamation was the formula behind the apostolic mission. The structure of the conversion stories seen in Chapter 1 showed this narrative pattern flowing through a number of conversion accounts that form the scope of this investigation.

In order to demonstrate the way this literary symbiosis between the miraculous and proclamation functions, we analysed, first, Luke's presentation of the supernatural and some of its literary roles and, secondly, his presentation of the missionary discourses and some their narrative functions. We have shown the way Luke sets both the miraculous and proclamation in a complementary relationship with each other in order to provide Christian mission with the strategic and indispensable balance that it requires. We illustrated this complementarity first, in Luke's characterisation of Jesus' mission and, secondly, in his portrait of the subsequent apostolic mission, including Paul's.

This chapter will further demonstrate in detail the balance between the miraculous and the missionary discourse in the Pentecost story. At the end of our analysis we will seek to suggest a distinctive narrative pattern of conversion within the Pentecost story.

As the structure of the conversion stories seen earlier shows, Pentecost is the first one in the series of the stories where the presence of miraculous phenomena and missionary discourses is clearly present, demonstrating Luke's clear intention, at the outset, to set it as a pattern for the subsequent apostolic mission. In 1:4-5 Jesus asks his disciples to stay in Jerusalem awaiting the promise of the Father, creating, as shown earlier, an internal Prophecy-Fulfilment scheme within which Jesus further promises the power of the Spirit (1:8). Importantly, the coming of the Spirit on the apostles is directed precisely towards a worldwide witnessing—to move far beyond the confines of geographical particularity (1:8). The apostles do start from Jerusalem, but gradually move out to other areas such as Judea and Samaria and continue witnessing until the apostolic witness reaches Rome (Acts 28). This centrifugal movement of their witnessing is possible, however, only after the infusion of the Spirit, that is, the supernatural power to witness. Except for Peter's brief allusion to it in the Jerusalem plenary session (11:15,17) and in the Jerusalem Council (15:8,9), the event is not recounted elsewhere. Nevertheless, its importance is seen primarily in the way it puts forward an evangelistic pattern, by presenting the miraculous and proclamation, not as two mutually exclusive opposites, but as the two ends of the same spectrum, which eventuate a mass conversion in a totally Jewish context.

While all commentators recognise the import of Pentecost as a decisive starting point towards universal mission in the narrative of Acts, only a few of them accord due importance to the miraculous and proclamation combination manifested in that event.[1] The position of Pentecost as the starting point of a distinct class of conversion stories and its theme mark its critical importance and the need for its detailed study. This is reiterated when we discuss further the narrative context of Pentecost below. Before demonstrating how the components of Christian mission in Acts—the miraculous and proclamation—function together in literary reciprocity, certain things need to be clarified.

The present chapter does not evaluate Pentecost as a psychological or sociological phenomenon nor study any ancient or modern story that resembles it. The chapter also does not attempt to determine the sources or traditions, which Luke may have referred to in its composition. The focus of the chapter is not historicity but Luke's literary presentation of Pentecost. We first study the literary context of Pentecost and then exegete Acts 2:1-41.

---

[1] For instance, I.J. Martin, ("Glossolalia in the Apostolic Church", *JBL*, 63, [1944], 123-30, esp.128) holds that "Had the performance (speaking in tongues) been allowed to continue at Pentecost, the new faith would have suffered reproach and misunderstanding. Peter, realizing the danger, promptly saved the day for the faith by speaking in intelligible Aramaic, which the polyglot crowd understood...."

THE NARRATIVE CONTEXT

Pentecost is set immediately in the context of the words of the risen Jesus to his disciples. After his resurrection and until his ascension, Jesus instructs his disciples through the Spirit (1:2b). Right at the outset, Luke gives his readers the privileged knowledge that the immediate narrative audience (i.e., the disciples) lacks. Whereas the readers know that it was through the Spirit that Jesus gave instructions to his disciples, the disciples themselves will have to wait a little longer for this revelation. The appearance of the Spirit here in conjunction with the giving of instructions functions as a precursor to the later association of the Spirit's coming with inspired speech (e.g., ἀποφθέγγεσθαι, 2:4,14) and prophecy (vv.16ff.). Here Luke begins to show the way he would accord proclamation the functional primacy in the subsequent narrative. Further, Jesus asks his disciples to "*wait for the promise of the Father*" (1:4; cf. Lk. 11:13; 24:49). Since it is not immediately obvious what this promise of the Father is, it stokes anticipation and retains it in the disciples until Jesus himself resolves it later. Since the readers have the full text before them and maintain a faster narrative pace, they know well before the disciples what the promise of the Father is. Therefore, they await the actual event of Pentecost.

The suspense aroused by Jesus' initial command to wait for the promise of the Father (1:4) is cleared when he himself discloses who the promise of the Father is: "*...be baptized with the Holy Spirit...*" (1:5; cf. Lk. 3:16).[2] Now it is clear to the disciples that Jesus' earlier reference, in the narrative, to the promise of the Father is actually about the Spirit.

However, some actual readers may be baffled by the expression of being baptised with the Spirit, since baptism is generally associated with immersion in water; they may not know how this relates to the infusion of the Spirit. Howard Marshall explains that the baptism language here metaphorically points to the coming of the Spirit (2:17f; 10:45).[3] This is correct particularly when the readers compare πνεύματι βαπτισθήσεσθε ἁγίου in 1:5 with δωρεὰ τοῦ αγίου πνεύματος ἐκκέχυται in 10:45. Thus, to be baptised with the Holy Spirit means to experience the outpouring of the Spirit. Luke is employing here a familiar language to explain the infusion of the Spirit. Further to his promise of baptism with the Spirit (1:5), Jesus promises his disciples "*You will*

---

2 The passive voice here clearly refers to the event for which the reader is being prepared. Cf. R.F. Zehnle, *Pentecost Discourse*, 102-03.

3 I.H. Marshall, "The Meaning of the verb 'To Baptize'", *EQ*, 45, (1973), 130-40.

receive power when the Holy Spirit has come upon you; and you will be my witnesses..." (1:8). Now the disciples know for sure that the express purpose of the Spirit's coming is to witness.

It is clear now that the Spirit is the gift that the Father promised (1:4) and that his coming is to empower the disciples for a worldwide mission (1:8). However, they know not when, where, and how the Spirit would come, and the accompanying manifestations. The only clue given is that it will happen "*not many days from now*" (1:5). This sustains the suspense and anticipation in the narrative, thereby accentuating its numinous quality. Moreover, this internal prediction creates a narrative need for its fulfilment; a narrative destination toward which events should and will move. The gift of the Spirit, whenever it is given, would be in fulfilment of what has been foretold in 1:4-5, 8 and would also point to similar experiences in future (4:31; 8:15-17; 10:44-47, etc.).

Thus, Luke situates Pentecost within an internal Prediction-Fulfilment scheme. It is the fulfilment of the promise of the Father, the power from on high, and the baptism of the Spirit in order to be witnesses to the end of the earth. The stage is now set to study the event of Pentecost.

THE EVENT OF PENTECOST (2:1-13)

First Luke introduces the narrative world of Pentecost, its characters, its location, and the events that constitute the incident. The event of Pentecost functions simultaneously at two levels. At one level, it is about the coming of the Spirit, fulfilling the earlier internal predictions. The narrative ends with those filled speaking in tongues. At another level, the simple event of the coming of the Spirit performs a higher narrative function by complementing the ensuing discourse. As readers move along with the narrative and listen to Peter's address, the way Pentecost functions at this higher plane, becomes clear to them.

Luke begins his description of Pentecost by introducing the community, "*...they were all together in one place*" (2:1). It is not clear, however, who were included in the gathering—whether the 120 believers (1:15) or only the twelve apostles (including Matthias [1:15-26]). The latter is likely since in the following events only the apostles are present (cf. 2:14). Moreover, the presence of ἐπὶ τὸ αὐτό (2:1; cf. 1:5; 14:1) implies the oneness and the concord of the apostolic community, which is later, referred to as κοινωνία (2:44-45; cf. 4:32-5:11, etc) characterised by the ὁμοθυμαδόν, referring to their single-minded harmony (2:46; 8:6; cf. 1:4; 4:24; 5:12; 15:25). By introducing the disciples as a company, Luke provides his readers with a collective testimony to the certitude of the experience of the Spirit and a verification of its interpretation that follows. It also presents Peter's interpretative speech (2:14-36) as a community enterprise (2:14).

Having described the community of the disciples, Luke introduces the advent of the Spirit by means of aural and visual signifiers.[4] The term "signifiers" is deliberately employed here, because they merely signify something supernatural behind the appearances, thus performing a revelatory function. As shown earlier, such prodigies are signs from the gods to communicate their intent and to guide human affairs.

Luke's employment of the aural metaphor of the rushing wind (πνοή) to introduce the phenomenon seems to be intentional, as it stands for the coming of the Spirit (πνεῦμα).[5] In the OT, as shown earlier, wind symbolises a Theophany (2 Sam. 22:16; Job 37:10; Ezek. 13:13). Although it is absent from the Sinai narrative in the OT, Luke's readers, who know Josephus, might recall that he records also noise (ἦχος) at Sinai (cf. Ex. 9:16): "there came strong winds...and declared God to be there present."[6] Such an amplification of the Theophany at Sinai would give the readers certain insights in whose light, if they know Josephus, they can understand Pentecost also as Theophanic.[7] Further, the fact that the sound came from heaven symbolises its divine origin. Although not certain, it is likely that here Luke has in mind the Graeco-Roman belief that the divine origin of an event makes it miraculous.

Following the aural phenomenon at Pentecost, the visual phenomena (tongues as of fire) prove tangibly that something extraordinary is taking place (v.3). As pointed out earlier, fire is a common feature in the OT Theophanies (Ex.

---

4 R.W. Funk, (*The Poetics*, 110-11) calls these "perception precipitators".

5 "For Greek-speakers πνοή and πνεῦμα are thoroughly related ideas." Cf. E. Haenchen, *Acts*, 167-68.

6 Josephus, *Antiq.*, III.5.2.(80); Philo. *Decal.* IX.33; X.46). Cf. I. Howard Marshall, "The Significance of Pentecost", *SJT*, 30, (1977), 347-69, esp. 354.

7 Cf. J.D. Kingsbury, "Reflections on 'The Reader'", 456.

19:18).[8] Luke's Theophanic language gives his readers the privileged knowledge that the immediate narrative audience lacks. They realise the Theocentricity of the happening; and that through natural and ordinary means God communicates his will in an extraordinary way. It also affirms the divine presence in the happening.[9] Luke's intention here is to direct his readers' attention on God and his acts rather than on the event itself.

Luke describes a flame, divided into several tongues, resting upon everyone present. This performs an aetiological function, i.e., the descent of the Spirit is the cause of the impending worldwide mission of the apostles.[10] However, Luke would not want his readers to equate the wind and the fire with the Spirit. He is only using analogical language (ὤφθησαν αὔτοις...ὡσεὶ, v.3) to give verbal articulation to something ineffable.[11] When referring directly to the Spirit, he would employ πνεῦμα (v.4). The metaphors do not deny the reality of the phenomenon, but at the same time, they do not exactly represent the Spirit; therefore, the true nature of the miraculous phenomenon is by no means clear to the spectators. This inherent inexplicability in the 'miraculous' happening creates a sense of suspense in them and naturally necessitates an interpretative speech. However, those of Luke's readers, who know the Old Testament and have some prior knowledge of God's manifestations, would realise that, in their light, the phenomena of wind and tongues of fire in Acts 2 are certainly Theophanic. From the narrative audience's point-of-view, the ineffability of the phenomena at Pentecost further intensifies their miraculous quality and, hence, the strong need for a detailed exposition.

Having narrated the signifiers, Luke now discloses the signified: "*All... were filled with the Holy Spirit*" (v.4a). This information is immediately available

---

8 In Philo (*Decal*. [IX] 33; [XI] 44-49), the voice of God was changed into a flaming fire as the commandments were uttered (Cf. Marshall, "Significance", 354). The Theophanic language of both the images here does not advocate the view that the Pentecost experience is identical with the appearance of the risen Jesus to more than 500 brethren (1Cor. 15:6) as held by S. MacLean Gilmour ("The Christophany to more than Five Hundred Brethren", *JBL*, 80, [1961], 248-52; idem, "Easter and Pentecost," *JBL*, 81, [1962]), 62-66. On the contrary, C. Freeman Sleeper ("Pentecost and Resurrection", *JBL*, 84, [1965], 389-99) correctly holds that the Pentecost experience is a Theophanic experience.

9 J.D.G. Dunn, *Baptism in the Holy Spirit: A Re-examination of the New Testament Teaching on the Gift of the Spirit in Relation to Pentecostalism Today*, (Napierville, IL: Allenson, 1970), 11-13.

10 So Zehnle, *Discourse*, 118.

11 The phenomenon of fiery tongues appears only to the apostles (v.5) whereas the narrative audience (i.e., the spectators) is attracted only by the aural phenomenon (v.6).

to Luke's readers since they have the advantage of the whole text before them. In the mean time, the apostles also know that they are being filled with the Spirit, whereas the spectators have to await Peter's speech to disclose the meaning of the phenomena. Because of this, there is a narrative distance between the apostles whom Luke summarily calls " πάντες" (v.4) and other spectators (v.6).

In the context, Luke employs πίμπλημι to denote the filling of the Spirit (v.4).[12] He uses this term particularly where the Spirit inspires a person for a prophetic utterance (e.g., 2:4; cf. 1:41,67; 4:8,31; 13:9). His choice of this term here may be deliberate because the Spirit's outpouring immediately inspires speaking in other tongues and anticipates Peter's Spirit-inspired utterance (ἀποφθέγγεσθαι, v.14) as well as the later equation of tongues with prophecy (vv.16-17). Thus, Luke's readers are able to see Luke's keenness to accord an intrinsic prophetic import to the apostles' utterance.

The effect of the visual metaphor of tongues is immediately apparent when the apostles begin "*to speak in other languages* (γλῶσσα)*, as the Spirit gave them utterance*" (ἀποφθέγγεσθαι, v.4b).[13] This is Luke's objective proof of the Spirit's coming. Whereas according to Graeco-Roman historical understanding, an event becomes 'miraculous' when attributed to the gods, for Luke, the Pentecost phenomena are not just a matter of perspective or interpretation, but are an objective divine act, i.e., this is the only explanation possible to the occurrence, which is not challenged anywhere in the narrative. Thus, ἀποφθέγγεσθαι interprets γλῶσσα, which, in turn, is equated with prophecy later in the speech. ἀποφθέγγομαι in the OT mostly denotes prophetic or inspired speech (1Chron. 25:1; Ezek. 13:9,19; Mic. 5:12; Zech. 10:2).[14]

---

12 This is characteristically Lucan. Out of 24 references to πίμπλημι in the New Testament, 9 are found in Acts. Luke employs two other words for filling which have direct connection to the effect of the coming of the Spirit: a) πλήρης: This refers to a permanent endowment that becomes part of a person's character (Acts 6:3,5; 7:55; 11:24; cf. Lk. 4:1). b) πληρόω: This is used only once in Acts in the imperfect with reference to the Spirit. In Antioch the believers were being filled with joy and the Holy Spirit (13:52). The imperfect tense suggests a continuing process. Cf. Marshall, "Significance", 355.

13 Translation mine. The NRSV's translation ("*as the Spirit gave them ability.*") minimises the importance of the Spirit's inspiration here for utterance.

14 Cf. Haenchen, *Acts*, 178; Marshall "Significance" 357; Jackson & Lake, *Beginnings*, 18.

Further, Luke equates γλώσσα with διάλεκτος (v.8) proving that intelligible speech in different languages is meant.[15] Thus, he establishes the reality of the phenomenon of tongues for his readers. In the subsequent narratives, wherever he records the descent of the Spirit, where the recipients speak in other tongues (4:31; 8:15-17; 10:44-47), they might recall Pentecost and understand it as an event that symbolically foreshadowed the future proclamation of the word in other languages.[16] Some may hold that in the polyglot at Pentecost, there is a conscious reversal of the story of Babel,[17] but for Luke what is important is that Pentecost is not about overcoming linguistic barriers, but about being empowered by the Spirit for witnessing.

Thus, Luke presents the wind and the tongues of fire as miraculous, since they come from heaven; within the narrative, they demonstrate the actual coming of the Spirit. It is also the ultimate cause of a worldwide mission as Jesus envisions in 1:8. Since the readers have the whole text before them this may be obvious to them, but the narrative audience of Pentecost have to await Peter's speech.

AUDIENCE-REACTION TO THE MIRACULOUS

The aural and visual phenomena at Pentecost attract the onlookers (v.6),[18] whom Luke identifies as *"devout Jews from every nation..."* (2:5).[19] The catalogue of the nations (2:9-11) illustrates the phrase, ἀπὸ παντὸς ἔθνους (v.5) and catalyses a sequential reading for the readers. They can view the table of nations in light of ἕως ἐσχάτου τῆς γῆς envisioned in Acts 1:8 and understand

---

[15] BDAG, (201-02) defines Glossolalia as "speaking in marvellous, celestial languages." The Pentecost phenomenon is unlike what we read elsewhere about the "speaking in tongues" where it is taken to mean some kind of unintelligible utterances (cf. 1Cor. 12 and 14). See Robert H. Gundry, "Ecstatic Utterance", *JTS*, 17, (1966), 299-307, esp.300.

[16] Cf. Frank W. Beare, "Speaking with Tongues: A Critical Survey of the New Testament Evidence", *JBL*, 83 (1964), 229-46, esp. 237.

[17] For instance, Sleeper "Pentecost", 390; See also J.G. Davies, "Pentecost and Glossolalia", *JTS*, 3, (1952), 228-31 and William Neil, *The Acts of the Apostles*, (London: Oliphants, 1973), 72.

[18] The great sound (v.5) and the gathering of the crowd could not but have caught the attention and the intervention of the Roman soldiers. Cf. Zehnle, *Discourse*, 112.

[19] Tannehill, ("The Functions of Peter's Mission Speeches in the Narrative of Acts", *NTS*, 37, [1997], 400-14, esp.p.403, n.12) suggests that the Jews serve a dual function in the narrative: i) they represent Judaism as a whole, which is here being told about its Messiah; ii) they are distinct from other Jews because they were present when Jesus was condemned and crucified and bear some responsibility for these events.

it as pointing to Luke's witness motif.[20] From this point forward in the narrative of Acts, the apostles should set their eyes on the "ἕως ἐσχάτου τῆς γῆς".

Although in Acts 2 only the Jews are present, their presence from "*every nation*" (v.5) internally anticipates the future dissemination of the apostolic witness to all the nations, reiterating once again Luke's evangelistic motif.[21] Although the crossing of borders into Gentile territories will have to wait a little longer, Luke expects his readers to know that it will happen, because he has already demonstrated that what had been both internally (1:4,8) and externally (Joel 3:1-5 [LXX] predicted had come to pass (2:1-13). Therefore, if the purpose of the coming of the Spirit is to witness to the ends of the earth, as predicted and commanded by Jesus (1:8), Luke would want his reader to know that it will surely happen.

As the narrative progresses, the crowd gathers to see the happening; it hears the "apostles"[22] speaking in their own native languages. As stated above, this is not a miracle of hearing, but a clear intelligible speech.[23] Here lies the miraculous aspect of the phenomenon—what they heard was in their own dialects (vv.7-8). The glossolalia is even more miraculous, for the apostles were declaring the "μεγαλεῖα τοῦ θεοῦ" (2:11c; cf. Deut. 11:2; Sir. 36:8; Ps. 70:19 [LXX]).[24] Thus, Luke objectively establishes the reality of the coming of the Spirit and its effect. They would affirm, along with the devout Jews, that the apostles were, indeed, speaking of "*the mighty works of God*".

Through the events transpiring at Pentecost Luke makes his logic clear. When the Spirit descends on people and gives them utterance, it will be about his own mighty works and not some unintelligible and meaningless blabber. As

---

20 Luke does not show that the apostles themselves realised this. The crossing of borders is always due to some extraordinary event such as persecution (8:1-3) leading to the dispersion of the church into non-Jewish territories and clear divine guidance initiating new moves in mission (8:26-40), and visions (10:1-11:18), etc.

21 For instance, Samaritans (8:4-25); Ethiopian Eunuch (8:26-40); Gentiles: Cornelius (10:1-11:18) and the Philippian jailer (16:25-34), et al.

22 That they are apostles is known to the readers, but not to the spectators.

23 J.D.G. Dunn (*Jesus and the Spirit*, 151f.) suggests, "many present thought they recognized words of praise to God in other languages." The Western text reads here λαλουντας ταις γλωσσαις αυτων. James H. Ropes ("The Text of Acts" in *Beginnings*, III.2) suggests that this "is perhaps intended to make it clear that the speaking, not the hearing only, took place in these languages."

24 This anticipates the bestowal of the Spirit on Cornelius and his household resulting in μεγαλυνόντων τὸν θεόν: 10:46.

the readers advance through the whole of Acts, even where it is not explicitly stated, Luke expects them to recognise the "μεγαλεῖα τοῦ θεοῦ" wherever people similarly spoke in tongues (4:31; 8:15-17; 10:44-47, etc.). However, the devout Jews in the Pentecost account only partially recognise that the apostles' utterance was about the "mighty works of God." They will have to wait and watch whether Luke will expound his enigmatic phrase, "μεγαλεῖα τοῦ θεοῦ."

The suddenness of the event with no discernible cause or precursors, and the imperfect intelligibility of the 'apostolic' utterance lead only to confusion in the mind of some of the bystanders (v.12). Moreover, since Luke's expression "μεγαλεῖα τοῦ θεοῦ" (v.11) is only partially clear, the devout Jews wonder, "*What does this mean?*" (v.12; cf. v.7). Such expressions heighten the narrative moment.[25] Thus, everything happening in the event strongly anticipates a clear exposition of the event to know its exact meaning and its import, without which the event would be totally meaningless and the apostles would make themselves a laughingstock. Meanwhile, the heckling of some of the spectators further precipitates the need for an interpretation of the event.

Earlier it was shown that according to some Graeco-Roman approaches, one way of divesting an event of any miraculous connotation is to attach a pejorative label to it. Similarly, some in the Pentecost audience, whom Luke generally calls ἕτεροι (v.13)[26], attribute drunkenness to the polyglot. What is prophetic utterance about the mighty works of God to some is drunkenness to the others (ἕτεροι); their speech is meaningless; therefore, there is nothing divine or miraculous about the phenomenon.[27]

The attribution of a pejorative label to the phenomenon of glossolalia at this juncture in the Pentecost narrative seems to be a deliberate literary ploy by Luke to clarify two important points. First, in his scheme miraculous phenomena are crucial since they demonstrate the hand of God in advancing the Christian witness.[28] However, this crucial importance of the miraculous has only an instrumental value—it is important only insofar as it serves Luke's kerygmatic purpose. When they function on their own, as happens at Pentecost,

---

25 Metzger, *TCGNT*, 292.

26 It is not clear whether ἕτεροι are part of the diaspora Jews or native Jews. Robert Gundry ("Ecstatic Utterance", 304) thinks that the latter is the case. But this is not certain.

27 Conzelmann (*Acts*, 15, n. 18) reports that in Plutarch, (*Defect. Orac.* p.437 cd) the spirit which rushed into the body of the Pythia acted like wine.

28 Cf. H.C. Kee, *Miracle*, 220. Also J.A. Hardon, "Miracle Narratives", 311.

the miraculous can lead to wrong impressions. Sometimes people can and do form opinions and attitudes in relation to God's doings that are wrong and are exactly antithetical to what is intended, which need to be corrected. Secondly, such mistaken notions do not simply change automatically or with the passage of time. They have to be changed by a persuasive proclamation. As stated earlier, this is one main reason why Luke characterises the miraculous as functionally dependent on proclamation. Thus, Pentecost strongly anticipates and necessitates an explanatory speech.

We may sum up the developments here. The supernatural phenomena function as an attention-catcher and arouse in the narrative audience reactions of wonder, amazement, confusion, and even ridicule. As for Luke, it is the proclamation that can move the audience from mere reaction to a deeper response: "The crowd must remain ambivalent, because conversion...come(s) only as a result of the sermon."[29]. George Kennedy articulates succinctly the importance of the Pentecost speech as follows:

> "The great interest of this speech is that it is the first example of a type of Christian preaching in which a speaker seizes upon some occasion, situation, or sign and uses it as a way to lead into the proclamation of the gospel."[30]

Thus, the stage is set for Peter's discourse.

THE DISCOURSE (2:14-41)

As emphasised earlier, speeches are employed to construct a coherent picture, to interpret events and the Scriptures, and to exhort people to action.[31] We will see here that Peter's Pentecost speech does not simply report or explain an event but it is meant to illuminate the situation and interpret the meaning of the event for the spectators. This interpretive reading arises as an attempt to clarify obscurities of and to disclose the meaning hidden in the supernatural phenomena. The speech refers to what has just happened and to earlier historical events, particularly vis-à-vis Jesus and reveals their meaning.

---

[29] Conzelmann, *Acts*, 15.

[30] Kennedy, *New Testament Interpretation*, 117.

[31] Cf. Kennedy in his introduction to Stadter (Ed.), *Speeches in Thucydides*, xi; David E. Aune, *Literary Environment*, 91. See Dibelius, *Studies*, 139-40.

In order to heighten the moment and to reiterate the need for interpretation, Luke highlights the audience's ignorance and the preachers' clarification as follows:

The crowd...was bewildered... were amazed and perplexed, saying, "What does this mean?" But others sneered and said, "They are filled with new wine" (2:6,12-13).	Peter, "...this is what was spoken through the prophet Joel (2:14,16).

This leads smoothly from the narrative to the discourse. At this point, the narrator leaves the centrestage and allows the characters to take the floor to determine the course and the outcome of the story; to engage in the speech and to change their world by their words. Eventually, the way audience comprehends Peter's missionary speech, particularly vis-à-vis the supernatural event and the Theological and Christological import enshrined in it, but disclosed by the speech, will affect their final response to the apostolic witnessing. This strongly binds the discourse to the context and the event. In the context, Peter's missionary speech functions as a three-tier discourse as follows:

First Tier : Apologia (2:14-15)

Second Tier :The Interpretation

Pentecost as the fulfilment of Joel's Prophecy (2:16-21)
The Jesus-Kerygma (2:22-36)
Pentecost as linked to the Passion and Resurrection of Jesus (2:22-33)
Pentecost as the Confirmation and the Result of the Exaltation of Jesus as the Lord and Messiah (2:34-36)

Third Tier :Call to repentance and baptism (2:37-41)

Apologia
(2:14-15)

Peter's immediate response to the critics consists in refuting the charge that the apostles were drunk. Owning the responsibility and supported by the rest of the apostles (2:14), Peter offers a riposte—an alternative interpretation. Peter's speech here is not a subjective and isolated explanation, but a corporate exercise. It has the attestation of the apostles.[32] Within the narrative, what starts as a simple retort will evolve into a fully-fledged missionary discourse. However, this will not be an elaboration of the glossolalia, but an exposition of the event.[33]

Luke introduces Peter's defence again by ἀποφθέγγεσθαι (v.14; cf. v.4) to reinforce the inherent link between the coming of the Spirit and the resultant utterance. This also anticipates Luke's later linking of the event to prophecy (v. 18).[34] Taking his position like a Greek orator (σταθείς)[35], Peter demands the attention of the narrative audience, "*Let this be known to you...listen to what I say*" (v.14; cf. 2:22,29,37). By drawing the attention of the audience, he intends to transport the hearers into his time, space, and worldview, since he is the focal point for that moment.[36] At this juncture in the narrative of Pentecost, as seen earlier, the point-of-view changes from hyperdiegetic narration to intradiegetic narration—from the objective presentation of the narrator to the subjective interpretation of a character internal to the story, i.e., Peter. Once this happens, it becomes easy for the hearers to understand the occurrence from the speaker's viewpoint. Therefore, while the narrative audience watches Peter carefully as he discloses his mind, Luke's readers, already knowing what he is about to say, wait to follow him.

Peter's simple defence was that it was 9 o'clock in the morning and, therefore, too early to drink (2:14). His temporal explanation renders the counter-interpretation fallacious, for it does not consider the time of the day when intoxication is unacceptable. By explaining what the phenomenon is not, Peter also implies that the event has another explanation. This takes us to his interpretation.

---

32 This is also supported by Peter's inclusion of the other apostles "*all of us are witnesses*" (v.32). This takes the audience into the realm of the apostles. Later, although Peter has been speaking, the audience addresses the apostolic company, "*Brothers...?*" (v.37), signifying that they are beginning to see the Jesus-kerygma and its import from the apostles' viewpoint. The merger of apostolic and audience spaces has taken place in v. 29 (῎Ανδρες ἀδελφοί).

33 Luke T. Johnson, *The Acts of the Apostles*, (Sacra Pagina 5; Collegeville, MN: Liturgical Press, 1992), 53-54.

34 J. Panagopoulos (*Prophetic Vocation in the New Testament and Today*, [NovTSup.45; Leiden: Brill, 1977], 12-13) also emphasises that Pentecost is the example of prophecy proclaiming the word of God. Wherever it is done, it has prophetic character. Therefore, Peter's discourse is a Spirit-inspired prophetic utterance.

35 Haenchen, *Acts*, 178, n.1.

36 May ("Power of Speech", 55) suggests that deictics such as "here", "now", and "I" perform the function of shifting the reader or listener into the time and space of the speaking character, who becomes the centre of the world for that moment.

Interpretation
(2:16-36)

Basing his argument on prophecy, in this section Peter interprets that the phenomenon is not drunkenness, but the fulfilment of a prophecy.

Pentecost as the fulfilment of Joel's Prophecy
(vv.16-21)

Having stated that the phenomenon was not insobriety, Peter begins his interpretation of the event by affirming that far from representing drunkenness, the miraculous phenomena at Pentecost are the fulfilment of a prophecy (Joel 3:1-5 [LXX).[37] As shown earlier, by attributing the event to the Prophecy-Fulfilment scheme, Luke establishes a continuum between the present and the past, the reality of the present event and the truth of the following discourse from already accepted prophecies. By making an ancient prophecy contemporary to his hearers in the present while transporting them to the past, Luke establishes Pentecost not as an isolated happening, but as one in the long series of God's Promise-Fulfilment scheme.

The first thing we notice is Luke's nuanced alteration of Joel's prophecy. Peter's quotation follows the LXX generally, but makes a few alterations to suit the prophecy to the present context.[38] He alters Joel's "*...afterward*" (Joel 3:1 [LXX]) to "*In the last days it will be*" (Acts 2:17). Although he could not directly connect Joel's cosmic signs of the end time to Pentecost, its meaning for Luke is that the "last times" are already breaking into the present and the bestowal of the Spirit is its manifestation. Therefore, Pentecost does not merely resemble what Joel predicted, but this is it![39] Joel's prophecy is definitely not about speaking in tongues, but for the purpose of appropriating Joel's text to the present occasion, Luke takes two related but not identical phenomena—prophecy and speaking in tongues, as one and the same.[40]

---

37 May ("Power of Speech", 52), suggests that prophecies have a world-changing effect, for they are divine. Moreover, they demand from their audience intense engagement in the interpretive process (Ibid., 53).

38 This event forecasts such instances in the course of the church's mission. God promises to pour out the Spirit "*on all flesh*"(v.17) and the narrative traces the partial fulfilment of this promise in 8:15-17 (Samaritans) and 10:44-46 (Cornelius).

39 R.N. Longenecker, (*Biblical Exegesis in the Apostolic Period*, [Grand Rapids: Eerdmans, 1975], 70) calls this a "pesher" interpretation: "The 'this is that' fulfilment motif...is distinctive to pesher exegesis...."

40 Cf. Kirsopp Lake, "The Gift of the Spirit on the Day of Pentecost", *Beginnings*, V.111-21, esp. 111-12.

The narrative audience does not know the connection between Pentecost and Joel's prophecy. It is Peter's speech that establishes this link. Having done that, Luke brings out its universal scope—God's promise to pour his Spirit on "*all flesh*" (2:17), which he reinforces differently in 2:21 ("ὃς ἂν"). Does this include Gentiles as well? In the context of Pentecost, given the Jewish composition of the audience, God's promise to pour his Spirit on all flesh is only partially realised. However, as pointed out earlier, within the internal Prophecy-Fulfilment scheme of Acts, Pentecost does prophetically anticipate the incorporation of outsiders (e.g., the Samaritans [8:15-17]; the Gentiles: Cornelius and his household [10:44-46]), their response to the word, and receiving the Spirit. Importantly, these events take place in the presence of Peter and John (8:14) and in the presence of Peter and a group of believers from Jerusalem (10:44-45; cf. 11:15,17; 15:8). Since they themselves have experienced the coming of the Spirit, in these cases they will see the fulfilment of God's promise to send the Spirit on "*all flesh*", though in a limited sense. By this chain of similar outpourings of the Spirit on new people-groups, Luke clarifies what happens, or what should happen, when the word is proclaimed and accepted. This reiterates what we showed earlier in the structure of Acts that Luke is not so much concerned about demonstrating the actual geographical expansion of the Christian witness in 1:8 as about the universal outreach. In the context of Pentecost, the inclusion of '*all flesh*' within God's promise is the climactic point of Joel's prophecy upon which the greatest weight is placed. Moreover, by linking Pentecost to calling on the name of the Lord to be saved and to God's dealings with Jesus, Luke shows that God's promise to pour out the Spirit on '*all flesh*' also has salvific significance.

There is yet another nuanced alteration of Joel's prophecy in Peter's declaration that *"everyone who calls on the name of the Lord shall be saved"* (2:21). Whereas the "κύριος" in Joel refers to Yahweh, it anticipates the same term being applied to the Messiah in Acts 2:34 and to Jesus in 2:36. In other words, it is Jesus who saves everyone who calls on his name. This is how Luke wants his readers to understand this part of the prophecy. Such a shift from Theocentric soteriology to Christocentric soteriology is Luke's unique interpretation of this passage.[41] In addition, it makes clear that, for Luke, Christian proclamation is not just information about the Jesus story, but the declaration of the salvation contained in it by establishing the identity between the κύριος (v.21) and Ἰησους (v.22).[42] Thus, the proclamation of the Joel text denotes that the event

---

41 Richard J. Dillon, "The Prophecy of Christ and His Witnesses According to the Discourses of Acts", *NTS*, 32, (1986), 544-56, esp.549.

42 J.J. Kilgallen, "The Unity of Peter's Pentecost Speech", *The Bible Today*, 82, (1976), 650-56.

the spectators have just witnessed is actually the fulfilment of the prophecy about the Day of the Lord. Therefore, it is now the time to call on his name in order to be saved. This is not explicit to the immediate onlookers; it is the missionary speech, necessitated by and originating from the miraculous event itself, which makes it clear.

Given this twist in the speech, the immediate narrative audience might consider Joel's ὃς ἄν (v.21) as referring only to their fellow Jews. But the readers, because of their access to the whole speech and the text of Acts as a whole, will retrospectively realise that ὃς ἄν has universal connotation. It portends for them the expansiveness of those who call on the name of the Lord to be saved. Luke indicates this in many ways in the context: i) the notation, "*people from every nation under the heaven*" (v.5); ii) the enumeration of the countries of origin of those present (vv.9-22); iii) the Joel-citation emphasising the bestowal of the Spirit on "*all flesh*" (πᾶσαν σάρκα, v.17); iv) invitation to "*everyone*" (v.21), and v) the redemptive promise for "*all who are far away*" (v.29; cf. Isa. 57:19). The inclusion of ὃς ἄν within a missionary discourse reinforces its relevance and applicability of the Christian witness to anyone, whether Jewish or Gentile.

This is how Peter's speech interprets Pentecost vis-à-vis the prophecy for the narrative audience. But for the speech, the narrative audience would not have realised the connection between the event and its prediction by one of their own ancient prophets. By establishing continuity with the past, Luke provides his readers with a clear sense of direction on how to assess God's promises for the future.[43] Thus, Pentecost is, indeed, the fulfilment of Joel's prophecy through which God is offering the narrative audience, indeed, the whole of humanity, a soteriological provision in what he has done.

Having shown the connection between Pentecost and Joel's prophecy and the universal scope of God's offer of salvation, Luke proceeds to establish that this act of God cannot be fully comprehended apart from its intrinsic correlation to Jesus. The same God, who does not act capriciously but fulfils what he has promised, has acted in a special way in and through the person of Jesus. Importantly, had it not been for the speech, this link between Pentecost and its Christological import would have remained totally hidden to the audience.

---

[43] For instance, the fulfilment of the promise, "*I will pour out my Spirit upon all flesh*" (Joel 3:1; cf. Acts 2:17) in Acts 8:15-17 and 10:44-46.

The Jesus-Kerygma
(vv.22-36)

Although, in the first reading it may appear that the Jesus-kerygma in Peter's speech is an abrupt insertion,[44] by employing Joel's κύριος to refer to Jesus (cf. v.36), Luke shows a close connection between these two sections. Earlier we showed that Luke adds Christological specifics to his general portrait of God. What Peter develops in his speech about God at Pentecost is a microcosmic version of what Luke says in Acts as a whole, particularly about his dealings with Jesus. In the present, in Peter's speech, he will show the link between Pentecost and Jesus. Accordingly, he develops Peter's sermon into an exposition of Jesus' identity, setting him in relation to the prophetic tradition.[45]

Peter first presents God's dealings with Jesus. God had attested him by the various τέρατα καὶ σημεῖα that he had performed through him (v.22).[46] Peter puts them forward as objective demonstrations of God's attestation of Jesus. Peter's seeming appeal here to the hearers' knowledge of Jesus' story ("καθὼς αὐτοὶ οἴδατε" [v.22; cf. 10:37])[47] sounds a bit odd since Jesus' identity was known only to his immediate followers and not to all the Jews.[48] Therefore, καθὼς αὐτοὶ οἴδατε (v.22) should be considered more as an attention-seeker than as an appeal to the audience's historical memory, since the immediate narrative context does not evince any public knowledge of either Jesus' identity or his ministry.

Peter has already declared that the last days, forecast by Joel, have begun, evidenced particularly by the bestowal of the Spirit, accompanied by prophetic utterances, dreams, visions, wonders (τέρατα), and signs (σημεῖα) (v.19). These collectively represent the new age that Jesus had inaugurated. As seen earlier, Luke's hendiadys τέρατα καὶ σημεῖα clearly establishes Jesus as a miracle worker *nonpareil* (2:22; 10:38; cf. 1:1). Importantly, his signs and

---

44 For instance, Marshall, *Acts*, 74.

45 Cf. Acts 3:22-23; 7:37.

46 This means that the apostolic witness borne to Jesus is the active expression of the will and work of God (Soards, *Speeches*, 33). See also B.R. Gaventa, " 'You will be my Witnesses': Aspects of Mission in the Acts of the Apostles," *Missiology*, 10, (1982), 413-25.

47 cf. Barrett, *Acts*, 1.141.

48 A reading of Luke's Gospel shows that this is the case. Even John the Baptist wondered if Jesus was truly the "*one who is to come*" (Lk. 7:7:19); the Sanhedrin asked Jesus, "*If you are the Messiah, tell us*" (Lk.22:67; cf. 4:3,9). On the contrary, when Jesus asked, "*who do you say that I am*?", Peter confessed, "*The Messiah of God*" (9:20; cf. 24:19,21a).

wonders are due to divine causation (cf. v.17). This is important for the readers to realise since later in the speech Peter relates Pentecost also as God's work through Jesus. However, it first relates to the Jewish treatment of Jesus.

Pentecost as Related to the Passion and Resurrection of Jesus (vv.23-33)

So far, Peter has been logically arguing that Pentecost was the fulfilment of God's promise embedded in the ancient prophecy. He now expounds the Christological meaning ensconced in Pentecost since, for him, Pentecost can be best understood only in reference to God's dealings with Jesus. However, this Christological focus shows the contrast between God's acts and the acts of the Jerusalem Jews. This is how Luke links Pentecost to the passion and resurrection of Jesus.

The basic plot here is that although Jesus was God-appointed, the Jews had rejected and crucified him. As shown earlier, this is at once a tragedy and an irony. Instead of recognising Jesus as God's chosen one, the Jews had repeatedly rejected him (v.23).[49] Although the "lawless", i.e., the Romans, have actually put Jesus to death, Luke does not minimise the Jewish guilt in crucifying Jesus (v. 36; Cf. 3:18; cf. 13:27-29; 26:23).

Jesus' death on the cross seemingly contradicts his divine-attestation (2:19), but the scandal of the cross is overcome by the fact that it was all part of ἡ βουλή τοῦ θεοῦ (v.23; cf. 3:18). Such an employment of the device of cause-and-effect shows that it is God who ultimately determines Jesus' destiny, not humans. The seemingly free concerted action of the Jews and the Gentiles is indeed, part of God's foreknowledge, decision, and plan. Therefore, the cross is not a scandal.[50] If we relate Jesus' crucifixion to "*Everyone who calls on the name of the Lord shall be saved*" (2:21), then we may sense the direction of Luke's thought here. The cross is not a stumbling block, but the means of human salvation.

Meanwhile, inasmuch as the Jerusalem Jews were accomplices to their leaders in rejecting Jesus, the one attested by God himself, they have opposed God's

---

[49] See Tannehill, "Israel in Luke-Acts: A Tragic Story", *JBL*, 104, (1985), 69-85 for the tragic aspect of Israel in Luke and Acts.

[50] Haenchen, *Acts*, 180. There is a tension in the text here: if the crucifixion of Jesus is God's will, should the Jews be held culpable? Marshall (*Acts*, 75) suggests that this is a paradox of divine predestination and human freewill in its strongest form.

purposes. Peter's speech here performs an epideictic function by censuring the Jews for rejecting and crucifying Jesus and warning readers not to imitate the Jerusalem Jews.

Conspicuously Peter's charge here is appropriate neither to humanity nor to the Jews in general. This raises the question of the suitability of the speech to its audience as was expected in the Graeco-Roman tradition.[51] Within the narrative, Peter's accusation applies only to the Jews and their rulers at the time of Jesus' crucifixion (cf. 3:17). However, Luke does not indicate the precise sense in which his "target audience" should be understood. He addresses them differently at different times, but all the time widening their circle:

2:23	"You"
2:26	"The entire house of Israel"
3:17	"You...also your rulers"

This can be quite confusing, because as Jack T. Sanders holds[52], some readers might think that Luke was thoroughly anti-Jewish and, therefore, might develop a blanket notion that all the Jews were blameworthy for the rejection and crucifixion of Jesus. Certainly some in the narrative audience could plead innocent. In this sense, Frank M. Matera could be right in saying that according to Luke only the Jerusalemites and their leaders bear responsibility for Jesus' crucifixion. [53]

However, the readers' notion, represented by J.T. Sanders or by Conzelmann, that the Jews symbolise those who have rejected the Gospel and that they are the stereotypical enemies of the church[54], may be further reiterated by other incidents of rejection of the apostles and Christian preachers by the Jews in Acts. In particular, in the narratives about Paul in Acts, the Jews reject the Christian message repeatedly to such an extent that Paul is forced to turn to the Gentiles. In the end, it appears as if the Jews have lost forever the offer of

---

51 Cf. Thucydides, *HPW*, 1.22.2.

52 J.T. Sanders, "Who is a Jew", *NTS*, 37, (1991), 434-55, esp. 438. See also David P. Moessner, "The 'Leaven of the Pharisees' and 'This Generation': Israel's Rejection of Jews According to Luke" in Dennis D. Sylva (Ed.), *Reimaging the Death of the Lukan Jesus*, (Frankfurt: Hain, 1990), 79-107, 190-3.

53 F.M. Matera, "Responsibility for the Death of Jesus According to the Acts of the Apostles", *JSNT*, 39, (1990), 77-93. Also Craig A. Evans ("Is Luke's View of the Jewish Rejection of Jesus Anti-Semitic?" in Dennis D. Sylva (Ed.), *Reimaging the Death*, 29-56, 174-83) and L.T. Johnson, ("The New Testament's Anti-Jewish Slander and the Convention of Ancient Polemic", *JBL*, 108, [1989], 419-41) hold that only some Jews are guilty.

54 Conzelmann, *Theology*, 145.

salvation that Christian proclamation brings. Nevertheless, is this true? What is Luke's position regarding the Jews in Acts? Is he anti-Jewish? Are the Jews lost forever, especially after Paul's quotation and interpretation of Isaiah in Acts 28:23-28?[55]

There are two conflicting and totally incompatible views about Luke's characterisation of the Jews in Acts—negative and positive. The negative view holds that in the theology of Luke, after the end of Acts, Jews no longer have the opportunity to accept the Gospel and because of their total rejection of it, they have lost the offer of salvation. J.T. Sanders accuses Luke of 'anti-Semitism', particularly in light of Acts 28:27-30. Luke's interpretation of Isa. 6:9-10 in Acts 28:28 shows that for him, salvation is for the Gentiles and was never intended for the Jews. The cycle of rejection and further mission ends with rejection. For Luke, the Jews are irredeemably lost.[56]

The positive view, represented by Jacob Jervell, contends that Conzelmann and Haenchen are mistaken, because, "Luke does not describe a Jewish people who, as a whole, reject the early Christian message, and in which the believing Jews are the exceptions." Acts contains "numerous references to mass conversions of Jews."[57] On the other hand, Gentiles do not begin to be saved only after a Jewish rejection of the Gospel; rather, "from the beginning of the mission it is certain that, according to Scripture and in agreement with the missionary command, the Gentiles have a share in salvation."[58] Jervell adds that whatever the force of the final statement (28:28) is, it does not refer to the Jews *en masse*.[59]

In solution to the riddle of Luke's position regarding the salvation of the Jews, Jervell offers a mediating position or a division between "obdurate" Israel and

---

55 For a discussion on Luke's attitude to Jews, Gentiles and Judaism, see Christopher M. Tuckett, *Luke*, (New Testament Guides; Sheffield: SAP, 1996), 50-64, esp. 54-64.

56 J.T. Sanders, *The Jews*, 80-83, 297-99. For similar views see, H. Conzelmann, *Theology*, 80-83, 297-99; E. Haenchen, *Acts*, 691-92; idem, "The Book of Acts as Source Material for the History for the History of Early Christianity" in L.E. Keck & J.L. Martyn (Eds.), *Studies in Luke-Acts*, (London: SPCK, 1968/Philadelphia: Fortress, 1980), 259-65.

57 J. Jervell, *Luke and the People of God*, (Minneapolis: Augsburg, 1972), 44. See also R.C. Tannehill, "Rejection by the Jews and Turning to the Gentiles: The Pattern of Paul's Mission in Acts" in J.B. Tyson (Ed.), *Luke-Acts and the Jewish People*, (London: SCM, 1988), 83-101.

58 J. Jervell, *People of God*, 43.

59 Ibid., p.49, n.21 and p.63.

"repentant" Israel (i.e., Christians).[60] This renewed Israel is then composed of both Jews and Gentiles, that is who accept the Gospel. In fact, the addition of the Gentiles is part of the restoration of Israel.[61]

J.D.G. Dunn expresses the same note of optimism. He argues that any notion of final rejection is the first step towards anti-Semitism.[62] Acts 28:28 is not Paul's final turn away from and rejection of his people in favour of the Gentiles. It is no more final than the earlier denunciations. Dunn explains that the idea of 'the salvation of God' being known to 'the nations' is an allusion to Ps. 67:2 (Cf. Ps. 98:3; Isa. 40:5). Such passages express the thought of God's faithfulness to Israel as part of his universal saving concern for all nations. Salvation is for all people—Gentiles as well as Jews. Paul's turn to the Gentiles is part of God's larger scheme of salvation. Turning to the Gentiles does not imply rejection of Israel. It is a phase in the larger purpose of God.

The second view exuding optimism is tenable. To the scholarly views expressed above, we may also add Luke's notion of Divine Providence and his Prophecy-Fulfilment scheme, which the negative view stated above, obviously tries to negate or overlook. Luke's declaration at Pentecost, "*Everyone who calls on the name of the Lord shall be saved*" (2:21) is a prophecy that is realised immediately at Pentecost (2:41) and later in 4:4 where masses of Jews are converted (3000 and 5000). This prophecy (2:21) is a Lucan absolute for all times, whereas "*Let it be known to you then that this salvation of God has been sent to the Gentiles; they will listen*" (28:28; cf. Isa. 6:9-10) is not a prophecy, but one in a chain of similar statements. It follows a particular mission strategy in Acts, i.e., preaching first to the Jews and in the synagogue (18:4,19; 19:8) is followed by extended ministry outside of the synagogue. The earlier occasions (i.e., 13:46,51; 18:6, etc.) show that Paul's seeming giving up on the Jews is not final. Paul invariably starts with the Jewish synagogue, for instance, in 14:1: "*...Iconium, where Paul and Barnabas went into the Jewish synagogue and spoke in such a way that a great number of ...Jews...became believers*"). Similarly, in 17:1-2, 10-12 Luke records: "*These Jews were more receptive...welcomed the message very eagerly...Many of them therefore believed....*"

---

60 Ibid.

61 Ibid., 60. See also E. Franklin, *Christ the Lord*, 114; LT. Johnson, *Acts*, 476. Tuckett (*Luke*, 60), considers Jervell's view as good as the negative view.

62 J.D.G. Dunn, *The Acts of the Apostles*, (Epworth Commentaries; Peterborough: Epworth Press, 1996), 355-56. For reasons why it is hard to accuse Luke of anti-Semitism, see Tuckett, *Luke*, 62-64.

In addition to this positive portrayal of the Jews and their response to the Christian proclamation, the open ending of the book of Acts also leaves all the possibilities still wide open. Therefore, the same chain is most likely to recur. Here we are once again reminded of Dunn's resounding optimism.[63] Moreover, the all-inclusive tone of Luke's πάντα language elsewhere in Acts is one argument that one cannot totally rule out the possibility of a continued mission to the Jews even beyond 28:28, which (unfortunately) sounds final. First, God commands πάντας πανταχοῦ μετανοεῖν (17:30); cf. 2:38; 3:19). Therefore, Luke's reference to πάντας τοὺς εἰσπορευομένους πρὸς αὐτόν (i.e., Paul) could have included at least some Jews, and, therefore, Paul continues "*proclaiming the kingdom of God and teaching about the Lord Jesus Christ with all boldness and without hindrance*" (28:31). In the context, Paul's proclamation means nothing more than a continued proclamation to all—Jews as well as Gentiles. With this optimistic note, we now return to Acts 2, because the end of the Pentecost story will demonstrate that in Luke's scheme in Acts, the Jewish response to the Christian mission always is mixed. We will refer to this later in the chapter.

In the Pentecost account, while recording the Jewish rejection and crucifixion of Jesus, Luke also categorically states that in a divine contrast scheme, God raised Jesus up from the dead (2:24). Here we might recall other instances where he demonstrates the divine contrast scheme (3:15; 10:39-40; cf. 4:10; 5:30; 13:28-30, etc). This is another ironic situation where the readers may notice the Jewish subterfuge to do away with Jesus totally and its reversal—God raised him up. Peter elaborates that Jesus' resurrection is, in fact, the fulfilment of a prophecy and is the proof that he is the Messiah.

Basing his argument on Scripture, Peter refers to Jesus' resurrection (vv. 25-28; cf. 3:15; 10:40) by quoting Ps. 15:8-11 (LXX), which is regarded as a statement about the Messiah. Luke understands David's reference to the *Holy One* (ὅσιόν: Ps. 15:10 [LXX]) as referring to the Messiah. He argues that David could not have been talking about himself since he died and was buried (v.29), which is a tangible proof of his permanent dead-state.[64] If, then, David was not speaking about himself, it follows that he must have been speaking prophetically regarding the Messiah who would be his descendant (2:31). Instead of being abandoned to Sheol, the Messiah would be raised from the

[63] See also Dunn, *The Partings of the Ways between Christianity and Judaism and their Significance for the Character of Christianity*, (London: SCM/Philadelphia: Trinity Press International, 1991), 151.

[64] William S. Kurz, "Hellenistic Rhetoric", 184.

dead. Now Peter's logic is clear. The OT prophesied that the messiah would rise from the dead. God raised Jesus from the dead (v.24) and, therefore, it follows that he must be the Messiah.[65] Luke uses Scripture here as an interpretative tool and allows it to interpret itself and the parts to interpret each other and, thereby, build a consistent picture for the audience. In other words, Pentecost points to and confirms that Jesus did rise from the dead and that the bestowal of the Spirit is his action inasmuch as it is God's action.

Having established that Jesus was indeed the prophesied Messiah and, therefore, was raised from the dead, Peter now explains its connection to Pentecost, which is not obvious on the face of it.

Pentecost as the Confirmation and Result of the Exaltation of Jesus (vv.33-36).

Jesus' resurrection is, in fact, the exaltation to the right hand of God (v.33).[66] Being in that position of authority, he received from the Father the Spirit and has poured it out upon his people.[67]

Peter declares that the Spirit is the gift that Jesus received from the Father in virtue of his exaltation, which he has bestowed on his people (v.33).[68] Here Luke offers a double-consolidation of Jesus' exalted position in this section: polemically, Jesus, the one rejected by the Jews, is the Lord and Messiah (2:36); Pentecost is an argument for this. From all this evidence (οὖν, v.36), it is clear that the bestowal of the Spirit is the confirmation that God has made Jesus both Lord and Messiah (v.36).[69] All the Scriptural testimony and apostolic witness too attest the same. This conversely implies that Pentecost is the

---

65 Peter is not arguing that Jesus became Messiah by his resurrection, but rather that since the Messiah must rise from the dead, and because Jesus rose from the dead, it follows that Jesus was already the Messiah during his earthly life. Marshall (*Acts*, 77) points out two difficulties in this argument: i) the prima facie interpretation is that David was expressing his own hope of resurrection; ii) it is not clear that Ps. 132:11 refers to one specific descendant of David as being the Messiah. The likelihood is that Peter's listeners shared a belief that the passages about David's descendants included a reference to the Messiah in particular.

66 Although Luke distinguishes the ascension from the resurrection in his narrative, in the kerygma here the resurrection appears to be identical with the exaltation (Cf. Conzelmann, *Acts*, 21).

67 This may be an allusion to Ps. 68:18. J. Dupont cited in Marshall (*Acts*, 78).

68 In 3:1-10, the healing of the paralytic is the visual demonstration of Jesus' glorification (3:13).

69 Other instances where the true identity of Jesus is declared are 3:13,14,15,20,22,26; 10:36,42.

confirmation of Jesus' Messiahship and the result of his exaltation.[70] Therefore, "The 'evidence' of the veracity of this argument is the Holy Spirit."[71]

The title "Lord" in 2:36 is Luke's own faith declaration[72] indicating a common conviction about Jesus since later it becomes "*the Lord Jesus*" or "*the Lord Jesus Christ.*" (2:36, 8:5,12,22; 10:16,36; 16:31)[73] This explains why Luke interchanges κύριος for God or Jesus, especially in the OT *testimonia*. In establishing that Jesus is the Lord, Luke wants the audience to understand "*Everyone who calls on the name of the Lord shall be saved*" in 2:21 as referring to none other than Jesus himself. This is the main thrust of Luke's presentation of Jesus based on the Pentecost occurrence. This is what the Pentecost crowd in Acts 2 witnesses, but this is not readily obvious to them. It is disclosed progressively by the missionary discourse.

Luke does not explain the title ὁ Χριστός (v. 31,36,38) or the precise sense in which it should be understood in Acts. He takes it for granted that the Jewish audience knew the meaning hidden in the title and the implications of acknowledging him as such.[74] As stated above, Luke's focus here is on presenting Jesus as the fulfilment of the Jewish messianic expectation. In addition, it sets him in conformity to the Jewish Scriptures. Thus, the narrative audience has all that is needed to accept Jesus as the final and complete instrument of God and as the fulfilment of the OT promise (2:31-2,36; 3:20; 8:5,28).[75]

Pentecost is not just about the wind and the tongues of fire. It is primarily about God and his dealings with Jesus. All along God is invisible, and yet, ubiquitous and is recognised in what he has done in and through Jesus. Jesus'

---

70 Jesus' exaltation should not be viewed as adoptionism as if Jesus was made κύριος and Χριστός only through his resurrection. The main thrust of Luke's argument is to set forth God's action in contrast to the Jewish treatment of Jesus and not to reflect on the time of installation. Cf. Conzelmann, *Acts*, 21.

71 Soards, *Speeches*, 36.

72 C.F.D. Moule, "The Christology of Acts" in Leander E. Keck & et al, (Eds.), *Studies in Luke-Acts*, 159-85, esp. 160-61.

73 Cf. Franklin, (*Christ the Lord*, 53) suggests that calling Jesus as "Lord" is an expression of faith and common allegiance to him.

74 In his Gospel (24:26) Luke clearly indicates that to be the Christ necessarily means to suffer and thus to enter into glory. True, Jesus was the Christ even at his birth (2:11), but "still he had to become the Christ by performing the messianic role foreordained by God" (Zehnle, *Discourse*, 68).

75 See also O'Neil, *Theology*, 119-20.

mighty works (2:22), his death (2:23), his resurrection (2:24,32), the bestowal of the Spirit (2:33-34), his exaltation as Lord and Messiah (2:36), are all God's works. He has reversed the intent of the Jews to do away with Jesus (cf. 3:33-35), and exalted him (2:33-35). Pentecost strongly emphasises that the repeated employment of accusatives referring to Jesus, namely "Jesus" (2:22), "this one" (2:23), "this Jesus" (2:32), "him both Lord and messiah, this Jesus" (2:36) is Luke's rhetorical ploy "to make Jesus vividly present to the audience as a special kind of person."[76] This also discloses the irony in the whole story, i.e., the Jewish rejection of Jesus cannot stop his exaltation; rather, it leads to it. What the Jews have done to Jesus is a deliberate attempt to undo all that God had intended. This brings out the terrible nature of the guilt of the Jews in crucifying Jesus, exacerbating the need to repent.

Call to Repentance and Baptism (2:37-41)

The Theological and Christological content of Pentecost is missionary since, as seen earlier, it comes with certain demands and expectations of appropriate audience response. The accusatory note and the persuasive force in Peter's speech evoke feelings of guilt in the audience and persuade them to act at the same time. We have already pointed out the exhortative or the persuasive function of the missionary speeches. This recalls, for instance, the emotional make up of the Spartans, characterised by constant terror of Athens, which the Corinthians exploit to conscript them for war with Athens.[77] Similarly, the persuasive function of Peter's sermon reminds us of the speeches in Thucydides which, more than being vehicles for expressing a particular viewpoint, are attempts at persuasion.[78] Likewise, Luke builds up Peter's speech to a convincing climax with a view to producing the effect referred to in the following verse.

The listeners are "*cut to their heart*" (v.37), since they have rejected and crucified Jesus, their Lord and Messiah. They interrupt Peter and ask τί ποιήσωμεν (v.38) to remedy the situation. Such interruptions heighten the significance of the moment, the crime of the Jewish audience, and what follows;

---

[76] Tannehill, *Narrative Unity*, 1.41.

[77] Thucydides, *HPW*, I.68-71.

[78] Cf. Thucydides, *HPW*, I.68-71; III.36-49; S. Hornblower, *Thucydides*,, 163-4. Also Josephus, *War*, II.16.4.[345-401]). Luke's persuasion takes place in a religious sphere. The other difference is that whereas in Thucydidean debates two parties approach the same problem from two different perspectives, thereby giving options for the audience to choose from, in Luke there is only once course of action that the audience can take.

they accentuate the dramatic complexion of the present moment (cf. 10:44),[79] and also form a recognition scene "where...persons who have acted blindly against their own best interests suddenly recognize their error."[80]

If what the narrative audience knows, sees, and hears (2:22,29,33) is an especially convincing basis for Peter's argument[81], certainly it has accomplished its missionary purpose. The reminder of the Jews' rejection of Jesus underscores the importance of conversion. Therefore, in response to the audience-initiative, Peter demands from them the ideal response under the circumstances.

First, Peter commands the respondents to repent (μετανοήσατε, v.37-38). A call to repentance is an essential constituent of the apostolic proclamation. In the context of conversion (3:19-26; 8:22; 10:43), as seen earlier, it refers to the inner decision to turn, and to make a complete break with the past,[82] to adopt another view, and therefore, to regret the prior viewpoint.[83] The fact that Peter's invitation is in the imperative (μετανοήσατε: aorist imperative) proves that under the circumstances, repentance is the most urgent task, which the hearers must undertake immediately. Therefore, the speech summons the Jews to repent for their rejection and crucifixion of Jesus, and points to a new phase characterised by accepting Jesus as the Lord and Messiah. This is not explicit in the text, but Luke would expect his readers to make such logical associations.

Secondly, Peter commands the hearers to be baptised in the name of Jesus (v.38). This immediately concretises the audience's repentance. Moreover, the fact that it is in the singular (βαπτιθήτω ἕκαστος ὑμῶν) indicates that it is specifically directed to the individual members of the crowd. Baptism, therefore, is a sign of the individual's response to Christian witnessing although its demand to convert has a collective appeal.[84] This baptism should be administered in the name of Jesus, marking the beginning of a new relationship, in that, when the respondent is baptised in the name of Jesus, he/she comes to

---

79 Conzelmann, (*Acts*, 22) suggests that this is a literary device. See also Aune, *Literary Environment*, 127. Similar interruptions are seen in 3:26/4:1; 10:43/10:44.

80 Tannehill, "Mission Speeches", 403-04. Haenchen (*Acts* 183, n.5) reminds that here there is no anti-Judaism, but only an attempt to show the man who is to come to faith in Jesus that he is guilty of Jesus' death.

81 Cf. Tannehill, *Narrative Unity*, 2.41.

82 Also C.K. Barrett, *Acts*, 1.203.

83 So also Richard J. Sklba, "The Call to New Beginnings: A Biblical Theology of Conversion", *BTB*, 11, (1981), 67-73, esp. 67.

84 Cf. Barrett, *Acts*, 1.153-4.

belong to him.[85] It immediately, but partially, fulfils calling on the name of the Lord, envisaged of everyone, to be saved in 2:21. Further, Luke's pairing of repentance and baptism might mean that the former is an element of the latter or that repentance should necessarily issue in baptism and that baptism presupposes repentance.

Pentecost is the only occasion where baptism is explicitly demanded of the audience. In other places, Luke shows it as a natural corollary to conversion, though not explicitly stated; in some other places, it is due to the audience initiative. Nevertheless, in almost all the conversion stories we have recorded, Luke shows it as the most common response of people to Christian witnessing. As discussed above, Luke would want his readers to accept baptism in the Pentecost story as evidence of repentance and believing and as a sign of conversion and new life.[86] It is an external demonstration of the internal transformation in response to the demand to repent.

The first blessing issuing from the audience's response of repentance-baptism is the ἄφεσις ἁμαρτιῶν, which is predominantly a Lucan concept (2:38; 10:43; cf. 5:31; 13:38; 26:18). It is the central benefit of accepting the word, repenting, and being baptised. As shown above, for Luke, being forgiven of sins means to be saved.[87] For the readers this might be further reinforced if they know Luke's Gospel where he explicitly connects forgiveness of sins to salvation in Zechariah's prophecy "τοῦ δοῦναι γνῶσιν σωτηρίας...ἐν ἀφέσει ἁμαρτιῶν" (1:77).

The second blessing of conversion is the reception of the Holy Spirit (v.38). Nevertheless, nowhere does Luke give his readers adequate information whether the coming of the Spirit precedes or follows baptism. Perhaps he is not concerned so much about the sequence of receiving the Spirit as about the fact and the necessity of receiving the Spirit (2:38; 8:35-38; 10:44). What matters most for Luke in Pentecost is that the respondents should receive the Spirit as an indication of repentance and forgiveness of sins (cf. 10:44-48).

The promise of the forgiveness of sins and the gift of the Spirit is also for those who are far away (v.39). Luke may have had in mind the other Jews who are

---

85 Ibid., 1.154.

86 Cf. Joel B. Green, "'Salvation to the End of the Earth' (Acts 13:47): God as Saviour in the Acts of the Apostles" in Marshall, et al, (Eds.), *Witness to the Gospel*, 83-106, esp. 104.

87 So also R.E. Brown, *The Birth of the Messiah: A Commentary on the Infancy Narratives in the Gospels of Matthew and Luke*, rev. edn., London: G. Chapman/New York: Doubleday, 1993, 373.

still in diaspora, while at the same time prophetically including the distant Gentile world (παντὸς ἔθνους, v.5) as well.[88] The OT employs the phrase "far away" metaphorically. For example, Isa. 46:12 refers to people being "*far from deliverance*". Similarly, in Isa. 59:11, people wait "*for salvation, but it is far from us*" and "*righteousness stands at a distance*" (Isa. 59:14). Although the "deliverance" and "salvation" in Isaiah may carry political overtones, by employing Isaianic language in the context of conversion, Luke accords it salvific significance. In view of Luke's predilection to make nuanced alterations, we might say that in Acts (2:39) Luke employs "far away" as meaning being beyond salvation. Therefore, the πάντα ἔθνη are well within the scope of the forgiveness of sins and the gift of the Spirit.

The third demand that Peter places before his audience is "*save yourselves*" from the wicked generation (σωθῆτε...σκολιᾶς, v.40).[89] The phrase σωθῆτε becomes meaningful in light of Acts 2:21 where Peter declares, "*Everyone who calls on the name of the Lord shall be saved.*" The passive use of σωθήτε in 2:40 may be taken to mean that the audience should save themselves (intransitive). However, since we have already shown that it is God who alone saves, in the context, salvation is not possible except by calling on the name of the Lord. Therefore, "σωθῆτε" can only mean that the hearers must "Accept...salvation"[90] unlike their unrepentant Jewish contemporaries. Luke calls such persons, "σῳζομένους" (v.47). The passive voice here implies an external agent, thus ruling out the question of saving oneself.

Through all that has been going on so far, both in the narrative and in Peter's missionary speech, Luke demonstrates that the apostles read the situation correctly and made use of the events of Pentecost as a starting point. Secondly, Luke points out the benefit of both the adequate knowledge of and the appropriate use of the Scriptures at the right time (Peter recollected Joel's prophecy and applied it appropriately to the present context). Thirdly, a straightforward presentation of God and what he has done in and offers through Jesus (e.g., salvation; cf. 2:21) is powerful enough to evoke in people the right kind of responses, such as repentance and searching for forgiveness of sins. Fourthly, Christian proclamation necessarily contains missionary elements that challenge the narrative audience for an action such as repentance and baptism, etc.

---

88 Cf. Isa. 49:1,12; 57:19.

89 Cf. Deut. 32:5; Ps. 77:8 (LXX).

90 Barrett, *Acts*, 1.156.

In the end, Peter's speech fulfils its rhetorical intent; the narrative audience is persuaded. As shown in Thucydides' speeches above, at Pentecost Peter"does not merely express a personal opinion, but strongly impacts on the narrative audience to decide for a particular course of action. Therefore, his call to repentance receives an overwhelming response (vv.41-7). Three thousand people accept (ἀποδέχεσθαι)[91] Peter's proclamation of the word and are baptised. Later the narrator calls them the "οἱ πιστεύοντες" (v.44). We have already taken the position that the actual audience response in the narrative in Acts is the conceptual equivalence to what is demanded in the speech. Therefore, at Pentecost, accepting the word presupposes repenting and believing, and conversely, believing presupposes accepting the message proclaimed, and repenting. The Jewish audience received the word, convinced that something supernatural had occurred, and accepted the Theological and Christological claims hidden in it, but ultimately disclosed by the missionary discourse. They were persuaded that Peter was "believable" (cf. v.47) when he proclaimed that the event was the actual fulfilment, within the narrative, of the divine promise through the prophet and that it meant that Jesus was truly their Lord and Messiah. Therefore, their baptism concretely expresses that they have been persuaded to accept Jesus as such.[92]

At the end of the Pentecost narrative, we see clearly a neat linear progression of the story towards the conclusion. Therefore, we may refer to the conversion at Pentecost as following a "*Linear Narrative Pattern of conversion*" as the following diagram demonstrates:

Linear Narrative Pattern of conversion

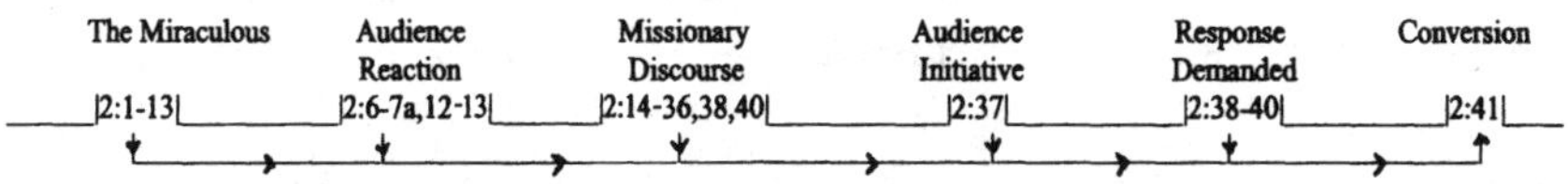

Having analysed the Pentecost story and demonstrated the way Luke portrays the balance between the miraculous and proclamation as an effective means of Christian witnessing that has resulted in mass-conversion, we may now sum up the narrative functions of the Pentecost story.

---

91 This is a hapaxlegomenon in Acts. Elsewhere Luke employs a simple δέχεσθαι (8:14; 11:1).

92 Cf. Barrett, *Acts*, 1.160.

NARRATIVE FUNCTIONS

New Directions

The outpouring of the Spirit on the apostles at Pentecost, followed by the missionary discourse results in 3000 people witnessing the supernatural phenomena (2:1-13) and hearing Peter's message (2:14-36), and becoming the οἱ πιστεύοντες (2:37-41, 44). By giving birth to such a powerful evangelistic pattern—the miraculous + proclamation= conversion—Pentecost shows new directions for effective and successful apostolic mission in Acts. A close reading of the whole of the book of Acts shows that the Pentecost story is the first in the long series of such stories where Luke builds the Christian mission around "the miraculous + proclamation = conversion" pattern. We have been emphasising this since the beginning of our study.

The immediate narrative setting of Pentecost retrospectively connects the event to Acts 1:8, where Jesus commissions his disciples to be his witnesses, where Luke provides glimpses of Jesus' universal vision—the witnesses have to reach the ends of the earth, not Rome. In the phrase "*the ends of the earth*" (1:8), Luke's readers see a destination, an ultimate goal towards which the witness should move. Through Pentecost, Luke conveys his claim that it requires nothing less than the supernatural means—the miraculous and proclamation—to accomplish this. Thus, Pentecost sets on course a distinct type of mission, which emphasises both the need for and demonstrates an integrated approach to Christian mission—a balance between spectacular events and proclamation. All the other conversion stories that we have identified in Acts, where Luke demonstrates a similar balance, are but reflections of what Luke effectively demonstrates in the Pentecost episode.

Moreover, the fact that the events surrounding and immediately following Pentecost take place in Judea also suggests a new direction in the spread of the Christian witness. What starts with the Jews is not for them alone; it is actually for πᾶσαν σάρκα (2:17)—"*all flesh*". Within the narrative framework of Acts, Pentecost anticipates a limited fulfilment of this promise in terms of reaching out to the Samaritans (8:4-25), the Ethiopian Eunuch (8:26-40), and the Gentiles (e.g., 10:1-11:18). The various conversion texts given earlier demonstrates in detail how the whole of Acts resonates with Luke's motif of mission to "πᾶσαν σάρκα. In light of this, Luke's readers might read the catalogue of the nations in 2:9-11, not necessarily literally, but definitely as pointing to regions and horizons beyond one's own geographical immediacy. Therefore, the onus of carrying on the mission to the different ends of the earth that Pentecost has set on course continues till the end of the book of Acts and goes far beyond, employing the same principle—the complementarity between the miraculous and proclamation.

Construction of a Theo-Christocentric worldview

Pentecost exemplifies Luke's vision of investing Christian mission with divine-authenticity. It is a demonstration of the way God intervenes in the human realm, particularly vis-à-vis the Christian mission.

Pentecost demonstrates that God is the principle and the source out of which Luke evolves his arguments for universal mission. Peter begins his missionary speech with the solemn affirmation, "*God declares*" (2:17). The Joel text, which he quotes, does not have this phrase. This evidences Luke's predilection to identify God's work as the basis of his argument for mission. In the context, God's performance requires the events of Pentecost, the proclamation of μεγαλεῖα τοῦ θεοῦ, and Peter's sermon. In the end, Luke is not surprised at the result of this Theocentric action. He states the conversion of the 3000 only as a matter of fact. That is why he similarly builds Philip's Samaritan mission (8:4-25) on God's performance, seen both in the signs and wonders he performed (8:6b-7) and also in his proclamation about the kingdom of God and the name of Christ (8:5b-6a, 12). Although Luke does not specify the number of conversions, in Samaria, he summarily states that the Samaritans "believed" and "were baptised" (8:12). In the same way, while reading Luke's other conversion accounts, his readers will look for the same divine-focus in them and view conversions solely as God's prerogative. As stated above, within the narrative world of Acts, Pentecost is a limited fulfilment of God's promise to pour out his Spirit on "*all flesh*". This is God's way of promising to pour his Spirit on the Samaritans, and the Gentiles, and eventually on everyone who believes likewise.

Moreover, Pentecost unfolds the Christological focus intertwined with the Theological theme. It shows the readers that God, who is faithful to fulfil his promises, has acted in a unique way in Jesus, attested him through his signs and wonders, raised him from the dead, and exalted him as the Lord and Messiah. The fulfilment of God's promise, i.e., the bestowal of the Spirit is, in fact, the result and confirmation of Jesus' exaltation. In him, Luke's readers meet God.

In sum, we may say that to speak of God, for Luke, is to make a Theological assumption about Christ. First, God is the foundation and the source of this worldwide mission of witnessing that combines the miraculous and proclamation. Secondly, he has made himself known in Jesus, the Lord and Messiah, who, as a metanarrative, overarches all other stories and thereby provides a Christological basis for repenting, believing, and turning to God. This is what Pentecost and the other conversion stories in Acts strongly espouse.

Confirmatory Patterns

Pentecost also demonstrates a definite response matrix in terms of audience-responses. First, the formulaic question "τί ποιήσωμεν" (2:37; Cf. 16:30: τί...δεῖ ποιεῖν ἵνα σωθῶ) at Pentecost anticipates implicitly in the other conversion stories too a similar initiative from the audiences. When there is such an audience-initiative, Luke shows that the response to be demanded is 'repentance' and 'baptism' (2:38). He demonstrates almost a similar pattern in Acts 3 too. Although, there is no audience-initiative, Peter exhorts his hearers to *repent and turn to God* (3:19-20). At the end of an effective witnessing through the miraculous (3:1-10) and proclamation (3:12-26) and appealing for a definite response, those who witnessed the miracle, heard the word, and *believed*, numbered 5000 (4:4).

Further, the post-conversion scenario in Acts 2 also demonstrates a confirmatory pattern. In Acts 2, the primary effect of the complementarity between the miraculous and proclamation is accepting the message and believing (2:41,44), and the secondary effects of such a response to Christian witnessing are devotion to the apostles' teaching and fellowship, breaking of bread and the prayers (vv.42,46-47), and an economic 'koinonia' (v.45). Luke does not explicitly state that this was the outcome in all his conversion stories. However, as seen above, the presence of groups of believers in different places might presuppose such a post-conversion community that is devoted to the apostles' teaching, fellowship, breaking of bread and prayers and also the economic 'koinonia'. Thus, Luke shows the way the early church in Acts provided a definite pattern of follow-up to its converts, particularly in terms of nurturing them in the word and fellowship and providing them with a 'plausibility structure' to sustain their conversion.

CONCLUSION

While scholars have long recognised the importance of Pentecost, they have not sufficiently pointed out the interpretive reciprocity that exists between the miraculous and proclamation in the apostles' witnessing. By contrast, this chapter has demonstrated, with reference to the Pentecost story, that Christian mission in Acts has been phenomenally successful, primarily because of its ability to combine both the miraculous and proclamation as one integrated whole. Also, as the first in the series of conversion accounts that combine the miraculous and proclamation, the Pentecost account establishes precedents and contributes certain themes that receive varying degrees of repetition in the narrative of Acts.

Within the unfolding plot of Pentecost, Luke inserts Peter's discourse as an action intended to interpret the miraculous event, to influence a particular narrative audience to correct a wrong point-of-view and to challenge them for a responsive action. In other words, the missionary speech eventually activates certain responses from the audience by invitations (vv.38a, 40b) and by issuing promises (v.38). The speech not only interprets the occurrence, it causes something to happen—it causes the audience to realise its mistakes and repent, which is implied by its baptism.

Although Luke does not explicitly articulate this, in the Pentecost story we begin to see his logic behind the complementarity between the miraculous and proclamation as follows: The miraculous phenomenon necessitates and makes possible a proclamatory situation; the missionary speech interprets the 'event' as divine in origin and, therefore, miraculous, and abstracts the hidden message from the miraculous events in order to orient the audience towards the Theological and Christological emphases hidden in the supernatural occurrence. In turn, the miraculous confirms the word proclaimed as God's word. Thus, Luke interweaves both the miraculous phenomena and the speech in such a complex way that one does not function without the other. The miraculous anticipates and depends on the speech for interpretation; in turn the speech depends on the miraculous for confirmation and for persuasive proclamation. When such a miraculous confirmation takes place, the speech can be more persuasive in order to motivate the audience for an action that has salvific consequences. The result of such a mutual interpretative interaction is seen in the denouement of the Pentecost story—the conversion of the 3000 (2:41).

Although it is not as simple and straightforward as in Pentecost, this seems to be Luke's formula behind all the conversion stories. The next chapter is a detailed demonstration of this principle in the Cornelius story.

6

THE MIRACULOUS AND PROCLAMATION IN THE CORNELIUS STORY

INTRODUCTION

Our position so far has been that according to Luke, the integration between the miraculous and proclamation is the principle behind the growth of the Christian witness in Acts. We, therefore, singled out all the instances in Acts where Luke demonstrates this complementarity between the miraculous and proclamation in turning people to God, and illustrated it first, in Jesus' own mission and secondly, in the apostolic mission. The previous chapter demonstrated in detail the complementarity between the miraculous and proclamation in the Pentecost story—in a totally Jewish context—resulting in a *Linear Narrative Pattern of conversion* and the conversion of 3000 people (2:41). The purpose of the present chapter is similarly to demonstrate in detail the same complementarity between the miraculous and proclamation in the conversion of Cornelius, a thoroughgoing Gentile, and to identify a distinct narrative pattern of conversion within this story.[1]

---

[1] Some important studies on the Cornelius story are: M. Dibelius, *Studies*, 109-22; M.A. Plunkett, "Ethnocentricity and Salvation History in the Cornelius Episode (Acts 10:1-11:18)" in K.H. Richards, (Ed.), *SBLSP 1985*, (Atlanta: Scholars, 1985), 465-79; B.R. Gaventa, *Darkness to Light*, 107-29; R.C. Tannehill, *Narrative Unity*, 2.128-45; D.L. Matson, *Household Conversion*, 86-134; Ronald D. Witherup, "Cornelius Over and Over Again: 'Functional Redundancy' in the Acts of the Apostles", *JSNT*, 49, (1993), 45-66; Edith M. Humphrey, "Collision of Modes? Vision and Determining Argument in Acts 10:1-11:18" in Robert B. Robinson & Robert C. Culley (Eds.), *Textual Determinacy*, Vol. II, (Semeia 71; Atlanta: Scholars, 1995), 65-84.

THE CORNELIUS STORY

The Cornelius story is one of the longest narratives in the book of Acts.[2] As a 'repetitive narrative'[3], it appears at least four times in Acts indicating its paramount importance to Luke (10:1-48; 11:1-18; 15:7-11, 13-21), thus, qualifying itself as the most often repeated conversion account in Acts. Further, for the Jerusalem Council, it is the threshold of the Gentile mission;[4] Tyson calls the Cornelius event the 'center piece' of Luke's treatment of the Gentile mission.[5] The story underscores God's act of offering salvation to the Gentiles without discriminating them from the Jews: "*God had...opened a door of faith for the Gentiles*" (15:14; cf. 14:27). That the conversion of Cornelius represents all this speaks for its significance.

Further, just as Pentecost revolves around the supernatural phenomena and the missionary discourse, the Cornelius episode too, hinges on the vision and discourse combination. The intricate interplay and reciprocity between the miraculous and proclamation in the Cornelius story is something that many scholars fail to take notice of and hence miss its real significance and consequence.[6] Moreover, as an account replete with resonances for Gentile mission, the Cornelius story plays a paradigmatic role.[7]

Further, all of Cornelius' credentials (10:2, 22, 35) qualify him as the 'ideal convert'. However, "He is an 'ideal convert', but from whose perspective?" Definitely, the Jews did not accept him as such. Despite all his virtues and good will towards the Jews, Cornelius remains unknown to them. Even his

---

2 G.A. Krodel, (*Acts*, 187) points out that sixty-six verses devoted to the Cornelius story are more than the three conversion stories of Paul put together (forty-three verses).

3 See Mark Allan Powell, *What is Narrative Criticism?*, 39.

4 Richard J. Dillon (*From Eye-Witnesses to Ministers of the Word*, [AB; Rome: Biblical Institute Press, 1978], 190) observes "the Cornelius sequence is full of resonances of the dominical program for mission...." Stephen G. Wilson (*The Jewish and the Gentile Mission in Luke-Acts*, [Cambridge: CUP, 1973], 259) notes, "According to Luke, Cornelius was the first and decisive convert from the Gentile world".

5 J.B. Tyson, "The Gentile Mission and the Authority of Scripture in Acts", *NTS*, 33, (1987), 619-31, especially 624.

6 For instance, Gaventa, *Darkness to Light*, 96-122.; Matson, *Household Conversion*, 86-134.

7 Many scholars do correctly hold that the conversion of Cornelius and his household is paradigmatic of Gentile conversion in Acts. For example, Philip F. Esler, *Community and Gospel*, 161-62; S.G. Wilson, *Luke and the Law*, (Cambridge: CUP, 1983), 72; R.W. Wall, "Peter, 'Son' of Jonah: The Conversion of Cornelius in the Context of the Canon", *JSNT*, 29, (1987), 70-9-; J. Jervell, "The Church of Jews and Godfearers", in J. B. Tyson, (Ed.), *Luke-Acts and the Jewish People: Eight Critical Perspectives*, (Minneapolis: Augsburg, 1988), 11-20, esp. 12-13.

conversion did not really matter to the Jews (11:1). For them Cornelius is just a Roman centurion (10:1)[8]; he belongs to τὰ ἔθνη (11:1), which is the *terminus technicus* for Gentiles in Acts.[9] Moreover, he is ἀλλόφυλος (10:28) and uncircumcised (ἀκροβυστίαν ἔχοντας, 11:3; cf. 10:22,35,45; 11:1,18). All these collectively establish Cornelius' Gentile identity, which later becomes the bone of contention between Peter and his Jerusalem detractors (11:3). These developments in the narrative are important for our study. Although Cornelius is from Caesarea, a Judean territory, he is a Gentile essentially. Therefore, this Gentile conversion story, qualifies for a separate study. But before demonstrating the way the miraculous and proclamation function together as an integrated whole in the Cornelius story, certain matters need clarification.

The Cornelius conversion story is not studied from psychological or sociological perspective; nor is it evaluated from the perspective of any ancient or modern story having resemblance. Further, we will not attempt to determine the historical veracity of the Cornelius story or the tradition that might lie behind it.[10] Instead, we seek to answer only certain literary questions such as "How do the visions and speeches, both direct and recapitulative, function together in the Cornelius story? How do the recapitulations shed light on the earlier visions and on Cornelius' conversion? How does the story function and how does it lead the readers to read the story? Is there any perceivable narrative pattern of conversion within which the Cornelius story operates?"

In order to answer these questions, we first establish the narrative context and then focus particularly on the link between the visions, Peter's discourse, the descent of the Spirit, and the subsequent recapitulations. After discussing the literary functions of the account of Cornelius' conversion, we will attempt to suggest a distinct narrative pattern of conversion within the Cornelius story.

---

8 Readers knowing Luke's Gospel might remember the centurion who sent messengers to Jesus with a request for help (7:1-10) and also the Centurion who confessed the innocence of Jesus at the crucifixion (23:47).

9 Cf. Karl Ludwig Schmidt, "ἔθνος in the New Testament", *TDNT*, II.369-72, esp. 370.

10 See. Dibelius, *Studies*, 109-22.

THE NARRATIVE CONTEXT

Earlier we have shown that Acts 1:8 programmatically sets forth the course of the mission of the apostles: [11] Although, in the process of executing this divine mandate, the story of Cornelius functions as an important watershed, Luke does not present this event in the immediate context as the beginning of the Gentile mission starting from Antioch in 11:19-21. In fact, only retrospectively is the Cornelius event interpreted as the starting point of the Gentile mission (11:1; cf. 15:14). Within the narrative framework of Acts, it is the martyrdom of Stephen that initiates the Gentile mission (8:1,4; cf. 11:19). The linguistic correlation between 8:4 and 11:19 clearly shows that the Antiochian mission (11:19) continues from the dispersal in 8:4.[12]

8:4: Οἱ μὲν οὖν διασπαρέντες διῆλθον εὐαγγελιζόμενοι τὸν λόγον.	11:19: Οἱ μὲν οὖν διασπαρέντες...διῆλθον... λαλοῦντες τὸν λόγον τὸν

Cornelius' story does not usher in the Antiochian mission and, therefore, could fit well anywhere without disrupting the narrative flow.[13] Yet, by deliberately placing the story immediately before the Gentile mission, obviously Luke wants to present it as the introduction to the full-scale Gentile mission.

Further, Peter's ministry in Lydda and Sharon and Joppa (9:32-42) brings him geographically closer to Caesarea. While at Joppa God commands him in a vision to go to Caesarea to preach (9:43-10:1ff). Luke's introduction of a journey motif here by introducing διέρχεσθαι (9:32) to explain Peter's journey to Lydda demonstrates the centrifugal movement of the Christian witness from Jerusalem. These geographical locations are crucial for the story as they create links in the narrative[14], necessary for consistency and sequence in the story.

The journey motif that Luke employs here will be further reinforced for those readers who know Luke's Gospel where the same διέρχεσθαι language occurs

---

11 R. Brawley (*Luke-Acts and the Jews*, 28-50) argues that a strict reading of Acts 1:8 as programmatic of a geographical expansion is not possible on the basis that there is no natural transition from one region to another. However, Brawley overlooks the fact of divine providence in Acts that leads to the outward movement of the witness from Jerusalem, to neighbouring areas, and finally to Rome.

12 Tannehill (*Narrative Unity*, 2.146) notices that this verbal link presents the developments in Antioch as "the continuation of the gospel's spread resulting from the scattering of believers by the persecution at the death of Stephen."

13 Ibid., 2.147.

14 Tannehill, *Narrative Unity*, 2.124.

in the context of preaching the Gospel (Lk. 5:15; 9:6; 19:1,4). In Acts too it occurs frequently in the context of the disciples' passing through different regions preaching the word, and also in Paul's missionary journeys.[15] By introducing this term, Luke effectively demonstrates the outward movement of the Christian witness and its universal perspective envisioned in Jesus' commission in 1:8.[16] Luke's introduction of Peter at the end of Acts 9 leads to the events in chapter 10. In the context, Peter's subsequent "crossing of borders" to enter the Gentile domain (10:48) is foreshadowed in his willingness to stay with Simon, the tanner, in Joppa (9:43). The narrative context shows the way Peter is being drawn into the divine-ordained course of mission to the Gentiles (10:5-6, 17-18).

Further, Peter's citations from Joel at Pentecost made it clear that in the last days God would pour out his Spirit upon πᾶσαν σάρκα (2:17). As pointed out already, for Luke, this foreshadows the mission to the Gentiles[17] and also fulfils, in a qualified sense, the internal prophecy about the offer of salvation to all (2:21), and anticipates the "Gentile Pentecost" in 10:44-48. These emphases point in the direction of those presently '*far away*' (2:39).[18] In these ways, Luke shows the emergence of the Christian witness as increasingly Gentile-focused.

Within this scheme, the readers may have already noticed a chain of conversions, starting from Pentecost, leading up to Cornelius' conversion: the conversion of the 3,000 (2:41), of the 5,000 (4:4), in Samaria (8:12-14), of the Ethiopian Eunuch (8:38), and Saul (9:1-19). In these cases, Luke describes the successful advance of the Christian witness, particularly through the combined operation of supernatural phenomena and proclamation.

Besides these concrete examples, in the immediate context, Luke's summary statements also create an atmosphere of conversion. Immediately after the mass-conversion at Pentecost, Luke states, "*Day by day the Lord added to their number those who were being saved*" (2:47b); similarly, in 5:14, "*More*

---

15 8:4,40; 9:32,38; 10:38; 11:19; 13:6,14; 14:24; 15:3,41; 16:6; 17:23; 18:23, 27; 19:1,21; 20:2,25.

16 Allison A. Trites (*The New Testament Concept of Witness*, [SNTMS 31; Cambridge: CUP, 1977], 140) argues that Acts 9:15 too provides a further description of the missions programme once it moves outside Palestine. The readers knowing Luke's Gospel might recollect Lk. 24:47 where Luke mentions preaching to τὰ ἔθνη.

17 Cf. F.F. Bruce, *Acts*, 61.

18 πᾶσιν τοῖ εἰ μακράν in the context clearly has Gentiles in picture. Cf. J. Jervell, *People of God*, 57-58.

than ever believers were added to the Lord, great numbers...." All these accounts create an air of expectancy and anticipate the conversion of Cornelius. In other words, the context is filled with Theological significance, because God is intervening decisively in the spread of his word in fantastic ways. He is about to incorporate a special kind of "Gentile" into the community of believers.

After establishing the narrative context, we consider the different aspects of Luke's presentation of the Cornelius account, namely the characterisations, the visions, the speech, the recapitulations of the visions, both internal and external, and the conversion of Cornelius' household, symbolised by the descent of the Spirit. The first thing we notice in the Cornelius episode is Luke's characterisation of Cornelius and Peter, the chief human actors.

CHARACTERISATIONS

The two principal characters in the present episode are Cornelius and Peter. Peter's fellow believers from Joppa and Cornelius' delegates to Peter (10:6) are only minor characters (10:44).

Luke characterises Cornelius positively, highlighting his piety and stature as a God-fearer. He describes his character by means of certain adjectives, which we identified, in Jakob Lothe's term, as "Direct Definition".[19] Luke describes Cornelius as εὐσεβὴ καὶ φοβούμενός τὸν θεόν (10:2; cf., v.7) which is later repeated by Cornelius' emissaries (v.22). Thus, there occurs a convergence of both the hyperdiegetic and intradiegetic points-of-view, as stated earlier. Cornelius is also an 'upright' man (δίκαιος 10:22). Both the narrator and the angel testify that the piety of Cornelius consists in almsgiving and prayer (10:2,4)[20], paralleled only by the prayer and charity of Peter and John (3:1-7). Thus, Luke presents before his readers a special "Gentile" whose religious propensities make him naturally receptive to the Christian proclamation. In this sense Luke expects his readers to consider Cornelius as the representative of all those who are similarly religiously disposed and are receptive to God's offer of salvation. This is further reinforced when Peter draws a Theological conclusion based on Cornelius' characterisation: "*...in every nation anyone who fears him and does what is right is acceptable to him*" (10:35; cf. 10:2,4,22,30).

---

19 Lothe, *Narrative in Fiction*, 81.

20 The readers may associate Cornelius' almsgiving to the charitable activities of Tabitha (9:36,39).

Since Luke portrays Cornelius as a type to be imitated by religiously inclined persons everywhere, the readers are predisposed to view Cornelius favourably, to identify with him and to move along with the action in the narrative, to meet Peter, to hear his message, and eventually to know the contents of his message of salvation. Thus, in Cornelius, Luke presents an imitable character, a role model in terms of religious dispositions. Later, Cornelius' implicit obedience in executing the Spirit's directive (v.8) sets an example for all the subsequent responses to the Spirit's promptings. This basic characterisation of Cornelius remains constant throughout the story, apart from certain other descriptions. Therefore, we earlier called him a 'flat character' (e.g., v.21). We have also pointed out above the picture of Cornelius from the viewpoint of the Jews and its relevance for our present study.

The other major character in the Cornelius story is Peter. Although Luke does not employ adjectives to describe Peter, up to this point he has characterised him with a flawless pedigree, which exemplifies his character. This, in Lothe's term, is "Indirect Presentation."[21] Earlier we also called Peter a 'round character' who develops and changes as the narrative progresses. A necessary aspect of such a character is his/her speech;[22] therefore, Peter's speeches perform a characterising function (2:14-36; 3:11-26; 10:34-43; 11:4-17; 15:7-11). Besides this, he leads the eleven (1:13); speaks for them (1:15); teaches and preaches throughout Jerusalem and Samaria (1:12-8:25), and suffers for the sake of the word (4:1-4; cf. 5:18,27-32,40-41; 12:3-5). Therefore, he is an ideal apostle, disciple, and a preacher.

Given their privileged knowledge, Luke's readers carefully observe what is happening in the text. They notice how both Cornelius and Peter, unknown to each other, do God's will in their own way and become major turning points in the advance of the Christian witness. In this story, Peter and Cornelius, a pure Jew according to the Law and a religiously disposed Gentile, are brought together to inaugurate the Gentile mission—a new phase in the movement of the Christian witness towards its final destination. Collectively, Peter and Cornelius function together as "action-initiators" by setting the action in motion based on their specific character idiosyncrasies and experiences.[23]

The next thing noticeable about Cornelius and Peter is that they are visionaries (10:1-8, 9-16). In a very real sense the entire story is dominated by the crisis precipitated by the twin-visions of Cornelius and Peter.

---

21 Lothe, *Narrative in Fiction*, 82.

22 Ibid., 82.

23 Ibid., 75.

THE VISIONS

Earlier we pointed out that according to Graeco-Roman popular religious experience, the gods could appear in person to communicate a message and also to either equip or commission individuals for a task. Likewise, we also showed from the OT the importance accorded to visions, dreams, angelophanies and Theophanies, as God's means of revealing his glory, of communicating his will, and of commissioning people for a particular task. In keeping with this contemporary literary ethos, Luke also quite freely introduces angelic appearances, visions, and dreams into his narratives in Acts.

From the middle section of Acts, Luke introduces the Gentile mission as emanating solely from God's plan, communicated through visions to different people at different times. Such visionary experiences are placed in the narrative in order to demonstrate God's will regarding universal salvation, and to guide his witnesses in fulfilling this will.[24] They either confirm God's guidance in the present or predict the future course of God's intentions and guide the visionaries in their immediate actions.[25] Although all these visions are important in themselves, only the parallel-visions of Cornelius (10:3-6) and Peter (10:9-16) are particularly important for our present study. Luke highlights them so much in the Cornelius story that he appears to emphasise them almost to the exclusion of human participation.[26]

However, this fear is rather unfounded. In the progression of the Cornelius story Luke clearly shows that God's initiatives in Gentile conversion are brought to fruition only when complemented by human response and action. Luke's express purpose behind constructing a complementary-vision scene is to bring both Peter and Cornelius into the same plot. Here Luke's readers might recollect other such parallel-vision stories in Acts, for example Saul's and Ananias'

---

24 Luke records visions in Jerusalem (2:3; 5:19-20; 12:7-11,23; 22:17-21; 23:11); on the Damascus road (9:3-6; 22:6-8; 26:13-18); in Joppa (10:3-7, 10-16; 11:5-10); Caesarea (10:30-2; 11:13-14); Troas (16:9-10); Corinth (18:9), and on board ship near Crete (27:23-4). See also the Table of Miracles in Acts (Row II) in chapter 3 in the book.

25 J.S. Hanson ("Dreams and Visions in the Graeco-Roman World and Early Christianity," *ANRW*, II.23.2, pp. 1395-427, esp.1413) remarks that in the ancient literature, "dream-visions are not merely decorative, but function to direct or redirect the movement of the narrative." He elaborates further, "the dream-visions provide the motivation for the actions of the main actors in Acts, clearly showing how the author makes use of this form in his literary work" (Ibid., 1422).

26 E. Haenchen, *Acts*, 362.

(Acts 9:1-19).[27] If the readers know Luke's Gospel, they might also remember the parallel visions involving Zechariah and Mary (Lk. 1:8-56). In these stories, the vision experiences are juxtaposed with the successful completion of an act of God through one human agent complemented by the faithful response of another.

However, the vision-scenes in the Cornelius story contain certain problems. They start with the vision of Cornelius (ἐν ὁράματι, 10:3) who initially reacts with fear (φόβος, 10:4). Meanwhile, Peter is also given a vision (ὅραμα, 10:17,19) while in ἔκστασις (10:10). He is commanded three times to ignore the dietary laws (Cf. Lev. 11; 20:25-26) and eat what has so far been considered unclean (10:13-16). That these visions clearly disclose God's plans is evident from the fact that Cornelius is instructed by the angel to send for Peter (10:3), which is later recollected as a revelation (ἐχρηματίσθη, 10:22). Nevertheless, in the main narrative, he is not told the meaning of his vision; also, he does not know why he should request Peter's presence. On the other hand, Peter's vision does come with an explanation in the form of a directive to abandon the distinctions of food laws (10:15). However, its partial intelligibility leads only to perplexity (διαπορέω, 10:17). Therefore, Peter does not know "*what to make of the vision*" (10:17). Earlier in the Pentecost story, we noted that such an imperfect intelligibility of the miraculous leads only to perplexity. In the same scene in the Cornelius story, while Peter is still trying to understand the vision (διενθυμέομαι, 10:19a), he is told about the visit of Cornelius' messengers and is directed to go with them to Cornelius (10:19b-20). Just as he did not understand the full import and the meaning of his vision, he also does not know why he should go with them. Therefore, he asks Cornelius' emissaries, "*What is the reason for your coming?*" (10:21b).

Despite these problems, the coordination between the visions of Cornelius and Peter results in a major missionary advance to the Gentiles. In the Cornelius story, going beyond their mere presence, the complementary-visions serve to further the story. They are rehearsed repeatedly, as the actors come together. Speeches, both main (10:34-43) and recapitulative (11:1-17; 15:7-11), interpret these visions while the visions themselves function as constant referents in the speeches. Peter's reappraisals bring the action and thought of the story to an intelligible and intelligent conclusion. Importantly, interpretive details are

[27] The widely read readers might recollect *Joseph and Asenath* 19:7-8 (the confirmation of Asenath's vision by Joseph). See also Josephus (*Antiq.*, XI.321-39) records that Alexander and the high priest have separate dreams preparing them for the events to follow. Cf. Gaventa, *Darkness to Light*, 109.

often introduced into subsequent retellings of the visions at crucial junctures in the drama, which not only characterise interpretation as part of the natural unfolding of the events, but also heighten and enliven the story, as will be shown below.[28] This takes us to the consideration of repetitions in the Cornelius story.[29]

RECAPITULATIONS

The Cornelius story contains a complex network of visions and vision-recollections that are important to Luke since he interrupts their flow by one main speech and many recapitulations, both internal and external. The importance of the whole story will be known only at the end of all recollections in 11:1-18 and 15:7-21.

The main narrative of the Cornelius story (10:1-48) does not disclose the ultimate purpose of the visions, but the later retellings of the story make clear both their message and their final meaning. In the retold versions, interpretive details, absent in the main narrative, are added progressively, particularly in the autobiographical reconstructions by Cornelius (10:30b-33) and Peter (10:28b; 11:4-17; 15:7-11). Autobiographical reconstructions function as an aspect of "memory-work" shaping personal experience into a narrative and making a story out of personal experiences.[30] This adds authority to the event by establishing a link between "self-understanding" and the actual event as described by the objective narration.

In the Cornelius story, from the moment of the visions to Cornelius' conversion, the visions are sustained in the characters' memories. The narrative audiences (Cornelius' emissaries, Cornelius, and Peter) reconstruct the original account, although partially and subjectively, from their own perspective. The total picture of the Cornelius story "does not exist independently, but rather as versions perceived and manufactured by individuals."[31] This dependence on subjective point-of-view illustrate that interpretations are dynamic rather than fixed. Therefore, a complete configuration of the meaning of the event is

---

[28] Cf. Dibelius, *Studies*, 119, 166.

[29] M. Sternberg (*Biblical Narrative*, 365-440) explains repetitions as "redundancy". Witherup ("Functional Redundancy", 68, n.4) calls this Functional Redundancy.

[30] Cf. Laura Marcus, "The Face of Autobiography" in Julia Swindells (Ed.), *The Uses of Autobiography*, (London: Taylor & Francis Ltd., 1995), 13-23, esp. 13.

[31] Jane Unsworth, "Why does an author who apparently draws so much on autobiography seem committed to alienating the reader?: A Reflection on Theories of Autobiography with Reference to the Work of Janet Frame" in Julia Swindells (Ed.), *Autobiography*, 24-30.

possible only in the recreation of the main narrative. This basic dynamism preponderates the Cornelius story. However, how could the narrative audiences (Cornelius, his emissaries, and Peter) arrive at such interpretations that totally recast the story, since Luke himself does not provide any explanation, should be left to scholarly conjectures.

While some scholars attribute repetitions to different sources,[32] others think of them as examples of emphasis to reiterate the same message over and over again.[33] Some others designate it as stylistic variation.[34] However, as a narrative technique, repetitions serve as a "counterbalance designed to ensure a full and unambiguous reception of the message."[35]

Within a literary framework, repetitions appear in the form of expansion, ellipsis, change of order, grammatical transformation, and substitution.[36] Each of these, or any combination thereof, can be employed to reinforce the message by reducing anomalies as much as possible in order to optimise its receptivity. When we analyse the interaction between the visions, the speech, and the recapitulations, it will become clear that Luke follows this narrative strategy for the same reasons. As the present study progresses, that repetitions play a dominant role in determining the meaning, the import, and the interpretation of the entire story by way of "Internal Analepses"[37], i.e., by referring to an earlier point in the main story, will become much clearer. The following Table shows the visions and their retellings with modifications, change of order, substitution and additions.

---

32 E.g. Conzelmann, *Acts*, 80; Dibelius, *Studies*, 109-22.

33 Haenchen (*Acts*, 357) suggests, "This technique of repetition is one to which Luke always resorts when he wants to impress something specially upon the reader." See also S.G. Wilson, *Gentile Mission*, 177; Bruce, *Acts*, 268.

34 For example, Krodell, *Acts*, 203; F.F. Bruce, *Acts*, 221; H.J. Cadbury, "Four Features of Lucan Style", in L.E. Keck, and J.L. Martyn, (Eds.), *Studies in Luke-Acts: Essays Presented in Honor of Paul Schubert*, (Nashville: Abingdon, 1966), 87-102; L.M. Maloney, "*All that God had Done with them*"*: The Narration of the Works of God in the Early Christian Community as Described in the Acts of the Apostles*, (American University Studies, 7.91; New York: Peter Lang, 1991), 67.

35 Sternberg, *Biblical Narrative*, 368.

36 Ibid., 391-92.

37 Lothe, *Narrative in Fiction*, 54.

TABLE OF RECAPITULATIONS (TR)

(A) CHARACTERISATION

(Cornelius)

Main Narrative (Cornelius' Emissaries)	**Internal Recapitulation**
εὐσεβὴς καὶ φοβούμενος τὸν θεόν…ποιῶν ἐλεημσύνας… δεόμενος τοῦ θεοῦ διὰ παντός (v. 2)	δίκαιος καὶ φοβούμενος τὸν θεόν μαρτυραίμενός ὑπὸ ὅλου του ἔθνους τῶν᾽ Ἰουδαίων (v.22)

(B) VISIONS

Cornelius			Peter		
CI	CII	CIII	PI	PII	PIII
Main Narrative (10:1-8)	Internal Recapitulation	External Recapitulation-I	Main Narrative	Internal Recapitulation	External Recapitulation-II
(CI (a) …πέμψον ἄνδρας εἰ Ἰόππην καὶ μεταπεμψαι.. Πέτρος (v.5). (Response: ἀπέστειλεν αὐ τους εἰς τὴν᾽ Ἰόππην (v.8)	CII (a) Κορνήλιος… ἐχρηματίσθη ὑπος ἀγγέλου…μεταπέμψασθαι . σε…ἀκοῦσαι ῥήματα παρὰ σοῦ (v.22) (Cornelius' messengers to Peter).	(CIII (a). ἀπόστειλον εἰς Ἰόππην…μετάμεμψαι.. Πέτρον, ὃς λαλήσει ῥήματα πρὸς σὲ ἐν οἷς σωθήσς σὺ καὶ πα ὁ οἶκός σου (11:13b-14) (Peter to the Jerusalem brethren).	PI (a) Sheet-vision (10:9-16) (Response: "I have never eaten.anything that is profane or unclean(10:14) (Peter to the heavenly voice).	(PII (a) ὁ θεὸς ἔδειξεν μηδένα κοινὸν ἀκάρτον… ἄνθρωπον (v.28b) (Peter to Cornelius)	PIII (a) Sheet-vision + Voice "Get up...kill and eat" (11:7) + Peter's Response "...nothing profane or unclean has ever entered my mouth" (11:8) (Peter recollecting his vision at the plenary
	CII (b) …πέμψον…εἰς Ἰόππην…μετακάλεσαι… Πέτρος…πάντες…ἐνώπιον τοῦ θεοῦ πάρεσμεν ἀκοῦσαι πάντα τὰ προστεταγμένα σοι ὑπὸ του κυρίου (10:30b-33) (Cornelius to Peter).		PI (b) ἅ ὁ θεὸς ἐκαθάρισεν, σὺ μὴ κοίνου (v.15). (Heavenly voice to Peter).		PIII (b) ἅ ὁ θεὸς ἐκαθάρισεν, σὺ μὴ κοίνου (11:9)
			PI (c)The Spirit said...Three men are searching for you... go with them without hesitation.. ἐγὼ ἀπέσταλκα αὐτούς (10:19-20) (The Spirit to Peter) (Response: Peter meets them, 10:21a).		PIII (c) εἶπεν δὲ πνεῦμα… συνελθεῖναὐτοῖς μηδὲν διακρίναντα (11:12a).

(C) CORNELIUS' CONVERSION

Main Narrative	**External Recapitulations-III**
	(Jerusalem detractors, Peter, and James in both the Jerusalem plenary session and Jerusalem Council).
While Peter was still speaking, the Holy Spirit fell upon all who heard the word. The circumcised believers who hadcome with Peter were astounded that the gift of the Holy Spirit had been poured out even to the Gentiles, for they heard them speaking in tongues and extolling God (10:44-46).	(a) ...καὶ τὰ ἔθνη ἐδέξαντο τὸν λόγον τοῦ θεοῦ (11:1).
	(b) ἐπέπεσεν τὸ πνεῦμα τὸ ἅγιον ἐπ' αὐτοὺς ὥσπερ και...δωρεὰν ἔδωκεν αὐτοῖς ὁ θεὸς ὡς καὶ ἡμῖν πισεύσασιν ἐπὶ τὸν κύριον ' Ιησοῦν Χριστόν... (11:17a).
	(c) ...καὶ τοῖς ἔθνεσιν ὁ θεὸς τὴν μετά νοιαν εἰς ζωὴνἔδωκεν (11:18b).
	(d) ...ἀκοῦσαι τὰ ἔθνη τὸν λόγον τοῦ εὐαγγελίου καὶπιστεῦσαί (15:7b).
	(e) ...ὁ...θεὸς ἐμαρτύρησεν αὐτοῖς δοὺς τὸ πνεῦμα...οὐθὲν διέκρινεν μεταξὺ ἡμῶν τε καὶ αὐτῶν τῇ πίστει καθαρίσας τὰς καρδίας αὐτῶν (15:8-9).
	(f) ...διὰ τῆς χάριτος τοῦ κυρίου ' Ιησοῦ πιστεύομεν σωθῆναι καθ ὃν τρόπον κἀκεῖνοι (15:11).
	(g) ...ὁ θεὸς ἐπεσκέψατο λαβεῖν ἐξ ἐθνῶν λαὸν τῷ ὀνόματι αὐτοῦ (15:14).

Table 'B. Visions' above clearly lays out God's plan disclosed in two apparently unconnected visions. As stated earlier, supernatural phenomena such as visions demonstrate God's revelation of his divine plan. The hyperdiegetic narrator narrates the visions separately in the third person establishing objectivity for the readers (TR: CI & PI: Main Narratives). They are not subjective hallucinations, but verifiable parallel experiences in which God is "mysteriously" at work through the promptings of the Spirit (10:19; cf. 11:12). Later, Cornelius' retelling of his vision becomes a hermeneutical tool for Peter to interpret his own vision (TR: CII(b) Internal Recapitulation).

The Table also demonstrates that the climax of the twin-visions is Peter's missionary discourse (10:34-43), which is interrupted only by the descent of the Spirit (10:44-47). Moreover, the first (11:4-17) of the three external recapitulations (11:4-17; 15:7-11, 13-21) of the main narrative (10:1-11:18), consisting of Peter's defence in Jerusalem, powerfully reinforces the message of acceptance of the Gentiles. Throughout the process, the visions are being retold with modifications, additions, and reversing the actual order. For instance, in 11:1-18, Peter recapitulates his vision first and ends with Cornelius', whereas in the main narrative the order is in the reverse. It starts with Cornelius' vision (10:3-6) and ends with Peter's (10:9-16). Recapitulations are not simple repetitions, but reconstructions of the action and movement towards a convincing conclusion (e.g., 11:18: "*God has given even to the Gentiles the repentance that leads to life*"). Moreover, the visions are not repeated verbatim. There are considerable variations between the original visions and their retold versions, as important interpretive details are introduced within the second and third telling as part of the main visions. In addition, in the process of recapitulation characters such as Cornelius and his emissaries disappear in favour of an increased focus on Peter's character and his speeches. As we progress through the story, that these retold versions control the entire Cornelius episode will become increasingly clear. Therefore, the speeches and the reappraisals of the visions are absolutely crucial for the readers to arrive at the correct and comprehensive understanding of the events that lead to the denouement.

Cornelius' Vision and its Recapitulation

Although Cornelius' vision is narrated four times in the story (TR: CI, CII[a], CII[b], CIII[a]), the vision itself functions only as a catalyst to the subsequent reconstructions and the message, but nothing much is made of it.

The first record of Cornelius' vision (TR: CI: 10:1-8) is told in the third person from the perspective of the hyperdiegetic narrator, thereby establishing the objectivity of the event and its divine origin (ὅραμα, 10:3). Luke's use of ἐν ὁράματι (instrumental dative, 10:3) in Cornelius' vision emphasises its instrumental value in God's initiative here. We have already seen that such dreams and visions, in the OT, for instance, are God's instruments to communicate his message. Similarly, the unfolding of the Cornelius story shows the way God uses vision to instruct Cornelius to send for Peter to hear the message of salvation (cf. 11:14).

The first recapitulation of Cornelius' vision comes from his delegates with truncation, substitution, and expansion (TR: CII (a): Internal Recapitulation). Peter's question "*What is the reason for your coming*" (10:21a) prompts Cornelius' emissaries to recount a shorter version of the vision, but their added detail reinforces the narrator's earlier hyperdiegetic portrait of Cornelius' piety. However, subtle changes in their report reduce Cornelius' part in the enactment of God's plan. Cornelius is named and described as an upright and God-fearing centurion; yet, neither his prayerfulness nor his almsgiving is mentioned. Instead, the messengers sum up Cornelius' character by adding that he "*is well spoken of by the whole Jewish nation*" (10:22a). They also add the message of the vision: "*to hear what you have to say*" (10:22b). This development, absent in the main narrative (TR: CI [a]), helps the readers to consider Cornelius' initial vision as important, but only insofar as it catalyses Peter's speech.

This nuanced recapitulation shifts the focus from the visions themselves to the roles that Peter and Cornelius should play. The emphasis of the vision is on Peter's ensuing testimony, and, therefore, Cornelius is relegated to the role of a passive recipient of Peter's message. From this point forward, his presence in the story will begin to wane gradually until he disappears totally. In the latter recapitulations, the readers will remember him only in hindsight. Further, they may also notice a subtle thematic interplay in 10:22, where Luke employs ἔθνος to denote the entire Jewish nation, while using the same term generally for the Gentiles (e.g., 11:1),[38] thereby internally anticipating the later fusion of the Jew-Gentile identity: ἐξ ἐθνῶν λαὸν τῷ ὀνόματι αὐτοῦ (15:14).

The second recapitulation of Cornelius' vision is by an intradiegetic narrator, i.e., Cornelius, a character internal to the story, is giving his subjective account (10:30b-33) (TR: CII (b): Internal Recapitulation). This swing between hyperdiegetic and intradiegetic points-of-view, as stated earlier, establishes that while God's actions are objective, they have a subjective dimension at the same time. Moreover, it makes the accounts reliable and gives a balanced perspective to the reports.

In the second recounting, Cornelius gives a personal account of his vision, reinforcing the viewpoints of both the narrator and his own messengers, which

[38] Cf. Schmidt, "ἔθνος in the New Testament", 370.

emphasises that all that transpires is divinely coordinated. Apart from certain observations such as the hour of his prayer and the appearance of the angel (v.30), Cornelius repeats almost verbatim the content of the vision (vv.31-32), thereby reinforcing its reliability and objectivity. Furthermore, he adds, "*...now all of us are here in the presence of God to listen to all that the Lord has commanded you to say*" (v.33). This re-emphasises what Cornelius' messengers have already told Peter: "*to hear what you have to say*" (10:22b). The focus again is on "hearing" the proclamation. Cornelius has assembled his entire household together to hear all that God has commanded Peter to proclaim. The stage is thus set for Peter's discourse (vv.34-43). We will defer its discussion for a while.

The final version of Cornelius' vision (11:11-14) (TR: CIII (a): External Recapitulation-I) is the decisive amalgam of the details, their elaboration, and their Theological and soteriological import. It occurs in Peter's apologia in the plenary session in Jerusalem. Subtle changes again demonstrate that Cornelius' role in this entire story is only secondary to the proclamation. In this final retelling of Cornelius' vision, although his piety is highlighted, more importantly, he is not named. The highlight of this account is the Spirit's directive to Peter to go with Cornelius' delegates without making any distinction between the Jews and the Gentiles (11:12; cf. 15:10) for the express purpose of proclaiming "*a message* (ῥήματα)[39] *by which you and your entire household will be saved"* (11:14). This soteriological perspective is the new insight that is missing in the earlier accounts (10:22,33). The final retelling of Cornelius' vision highlights more the action of the Spirit and the importance of the message of salvation than Cornelius as a character. In fact, he totally loses his character specificity and becomes an anonymous τοῦ ἀνδρός (11:12).

Thus, interpretative recapitulations bring the Theological and soteriological import of the visions to the fore. The ultimate purpose of all that happens is the offer of salvation to the Gentiles. With this understanding of Cornelius' vision, we now turn to Peter's vision.

Peter's Vision and its Recapitulation

Together with its recapitulations Peter's vision is mentioned in TR: PI[a], PIII[b-c]: 10:9-16, 28 and 11:5-10 with an assertion that the vision occurred "three

39 The use of this term here is for reasons of stylistic variation. This is interchangeable with λό γος which represents the Gospel message (10:36, 44; 11:1 (λόγος) with 10:37 (ῥῆμα) and 11:14 ῥήματα).

times (10:16; 11:10) (TR: PI [a-c: Main narrative]).[40] The first of the reports (PI [a]) is told in the third person by the narrator, with a view to establishing objectivity, which is later verified by Peter's personal version (PIII [a-b]: External Recapitulation-II). In both the accounts, Peter is praying[41] while he experiences the ἔκστασις (10:10; 11:5). Both the reports mention a sheet-like object descending from above with all kinds of animals, followed by a heavenly instruction to "*Get up...kill and eat*" (10:13; 11:7). As shown earlier, such prodigies are signs from the gods to communicate and to guide human affairs. In addition, as stated earlier, the very fact that the object is descending from heaven shows its divine origin. In both places, Peter is horrified since it would be a grave violation of Torah.[42] Here the readers may notice a substitution in Peter's account of his response to the Spirit's directive:

"No Lord; for I have never eaten (ἔφαγον) anything that is common or unclean" (10:14).	"No Lord: for nothing uncommon or unclean has ever entered (εἰσῆλθεν) my mouth" (11:8).[43]

It is obvious that Peter's first refusal (10:14) emphasises his own advocacy of the food regulations while the second pertains to his general stance on commonness or uncleanness. The heavenly voice does not insist that Peter slaughters the animals and eats, but it does demand that Peter acknowledge God's sovereignty in determining purity demarcations (10:15).

Since the readers move along with the narrative, they might see that to eat unclean food is to cross the boundary that separates Peter (hence, all the Jews) from the Gentiles. That is precisely what God wants him to do, which Peter

---

40 According to R.E. Brown (*The Epistles of John*, [AB 30; Garden City, NY: Doubleday, 1982], 123), the "rule of three" was an ancient mnemonic device suggesting the Hebraic mentality of the superlative degree or as common notion that three represents the sufficient number of times to establish a principle or series.

41 In Acts 10:9 Peter goes up to pray at about "sixth hour." Since this is usually the time for lunch (Conzelmann, *Acts*, 81), his praying at this time emphasises his personal piety.

42 Cf. B.J. Malina, *The New Testament World: Insights from Cultural Anthropology*, (Atlanta: John Knox, 1981), 134-37. See also Walter Houston, *Purity and Monotheism: Clean and Unclean Animals in Biblical Law*, (JSOTSup., 140; Sheffield: JSOT Press, 1993), passim. On issues surrounding the notion of κοινός and καθαρός see J.D.M. Derrett, "Clean and Unclean Animals (Acts 10:15; 11:9): Peter's Pronouncing Power Observed", *Heythrop Journal*, 29, (1988), 205-21; D.L. Tiede, "Acts 11:1-18", *Int.*, 42, (1988), 175-80.

43 Peter's strong protestation puts him in line with the tradition of Daniel (1:8), Tobit (1:10-11), Judith (12:1-2), Judas Maccabees (2 Macc. 5:27), Eleazer (2 Macc. 6:18-31), and other faithful Israelites who refused to defile themselves with food prepared against Jewish dietary stipulations.

himself acknowledges in Cornelius' house (v.28). God is demanding the demolition of the boundary, which that distinction perpetuates; hence the command of the Spirit the second time, "*What God has made clean, you must not call profane*" (10:15b; 11:9). The last word comes from God, but Peter is yet to understand its full meaning.

There are two subtle changes in Peter's response above that influence the import and the meaning of the heavenly vision. One concerns food while the other concerns Peter's response to the vision. The second account is elliptical. Whereas the first account mentions that Peter was hungry and that the vision occurred while the food was being prepared, the second report omits this detail totally. Luke's intention here seems to be to accord food the function of an analogy, made clear, particularly by the visit of Cornelius' messengers. Their coming and the Spirit's directive to accompany them to Cornelius' house (10:19-20) is Peter's first clue as to the analogical role of food and, therefore, he would equate the 'unclean' food with 'unclean' Gentiles (10:28). The literal reference to food stops at this point in the narrative. From here, the metaphoric significance of food is given prominence. Subsequently, in hindsight, Peter recollects the reality of his experience on the basis of the visit of Cornelius' envoys (ἐξαυτῆς, 11:11). This perfect coincidence establishes for Peter the reality of his vision and also gives him the first hint about its meaning. The Spirit now clears the ambiguity of the vision when he tells Peter that God is at work in initiating this new venture. It was not Cornelius who sent out messengers, but actually the Spirit who "*sent them*" (10:20). The visitors add that Cornelius was told by an angel that he would receive a message from Peter.[44] Peter will discover the new dimensions of the directive, provided he goes with them to Cornelius. This is in keeping with what we have demonstrated earlier that sometimes God commissions people for a particular task in visions and dreams.

That Peter clearly understood the analogical nature of the food vision as referring to the Gentiles is obvious from TR: PII(a). Peter confesses to Cornelius' household, "*...it is unlawful for a Jew to associate with or to visit a foreigner* (ἀλλοφύλῳ); *but God has shown me that I should not call anyone (ἄνθρωπον) profane or unclean*" (10:28). Thus, Luke reiterates that when God intervenes and acts, one's wrong assumptions and value system have to be reoriented. It

[44] P.F. Esler (*Community and Gospel*, 94) observes: "In asking Peter to visit the house of a Gentile, the three men obviously thought they were likely to offend his Jewish sensibilities, for that is why they prefix their request with a statement of Cornelius' virtues...to make the notion of entering his house less shocking."

is further confirmed in Peter's address at Cornelius' house, "*I truly understand that God shows no partiality but in every nation* (ἐν παντὶ ἔθνει) *anyone who fears him and does what is right* (δικαιοσύνην) *is acceptable to him*" (10:34-5). Thus, the vision and the command effectively set on course what follows.

We can now see that Peter is beginning to be convinced that as a result of his vision and the command, God is initiating new possibilities for mission in an unprecedented way. It is not Peter's personal piety (v.9) that prepared him for this "giant leap" as it were, but the divine initiative and the Spirit's directive coupled with Peter's obedience, showing that divine intervention in human affairs overturns wrong assumptions, and challenges and refashions earlier notions. Thus, the inaugural scenes effectively establish and forecast how the subsequent events will unfold and operate under God's guidance. In this sense, the vision may be applicable to both food and people. In fact, only when it is applied to people does it become truly intelligible and meaningful. Thus, the food analogy is really about people.[45]

At the end of all the reconstructions of the Cornelius story, Luke emphasises that the conclusive point of the visions is not so much about inter-ethnic relations, as about the offer of salvation to the Gentiles (11:18). Thus, the visions of Cornelius and Peter in the main narrative and their recapitulations interface with each other and thereby make possible a deeper and comprehensive understanding of the visions. Such an intersection of the visions underscores the divine initiative in effecting the God-appointed rendezvous between Cornelius and Peter that leads to hearing the message of salvation and the descent of the Spirit (10:33)—the second supernatural event in the Cornelius story.

So far in the narrative the *vision directives* and *command-obedience* sequences result in bringing Peter and Cornelius closer together. The visions are also intrinsically interwoven with Peter's missionary speech, because the meaning of the vision is the starting point of Peter's speech. The whole of the Cornelius narrative attains its climactic point in this discourse, which, as stated above, serves to heighten the moment in the story. Thus, the stage is now set for Peter's address. First, a brief word on the suitability of the speech to its situation is in order.

---

[45] *The Letter of Aristeas* (315) uses the term "common" to describe 'common' men. R.J.H. Shutt, "Letter of Aristeas" in OTP, 7-34, esp. 33.

THE SUITABILITY OF PETER'S SPEECH TO ITS SITUATION

Scholars debate whether or not Peter's speech suits the situation.[46] However, the course of the visions and the focus on certain aspects of Jesus' ministry (10:37-41) renders the speech particularly relevant for a Gentile audience.[47] Moreover, linguistic links with Peter's initial comments on God's impartial acceptance of ἐν παντὶ ὁ φοβούμενος...καὶ ἐργαζόμενος δικαιοσύνην (v.35) and Cornelius' characterisation in 10:2, 22 (ὁ φοβούμενος, δίκαιος) attest to the suitability of the speech to the situation. In addition, as will be shown in the chapter, this progressive grasping of the earlier visions gives Peter a new insight, which functions as the starting point of his sermon (10:34). This again reinforces the suitability of Peter's speech to its occasion.

Further, the Theological underpinning in Peter's argument and its all-inclusive tone also suggests the relevance of the speech to its situation.[48] Peter's emphasis, in his speech, of the universal Lordship of Jesus (πάντων κύριος, 10:36) and of the offer of forgiveness of sins to everyone who believes (πάντα τὸν πιστεύοντα, 10:43) undoubtedly includes, in the context, Cornelius and his household as well. Thus, his speech is well suited to its occasion; its close reading provides certain important insights into the Cornelius story.

PETER'S ADDRESS (10:34-43)

In his speech, Peter connects the visions and the events in which he is involved by giving an account of his own vision and God's revelation ("*God has shown*": 10:28). He is visiting Cornelius to proclaim the good news only because of the divine revelation. As stated earlier, Peter interprets his food-vision

---

46 Dibelius (*Studies*, 111) regards the phrase, "ὑμεῖς οἴδατε (v.37) as "scarcely appropriate" to Cornelius, "who, although he knows something of the Old Testament...knows nothing about Jesus Christ." That this sermon is similar to others in Acts indicates that "Luke wants to show his readers what Christian preaching ought to be" (Ibid). ὑμεῖς οἴδατε is more an "attention seeker" than an appeal to the audience's prior knowledge.

47 For C.H. Dodd (*The Apostolic Preaching and Its Development*, [London: Hodder ... Stoughton, 1938], 28) the speech reflects "the form of kerygma used by the primitive church in its earliest approaches to a wider public...it is quite intelligible in the situation presupposed that some account of the ministry of Jesus should have been called for when the gospel was taken to people who could not be acquainted, as the Jews of Judea were, with the main facts."

48 Cf. E.M. Humphrey, "Collision of Modes?—Vision and Determining Argument in Acts 10:1-11:18" in Robert B. Robinson & Robert C. Culley (Eds.), *Textual Determinacy*, (Semeia 71; Atlanta: Scholars, 1995), 65-84, esp. 79-80.

cumulatively as God's means of teaching him not to regard any person common or unclean. This progressive grasping of the earlier experience gives a new insight, which now functions as the starting point of Peter's sermon and is developed in due course.

Since the missionary discourses and their literary functions in Acts have already been discussed in detail, here we highlight briefly some features of the speech for reasons of emphasis.

The periphrastic construction "᾿Ανοίξας...Πέτρος τὸ στόμα εἶπεν" (v.34) introduces Peter's speech in a dramatic way anticipating something extremely crucial and solemn. In other words, because of the emphases contained in the speech, whatever is going to follow depends entirely on what Peter is going to say. In his "message of salvation" (cf. 11:14) Peter offers certain insights about God, Christ, salvation, and mission as follows:

God	Shows no partiality; accepts people in every nation who fears him and does what is right; sent the message of peace; anointed Jesus of Nazareth with power and the Spirit; raised Jesus on the third day; chose the apostles as witnesses (10:34ff).
Jesus	Lord of all; preached peace; was anointed by God with the Holy Spirit and with power; went about doing good and healing all who were oppressed by the devil;God was with him; crucified and was raised by God; commanded the apostles to preach and testify that he is the God-ordained judge; everyone who believes in him receives forgiveness of sins through his name (10:36ff.).
Salvation	By believing in Jesus one receives *forgiveness of sins through his name* (10:43)
Mission	πάντα τὸν πιστεύοντα receives forgiveness of sins (10:43).

Peter starts with the declaration that he is beginning to realise (καταλαμβάνομαι) that God shows no partiality (10:34).[49] At the end of his speech, Peter and his companions will see for themselves that God is demonstrating his impartiality in a new and unprecedented way (10:44f.). Since God does not show favouritism, anyone who fears God and works righteousness is acceptable to him (10:35; cf. v.22). Here, the readers know that, it is Cornelius

49 Lev. 19:15 uses the same sense to forbid justice (on the basis of external appearance). Deut. 10: 17 declares that God is impartial (cf. *Psalms of Solomon* 2:18: R.B. Wright, "Psalms of Solomon" in OTP, 639-70, esp. 653.

who is meant, but they may also notice the character ellipsis here. The character Cornelius disappears, but his character-indicators, more than merely referring to him, come to typify anyone acceptable to God anywhere. We have already pointed out that Luke portrays Cornelius as a 'Flat Character' whose characterisation remains constant throughout the story. Therefore, he functions as a type.[50] Thus, the domain of acceptability to God is widened. Cornelius and all those whom he typifies are partakers in the fulfilment of God's promises through Jesus, the Lord.

As Peter expounds the Jesus-Kerygma and the Lordship of Jesus, the Christological rationale for Gentile mission is unshakeably established. Earlier, while analysing the missionary speeches, we showed that what God does is understood only when seen through the prism of Jesus. Therefore, in the present account too, Peter declares that Jesus is the "*Lord of all*" (10:36).[51] This is the new insight he has gained (10:36) based on his earlier visions, which now he proclaims to Cornelius' household. This, in fact, is the main statement of the verse.[52]

After having proclaimed that Jesus is the Lord of all, Peter gives a quick review of Jesus' ministry (10:37ff). Finally, he declares, "*everyone who believes in him receives forgiveness of sins through his name*" (10:43). This strongly reminds us of Peter's declaration in his Pentecost address, "*Everyone who calls on the name of the Lord shall be saved*" (2:21). The readers, who know Luke's Gospel, might also relate 10:43 to Lk. 24:47 where the forgiveness of sins and the name of Jesus are explicitly connected to each other.

Luke makes another important affirmation in Peter's speech: The only qualification required for salvation is 'faith': "*...everyone who believes in him...*" (10:43). In the narrative, this explicit reference to 'faith' in Jesus as the determinant of one's forgiveness of sins prepares the readers for the climactic declaration in Jerusalem (15:9).

---

50 E.M. Forster, *Aspects of the Novel*, 75.

51 Werner Foerster observes that "Lord of all" is an expression found in the classical religions. For instance, Zeus is "the Lord of all": Pindar, *Isthm.* 5:35 ("κύριος", *TDNT*, III, [1965], 1047). Richard Wünsch suggests that even in Hellenistic religions, this phenomenon could be seen. For example, at the birth of Osiris a voice sounds, "The Lord of all advances to the light" and that it was this expression that passed over into Judaism. (cf. Conzelmann, *Acts*, 83). The expression may have political meaning as well as in Epictetus (4.1.12): "Caesar, the lord of all" (Ibid).

52 Cf. Tannehill, *Narrative Unity*, 2.139.

The visions, divine commands and human obedience to them leading to the hearing of the word in the Cornelius' story, consummate in the second supernatural act, the descent of the Spirit. That this is a crucial aspect of the Cornelius episode is clear from the fact that in the later recapitulations it is used as a hermeneutical key to disclose the core of Cornelius' experience. We will discuss this later in the chapter.

THE SEQUEL TO PETER'S MESSAGE

The descent of the Spirit on Cornelius and his household is sometimes called, "The Gentile Pentecost."[53] This is not preceded by an audience initiative such as, "*What should we do to be saved?*" (2:37; cf. 16:30), followed by a demand from the preacher (2:38,40b; 16:31, etc). Peter has just proclaimed the work, crucifixion and the resurrection of Jesus, the prophetic testimony and the offer of forgiveness of sins. Then the Spirit spontaneously descended on the hearers. The very fact that the Spirit descended even in the absence of certain "formal stages", such as audience-initiative, response demanded and the actual audience-response, proves that the Gentile conversion is purely a divine act. The Gentiles now receive the Spirit just as the Jews have (10:45,47), thus binding the Gentiles together with the community of God's people (10:47). Therefore, Peter concludes that it is pointless to withhold baptism from those Gentile believers, particularly after the Spirit's descent that parallels the experience of the apostles at Pentecost (10:44-48a; cf. 2:38). Peter's decision to baptise Cornelius and his household is only in response to the work of the Spirit, not in answer to an appeal by himself (cf. 2:38) or by Cornelius' conscious choice (cf. 8:36). If the outpouring of the Holy Spirit is evidence to God's acceptance, then by means of water baptism Peter implies acceptance by fellow-believers (cf. 11:15a). Recollecting this moment, Peter will declare in the Apostolic Council that in cleansing the Gentiles' hearts by faith, God has made no distinction between peoples (TR: 'C. Conversion': *External Recapitulations*-III [e]).[54]

---

53 Bruce, *Acts*, 1.264.

54 One development that Luke's readers might notice here is that the Spirit comes on Cornelius' household even before they were baptised, unlike the Pentecost story, where the respondents to the Christian proclamation were promised the gift of the Spirit following their baptism (2:38,41). In Philip's Samaritan mission, Luke shows the gift of the Spirit, following water baptism (8:12). In other places Luke does not say whether the gift of the Spirit followed baptism or vice versa (8:36,38; 9:18; 22:16, etc). What Luke makes clear is that for him, the descent of the Spirit is more important than its sequence. If it is God's decision to send the Spirit on the believers, then he decides when it should happen.

Thus, visions make a proclamatory situation possible for both Cornelius and Peter and hearing the Jesus-Kerygma brings the former within the salvific fold. Barrett observes, "Luke...is thinking primarily of the Gentiles present, who, on the basis of nothing but the proclamation of Jesus, had manifestly been brought within the scope of salvation."[55] It is precisely the preaching of the message of salvation and its hearing, following the visions, that has resulted in the conversion of Cornelius and his household.

Summary

Luke strongly espouses that God has set in motion a movement of offering salvation that includes the Gentiles as well. It requires nothing less than God's own intervention by means of parallel visions and his commands that the human characters have to execute. Here Luke establishes the *avant-garde* nature of God's acts when they are complemented by human obedience. Their obedience to the divine-command is their first hermeneutical tool that establishes a strong link between the visions and Peter's address, dialogues and deliberations.

Had Luke concluded the Cornelius story at 10:48, the readers could not have gained a complete picture of the story. His reconstruction of the Cornelius account twice more (TR: 'C. Conversion': *External Recapitulations*-III [a-g]) gives them a total picture of what actually had taken place in the narrative. The first recapitulation appears in Peter's defence before the Jerusalem plenary session.

PETER DEFENDS CORNELIUS' CONVERSION (11:1-18)

Peter's speech in the Jerusalem plenary session (TR: 'C. Conversion': *External Recapitulation*-III [a-c]) recollects all the events reported so far in the narrative and, thereby, gives events their heightened emphasis. We discussed this under the visions of Cornelius and Peter and their recapitulations earlier in the chapter. Barrett considers the repeated narration of events as superfluous[56]; by contrast, this passage is the most important clue to interpreting all that had transpired at Cornelius' house. Here, Luke re-narrates the account from Peter's point-of-view with a shift in the perspective of the narrative. This is a well-known

[55] Barrett, *Acts*, 1.529.

[56] Ibid., 1.491.

rhetorical technique in Antiquity, namely *prosopoeia*.[57] As a character within the story, Peter gives his own version of the story from his point-of-view. The most obvious difference in the order of Peter's first reconstruction is that he starts with his own vision and finishes with Cornelius' vision. Such a reversal of order brings the crux of the matter to the fore as significant interpretive details are added to the happening all along. Since we have discussed this earlier in detail, we will not repeat the details here.

At this point in the narrative, Peter's Jerusalem critics (οἱ ἀπόστολοι καὶ οἱ ἀδελφοι, [11:1]) function as a judicial body to which Peter is answerable. Although they knew very well that the Gentiles (τὰ ἔθνη) have received (ἐδέξαντο) the word of God (11:1; cf. 8:14; 17:11), as stated above, what concerned them most was that Peter had entered (εἰσελθειν) the house of an uncircumcised person and had accepted hospitality (συμφαγεῖν: 11:3; cf. 10:27, 48). This is a gross violation of the Jewish dietary laws. Here the theme of eating with the uncircumcised may allude to 10:9-16 and so prompt the readers to recall the vision.

Through this plot Luke cautions his readers that it is possible that human jurisprudence may go off at a tangent from God's original purposes because of its failure to maintain the same perspective as God's. As we repeatedly emphasised above, Luke's narrative world is built around God and, therefore, in order to understand and appreciate fully what he records, the readers must necessarily share the same Theocentric worldview. Also in what follows, Luke expects them to see the indispensable corrective function of the speech, which brings out a positive affirmation of God's actions at the end (11:18) by highlighting implicitly the crux of the matter.

Responding to the accusation, Peter recounts the happenings starting from his vision until the descent of the Spirit on the Gentile believers. Most significantly, instead of answering why he ate with the Gentiles, he recounts only the descent of the Spirit. Peter has clearly understood—obviously from his earlier visions, the heavenly voice, the visit of Cornelius' messenger, and Cornelius' recollection of his own vision—that dietary laws do not figure at all anywhere in God's scheme. In his autobiographical reconstruction of the original event

---

[57] Daniel Marguerat, "Saul's Conversion (9,22,26) and the Multiplication of Narrative in Acts", in C.M. Tuckett, (Ed.), *Luke's Literary Achievement: Collected Essays*, (JSNTSup. 116; Sheffield: SAP, 1995), 125-55, esp. 138, n.31. See also W.S. Kurz, "Hellenistic Rhetoric ", 186; Aune, *Literary Environment*, 125-28. Earlier, we called the same idea as 'intradiegetic' narration, i.e., narration by a character internal to the story .

in the form of personal narrative, Peter articulates how perfectly Cornelius' vision interfaces with his message. He recounts Cornelius' vision in which the angel tells him to send for him (i.e., Peter) by whose 'words' (ῥήματα: 11:14) salvation will be received (11:13-14): "*He will give you a message by which you and your entire household will be saved*" (11:14). This particular soteriological aspect of the previous visions is the new dimension that is missing in the earlier two recapitulations (CII [a-b]).

After narrating the salvific nature of his message, Peter recollects (without reference to speaking in tongues—a supernatural phenomenon at Pentecost [2:4] and baptism) the coming of the Holy Spirit on the hearers as if to validate what he was saying (11:15; cf. 10:44-46).[58] From Luke's point-of-view, this experience, paralleling the Pentecost experience of the disciples (2:1-5), is the decisive determinant of the conversion of Cornelius' household and the equality of membership in the community of believers. For the first time in the Cornelius story, Peter recollects the words of Jesus that the believers will be baptised with the Spirit (11:16; cf. 1: 5; Lk. 3:16). Up to this point in the narrative of Acts, this is the third time the promise is being recalled.

The promise of the Spirit in Acts 1:5 is immediately recalled and reiterated in 1:8 ("*You will receive power when the Holy Spirit has come upon you*") and later in 2:38-9 ("*You will receive the gift of the Holy Spirit. For the promise is for you...*"). Here Luke is producing multiple layers of interpretation. First, the coming of the Spirit on the Gentiles (10:44-47) is in fulfilment of Jesus' own promise. Secondly, it attests to the internal Promise-Fulfilment scheme, or the testimony of the Scriptures. Thirdly, the recollection from the mouth of Peter, the apostle, adds to the event the apostolic attestation. Moreover, the presence of the other Jewish believers at Cornelius' house and their witness to the descent of the Spirit also provides a collective testimony to the certitude of the event and its verification. This is the key to the interpretation of the original event.[59] Thus, by means of triple-attestation, Luke seals the reality and the authenticity of the event. However, the Gentile-focus is the new dimension that he adds to what has been originally promised in the Jewish context (1:5).

---

[58] Dibelius (*Studies*, 110) points this out as an anomaly. In Acts 10:44 the outpouring of the Holy Spirit happened at the end of Peter's sermon. According to Acts 11:15 it happened just as he had begun to speak. There is no problem if this can be read as, "Even well before I finished my sermon..."

[59] Maloney, "*God had Done*", 76. She elaborates: "As Luke had prepared for the descent of the Holy Spirit on the apostles by preceding it with a word of promise from the Risen One...here he also connects the descent of the Spirit on the gentiles with this same promise, depicting Peter as remembering it at this very hour (11:16)" (Ibid., 82).

Luke clearly wants his readers to see the natural incorporation of the Gentiles into God's promise (cf. 8:17), which the Jerusalem brethren themselves will acknowledge at the end of the plenary session (11:18; cf. 15:8,14).

Peter's recapitulative speech recasts the main event in order to enhance its rhetorical force. He concludes that if God has masterminded all that has transpired so far, then refusing to obey his voice is to oppose his purposes (11:17). Further, since the Spirit's coming on the Gentiles happened in the presence of Peter and his Jerusalem companions, just as it had happened to them at Pentecost, nobody could deny its reality. Tannehill comments, "...A sequence of events led Peter to change his mind. Now his audience is being led through the same sequence of events so that they can appreciate and share Peter's new insight."[60] This further affirms our earlier finding that Peter's vision was more about offering salvation to the Gentiles than socialising with them.

So far, Peter has related in his speech the event from his point-of-view and, thus, revealed its central meaning for him. His mission to Cornelius, his missionary speech and the resultant descent of the Spirit—everything is directly dependent on God's doing, i.e., the visions. Most importantly, at the end of Peter's defence, the issue of hospitality has become totally a non-issue. Peter further strongly defends his position by binding the experience of the Caesarean Gentiles with that of the Jerusalem Jewish Christians. Both the Jews and the Gentiles received the Holy Spirit without any discrimination (11:15-16; cf. 1:4-5, 8).

Thus, the reappraisal effects a transformation in attitudes and values[61] as Peter has effectively persuaded his accusers. The conclusion to this whole section comes from Peter's detractors themselves (11:18). They glorify God, saying "*God has given even to the Gentiles the repentance that leads to life*'" (11:18; cf. 5:31). What has started as a mere apology has become a deliberative situation, which is now setting a precedent for future Gentile mission in an unprecedented way.

Summary

A detour from the original issue of eating with the Gentiles and the reversal of order of visions indicates that from Luke's point-of-view the real issue is

---

60 Tannehill, *Narrative Unity*, 2.144.

61 Cf. Carol P. Christ, (*Diving Deep and Surfacing*, [Boston: Beacon Press, 1980], 51-2).

Gentile-salvation. Peter's visit to Cornelius' house in obedience to the heavenly vision, the command, and proclaiming the salvific message (11:14) incontrovertibly establishes that God is masterminding the conversion of the Gentiles. This has strategic importance for future Gentile-mission, which is why it re-figures in the Jerusalem Council.

CONFIRMATIONS IN THE JERUSALEM COUNCIL (15:7-21)

Peter's Confirmation

Although scholarly opinion unanimously concludes that Peter's speech in 15:7-11 (TR: 'C. Conversion': *External Recapitulation*-III [d-f]) is directly related to the Cornelius story,[62] neither Cornelius' nor Peter's visions appear anywhere. Cornelius is not even named. Instead, the passage shows a series of substitutions and additions, which help the readers to interpret the events of the Cornelius story from the vantage point of its present objective truths, which have not been referred to so far.

Peter begins by briefly referring to his speech at Cornelius' house (15:7: διὰ τοῦ στόματός μου; cf. 10:34) with a view to highlighting solely the message and its Theological meaning. He refers only to what has been proclaimed, what has been heard, and believed: "...ἀκοῦσαι τὰ ἔθνη τὸν λόγον τοῦ εὐαγγελίου καὶ πιστεῦσαι" (15:7). This is the first time Luke is pointing out the 'faith' dimension in the Gentiles' response to Christian proclamation (cf. 15:9,11). The 'faith' aspect of the descent of the Spirit on Cornelius' household (10:44-47) would not have come out had it not been for Peter's speech recapitulating that original experience, now being referred to as a solution to a new crisis in the church. In his speech, Peter points out that the real decider of conversion is believing and nothing else (15:9,11). He recognises, as emphasised earlier, that 'faith' actualises the '*cleansing of the heart*.'[63] The outpouring of the Spirit and the subsequent baptism are heart cleansing as a result of faith-response (15:9) to what has been preached. Peter arrives at this principle from specific aspects of his past experience.

---

62 For example, Wilson, *Luke and the Law*, 71; Derrett, "Clean and Unclean", 205; Maloney, "*God had Done*", 137-72, esp. 138.

63 πιστεύομεν σωθῆναι (15:11) has been understood in different ways. Bruce gives different possible construals: i) "We believe we shall be saved" (aorist infinitive in future sense cf. 2:30; 3:18); ii) "we believe we have been saved," or iii) "we believe (so as) to be saved" (epexegetic infinitive), we are saved by faith. Bruce prefers the third reading because this was Peter's stand as is implied by Paul in Gal. 2:15f. (Bruce, *Acts*, 337).

Peter's overriding conclusion is that faith and the grace of the Lord Jesus alone can effect salvation for Jews and Gentiles alike (15:11; cf. 2:21; 4:12; 16:30-31). The impact of Peter's cogent reasoning, based on his earlier visionary experience, is received with a resounding silence (15:12a; cf. 11:18) creating a climactic suspense. Will the circumcision-loyalists (15:1) pose any clever rebuttal? This suspense heightens tension in the narrative leading to the second confirmation of the Gentile conversion by James.

James' Confirmation

James, in his summation (TR: 'C. Conversion': *External Recapitulation*-III [g]: 15:13-21) recollects the Cornelius event as the first (πρῶτον: 15:14) official Gentile conversion and underscores "*...how God first looked favorably on the Gentiles, to take from among them a people for his name*" (15:14). James does not evince any knowledge of the conversion of the Ethiopian Eunuch (8:26-40). From his perspective, the Cornelius event is the first official Gentile conversion.[64] This official declaration enhances the importance of the Cornelius story.

In his confirmation, James points out that it has been God who was at work in the Gentile conversion. Most importantly, he refers to the Gentiles as the λαός (15:14; cf. 18: 10), which is the *terminus technicus* for the chosen people of God. Ex. 19:5 and Deut. 14:2 refer to Israel as a special people selected for Yahweh himself from among the Gentiles.[65] In Acts, the language is similar, but the meaning is different: "*this* people for God's name comprises believing Gentiles" as well.[66] Through James, Luke confirms that there is Scriptural basis for the inclusion of the Gentiles into the community of the λαός (15:15-18; cf. Amos 9:11-12, [LXX]).[67] The "events (i.e., visions) directing Peter and Cornelius to each other and the subsequent coming of the Spirit have the same meaning for Gentiles as the election of Israel has for the Jewish people."[68] The descent of the Spirit on Cornelius' household is evidence that the God who chose Israel, continues to call a people for his name, now from Gentiles also. Had it not been for James' confirmatory speech, there would not have been this final sealing of the conversion of Cornelius and his household.

---

64 Nobody in the Jerusalem accrediting body, not even Peter and John—the apostles at the forefront after Jesus' ascension—seem to know about the Ethiopian Eunuch's conversion. Philip remains anonymous throughout.

65 Cf. Deut. 26:18f.; 32:8f; Ps.135:4 (LXX 134).

66 Bruce, *Acts*, 1.339.

67 The original account of the story of Cornelius does not adduce any scriptural basis for the conversion of the Gentiles. See Tyson, "Gentile Mission ", 619-31.

68 Tannehill, *Narrative Unity*, 2.186.

Summary

Luke's main thesis is that God's salvation is all-encompassing; it belongs both to Jews and Gentiles alike. Ultimately this is God's work and not that of human beings. The event of Cornelius' conversion and all the visions, the speech, the descent of the Spirit, and the recapitulations testify that it is God who has acted decisively in the conversion of the Gentiles.

However, from the main narrative about the Spirit's coming (TR: 'C. Conversion', I. *Main narrative*) it is impossible to conclude anything about Cornelius' conversion or the meaning of the Spirit's coming. The elements present in the Pentecost account are conspicuously absent in the Cornelius story: there is no audience-initiative; no demand placed before the audience in the discourse and no indication of actual audience-response in the narrative, and no reference to the blessings that follow conversion. Explanations of Cornelius' experience are inconclusive. Maloney, for instance, calls Cornelius' experience "Christianisation", since he and his household are already Godfearers.[69] From social sciences point-of-view, basing her argument on Richard Travisano's definition, Gaventa calls Cornelius' experience, "alternation"[70], which does not involve complete cessation from the past, but stems from it. Travisano defines "alternation" as

> "...changes of life which do not involve a radical change...but which are a part of or grow out of existing programs of behavior..."[71]

According to this definition, Cornelius' experience requires no rejection of the past, thought or action. However, as pointed out earlier, such social categories cannot be used too freely since they presuppose many things, which cannot be established from the text.

However, a narrative reversal, i.e., a reconstruction of the main event through different flashbacks (TR: 'C. Conversion': *External Recapitulation*-III [a-b, e-f]) helps towards, what Iser calls, "sequential reading" and "consistency building"[72], that is, building a total picture by reading back and forth. The

---

69 Maloney "*God had Done*", 83, n.2.

70 Gaventa, *Darkness to Light*, 148.

71 Travisano, "Alternation and Conversion as Qualitatively Different Transformation," in Gregory P. Stone & Harvey A. Farberman (Eds.), *Social Psychology Through Symbolic Interaction*, (Waltham, Mass.: Ginn-Blaisdell, 1970), 594-606, esp. 600-601.

72 W. Iser, *Act of Reading*, 119, 148-50.

missionary kerygma preached by Peter and the later cumulative understanding of the whole event give us some clues about what exactly constitutes Cornelius' experience from Luke's perspective. Luke presents it as follows:

10:36	"Jesus Christ...Lord of all"
10:43	"...Everyone who believes in him receives forgiveness of sins through his name"
11:17a	"If then God gave them the same gift that he gave us when we believed in the Lord Jesus Christ..."
11:18	"Then God has given even to the Gentiles the repentance that leads to life"
15:8-9	"And God...testified to them by giving them the Holy Spirit, just as he did to us; and in cleansing their hearts by faith..."
15:11	"...we will be saved through the grace of the Lord Jesus..."

The Jerusalem Council, functioning as the final validating body, makes certain definite conclusions about Cornelius' experience, reminding us Rambo's suggestion that ultimately conversion is what a faith group says it is.[73] According to it, the descent of the Spirit on Cornelius' household denotes faith in the Lord Jesus Christ (11:17a), repentance that leads to life (11:18), cleansing of hearts by faith (15:8-9), and salvation through the grace of the Lord Jesus (15:11). Luke would want his readers to understand these aspects as the constituents of Cornelius' conversion.

In the Cornelius episode, Peter's missionary speech and recapitulations are born out of the visions and the infusion of the Spirit. In the whole process, as seen earlier, the visions, the descent of the Spirit, the dialogues, the missionary speech, and the deliberations are organically interconnected to accentuate the moment of the story and finally to effect the conversion of Cornelius' household. By his recapitulations of Cornelius' conversion, his focus on the final unfolding of the visions, the coming of the Spirit, and the missionary kerygma, Luke proves how strategic this story is in the life of the early church and its mission.

After having analysed how visions and speeches, both direct and recapitulative, interface with each other and operate together in Cornelius' conversion, we now turn to the literary functions of the Cornelius story.

---

[73] Rambo, *Religious Conversion*, XIV.

NARRATIVE FUNCTIONS

That the story of Cornelius plays a crucial and important role in the narrative of Acts is widely recognised in the scholarly circles. On the basis of our study so far, we highlight particularly two literary functions, in light of Luke's conversion motif in Acts.

Divine Providence and Universal Outlook

In Peter's Pentecost speech, Luke has already forecast salvation for all humankind (2:21,39), while the audience was exclusively Jewish. Likewise, the reference to πρῶτον in Peter's Temple speech (3:26) also implies that God's salvation will definitely move beyond its present boundaries. However, in the Cornelius story he highlights the Gentile-salvation prominently. For instance, 10:34 refers to the fact that there are people who are acceptable to God even among the πᾶντα ἔθνει (10:28; cf. 10:45; 11:18). He complements this by stating that Jesus is πάντων κύριος (10:36) and that the prophets predicted forgiveness of sins to πάντα τὸν πιστεύοντα in Jesus (10:43).[74] Here readers might notice the expansiveness of Luke's concept of salvation.

The Cornelius story is Luke's demonstration that the ever-widening scope of salvation is God's doing. It shows that incorporating Gentiles into the community of believers was so inconceivable to the Jews that God himself had to intervene through visions, heavenly voice, and through radical changes in people (e.g., Peter) and through convincing speeches by his human instruments, to make this a possibility.

From the food vision and from God's threefold command to Peter to eat the unclean animals (10:9-16) Peter deduces that no person is unclean (10:28), and that the message of salvation (10:36-43) should be preached to the Gentiles (11:1). God dramatically confirms these deductions by orchestrating the whole situation to bring the word of salvation to Cornelius through Peter, in the midst of which, the Spirit descends to affirm his acceptance of the Gentiles (10:44). At the end of Peter's cogent argument in the Jerusalem plenary session, based on his earlier visions and the coming of the Spirit, the Jewish sceptics finally agree, "*So then, God has even granted the Gentiles repentance unto life*" (11:18). We have already referred to this. The immediacy of the coming of the Spirit as a sign and seal of salvation to the Gentiles, following the message of salvation,

---

[74] So also Soards, *Speeches*, 83,183, n.179.

speaks for the centrality of God's activity. Thus, salvation is a gift, now offered to the Gentiles—in fact, to everyone who believes in Jesus' name (10:43).

In the Jerusalem meeting, Peter refers to the Spirit's coming on the Gentiles (11:15-18) as he did in the beginning, while recollecting the beginning of the actualisation of the promise that came in Acts 2. This, in turn, echoes Joel (3:1-5 [LXX]) and the distribution of the Spirit. Through such thematic links, which indirectly reintroduce OT explanation by echo, Luke interweaves the issue of Gentile-salvation with the revelation of God's purpose of salvation for all humans for all times.

In Peter's speech at Cornelius' house, Luke alluded to Isa 52:7 in Acts 10:36: "*The word sent to the sons of Israel evangelising peace through Jesus Christ.*" This was God's promise through Isaiah, according to which Jerusalem's coming salvation would be displayed "*in the sight of all the nations, and all the ends of the earth will see the salvation of our God*" (Isa. 52:10). With Cornelius' conversion, what was foretold by the prophet begins to unfold further. In his speech, Peter realises that, if Jesus is indeed the "*Lord of all*" (10:36), then the conversion of the Gentiles is its necessary consequence—a realisation, which the other apostles in the Jerusalem plenary session affirmed (11:1-18; 15:6-8, 14-18). Cumulatively, the Cornelius story is Luke's demonstration that God, his ways, and his saving grace cannot be monopolised. If the Jews in Acts thought that circumcision will make one worthy of salvation (cf. 15:1), in Cornelius' story, Luke shows that it is God who certifies what makes one worthy of salvation (cf. 10:34-35), i.e., 'faith' in his name (10:43; cf. 15:11). Since God is open to all (10:34-35), his saving grace is also open to all (10:43). This is what the Cornelius' story authentically demonstrates.

Social Interaction as a Consequence of Conversion

Having shown in the Cornelius account that Gentile-salvation is inevitable because God has masterminded it, Luke further affirms, through the Cornelius story, that the unity of the people of God is consequent upon conversion.

The "Jew-Gentile Table-Fellowship" aspect of the Cornelius story is undeniably important[75], but to say that it is the end of all that God had set out to do through visions, heavenly voices, and the missionary discourse, is to minimise the magnitude of God's role in initiating Gentile-salvation, here microcosmically

---

[75] For instance, Matson, *Household Conversion*, 86,134 and P. Esler, *Community and Gospel*, passim.

represented by Cornelius' conversion. Social interaction can at best be a natural corollary to God's doing, i.e., conversion, but not its primary end. As shown earlier, for all his piety and favourable disposal towards the Jews, Cornelius is still an uncircumcised Gentile (e.g., 11:1). Peter's Jerusalem detractors thought that eating with Gentiles was more important than Cornelius' conversion. However, through Peter's speeches, both in the Jerusalem plenary session and in the Jerusalem Council, Luke reinforces the fact that God was accomplishing something qualitatively and teleologically different. The bestowal of the Spirit on Cornelius' household is evidence that God recognised in them faith in the Lord Jesus Christ (11:17a), offered them repentance that leads to life (11:18), cleansed their hearts by faith (15:8-9), and offered them salvation through the grace of the Lord Jesus (15:11). At the end of these deliberations and understanding of the reality and the Theological and Christological significance of the Gentile-salvation that God has accomplished, Luke shows the Jewish acceptance of Gentiles: "*God...looked favourably on the Gentiles* (ἐθνῶν), *to take from among them a people* (λαός) *for his name*" (15:14). Having accepted the Gentile-salvation, the Jerusalem Council had to draw a code of conduct that should govern the new community of believers, implying that if God had accepted the Gentiles—evidenced by the coming of the Spirit as a symbol and seal of Gentile-conversion (10:44)—what remains is the Jewish acceptance of the Gentiles as their brethren (vv.19ff.).

The quintessence of the Cornelius story is that God offers forgiveness of sins through Jesus' name to everyone who believes (10:43) and that he has given even to the Gentiles the repentance that leads to life (11:18). This is what the Cornelius episode primarily reinforces. Luke's point is not that at the end of the story, Jews and Gentiles sat and ate together, but that conversion can (and therefore, should) lead to the dissolution of barriers that be and thus, effect the unity of the people of God (ἔθνος=λαός, 15:14).

This is illustrated by a steady progression in the understanding of the Jew-Gentile unity, following the conversion of Cornelius' household; it happens in the retellings as shown below:

	Reference to the Gentiles ("Them/These/They")	*Reference to the Jews ("Us/We")*
10:47	"...these people..."	"...just as we..."
11:12	"Go with them..."	"no distinction between them and us"
11:15	"the Holy Spirit fell upon them"	"...just as it had upon us"

11:17	"God gave them the same gift"	"that he gave us"
15:8	"Gave them the Holy Spirit"	"just as he did to us"
15:9	"...no distinction between them"	"...and us"
15:11	"...just as they will"	"we will be saved..."

These references evince a new sense of mutuality that was absent in the earlier references to the Gentiles (e.g., κοινὸν/ἀκάθαρτον: 10:28; ἀκροβυστίαν ἔχοντας: 11:3). The coming of the Spirit, which symbolises the conversion of the Gentiles and effects the Jew-Gentile unity, conversely implies that had there been no conversion there would have been no such unity and social interaction. The Cornelius episode depicts clearly that it is not nationality or the observance of specific customs but 'faith' in Jesus alone that makes possible new relationships between the Jews and Gentiles.[76]

CONCLUSION

Cornelius' conversion story is complex. It does not follow a simple linear narrative pattern as the Pentecost account does. What is being stated in the main narrative is recounted many times throughout the story. Since these repetitions play an integral role in the interpretation of the story, the Cornelius story can be said to follow an "*Internal Analeptical conversion Narrative Pattern*", in that, it follows a retrospective-reference scheme.

The vision-recapitulations, directed towards providing the readers with a hermeneutical tool to understand the main events retrospectively, help build a coherent picture of the story. The visions themselves are carefully constructed to provide dramatic contours to the story through the way they are connected to the speeches. The impact of this insertion of interpretation into the action characterises interpretations as part of the natural unfolding of events. On the basis of the interfacing of the visions, their recapitulations, and their literary functions, discussed so far, we can present diagrammatically the different "Internal Analeptical Narrative Patterns" in Cornelius' conversion story as follows:

76 Does this mean that the Jews and Gentiles form one body of mixed races or will the Jewish and Gentile communities remain separate? Luke does not answer such sociological questions in Acts. His designations to the 'converts', either Jewish or Gentile, are μαθητής, Ἀδελφός, πιστεύοντες, and ἡ ἐκκλησία.

Internal Analeptical Narrative Pattern

Visions

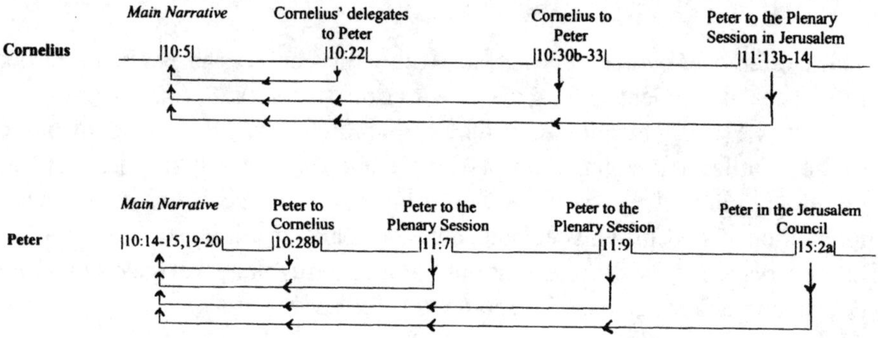

Conversion

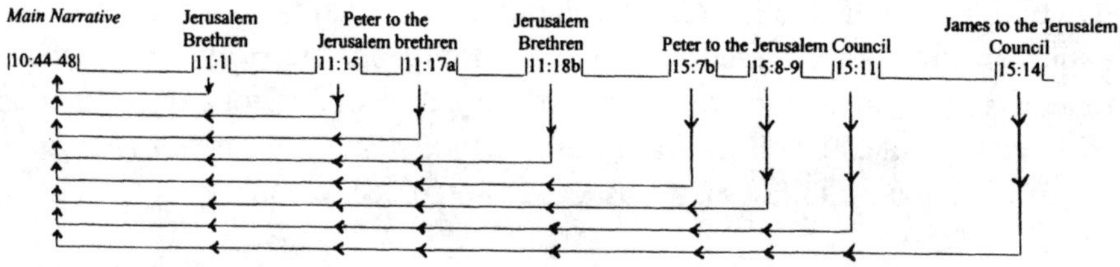

As the diagram shows, the twin-visions and the descent of the Spirit story become intelligible only through the speeches, which unfold events enacted by God and the human characters in the story. The speech and the interpretive details, inserted into the supernatural phenomena as the action develops in the retellings, enhance the moment and the significance of the miraculous occurrences. Their synthesis, in Luke's scheme, is the effective medium that achieves conversion in the apostolic mission in Acts, here microcosmically represented by the story of the conversion of Cornelius' household.

7

CONCLUSION

INTRODUCTION

The basic premise that governs this study is that conversion is achieved, in many cases in Acts, through the complementarity between the miraculous and proclamation, the two vital constituents of Christian mission.

Scholars have described Luke as a historian, theologian, and as a literary artist.[1] The strategies that Luke suggests as crucial means to advancing Christian testimony, which we have located at the end of our study, also show him as a mission strategist.[2] Through the intricate balance between the miraculous and proclamation—the taxonomy suggested in this study for Christian mission in Acts—their literary functions, and their control over the total narrative sequence in Acts in creating a believing community, Luke demonstrates their crucial importance to Christian mission.[3]

Through this taxonomy, Luke constructs a Theocentric worldview that becomes all-pervasive and all-determining in his conversion stories. This ideal situation assists in spreading the truth of God's providence, the Lordship of Jesus (2:21,36; 4:12, etc.), and God's plan of universal salvation (1:8).

Further, by linking his conversion motif with his vision of universal mission, Luke exhibits the signal importance of the theme of conversion to him. The

---

1 M.A. Powell, *What are They Saying about Luke?*, (New York: Paulist, 1989), 5-15.

2 So also H.C. Kee, *Good News to the Ends of the Earth: The Theology of Acts*, (London: SCM, 1990), 106.

3 Cf. R.J. Karris ("Missionary Communities", 96) suggests that Luke is writing for communities that are essentially missionary communities, that is, they send missionaries to the Jews and Gentiles.

complementarity he establishes between the miraculous and proclamation is his strategy to fulfil this motif. We identified this from the structure of Acts, his concept of divine providence, and the literary techniques he employs in Acts. The present chapter revisits the issues raised in chapter 1 in order to address each in turn, which will also summarise our findings. Finally, we will draw some implications for further exploration.

THE IMPORTANCE OF THE MIRACULOUS IN ACTS

In chapter 1 we grouped all the texts in Acts according to the way conversions take place in them and separated Group 'a' for a closer analysis because of the way this group of conversion stories identifies Luke's formula for effective Christian witnessing in Acts. The prominence of the miraculous in these stories raised the following questions: "What makes an event miraculous? Why is it important? What literary functions does it perform?"

In chapter 3 we showed that the demonstration of God's providence and power (e.g., 3:1-10) and the Theological and Christological meaning contained in it (e.g., 2:14ff) make an event miraculous. This description of the miraculous also shows its importance; it lies in the fact that it is a demonstration of God's providence, through which Luke shows that God is at work in the events that he records and thus, they have the stamp of divine necessity (δεῖ) and divine sanction.

Therefore, Luke interweaves his vision of a worldwide mission with his notion of the divine δεῖ. It was foretold by Jesus (e.g., 1:8); it conforms to scriptural prophecies (e.g., 2:21); and it is authenticated by God at critical junctures by the signs and wonders that he performs through Jesus (e.g., 2:22) and through his witnesses (e.g., 3:12ff.). Further, as seen in Graeco-Roman popular understanding and in the OT, Luke also punctuates his narratives in Acts frequently with visions, angelophanies, and heavenly voices to show the way God sometimes guides his witnesses and sometimes commissions some for a particular task. The Cornelius story demonstrates the all-controlling presence of visions given to both Cornelius and Peter (10:3-6, 9-16) that initiates a wholly new phase in Christian mission—the mission to Gentiles—now represented by Peter's Caesarean mission. This is evidence that God is directly involved in not only communicating his will, but also providing his witnesses with definite supernatural guidance. Going beyond the Cornelius story, we have also seen how Luke characterises Paul's mission by visions and angelic appearances, sometimes to guide him about the future course of action. Thus, the miraculous serves as an interpretive key to the events, both in the present and in future. It demonstrates the divine origin of the events that Luke narrates and confirms the word proclaimed at the same time. The readers are, then, able to see that every event that happened in the course of the movement of the Christian testimony towards its final destination necessarily falls within the jurisdiction of ἡ βουλή τοῦ θεοῦ.

The study of the miraculous in Luke's contemporary literary environment identified three strands of thought running parallel: a) Scepticism; b) acceptance of events as mediums of communication from the gods and c) subordination of the miraculous to morality and wisdom. By contrast, the events that Luke records in Acts are God's doings and, therefore, are objectively miraculous, that is, they are not a matter of perspective or individual interpretation. The only explanation possible is that they are God's acts in demonstration of his providence and power.

Moreover, within Luke's Theocentric worldview, the supernatural phenomena function as persuasive tools. This is seen, first, in the way the miraculous operated in Jesus' ministry. Peter reminds the audience at Pentecost that Jesus was a "*man attested...by God with deeds of power, wonders, and signs that God did through him...*" (2:22). Secondly, the supernatural phenomena also characterise the apostles' ministry and their co-workers (e.g., 4:22; 8:6). The δυνάμεις of Jesus are followed by those attributed to Stephen, Philip, and Paul (6:8; 8:13; 19:11). These mighty works authenticate and confirm the Christian proclamation. After one such miraculous occurrence Luke notes the frustration of the enemies of the apostles when they encounter the indisputable evidence, in that, the miraculous confirms the apostolic proclamation as God's word (e.g., 4:16). Just as God bore witness to Christ by external signs and miracles (e.g., 10:38), so he bears witness to the apostles in similar manner (e.g., 5:32).

This powerful confirmatory function is particularly evident in Acts 14:3. Paul and Barnabas remained for a long time in Iconium, "*speaking boldly for the Lord, who testified to the word of his grace by granting signs and wonders to be done through them.*" Thus, Luke presents a situation in the early church where, to the word proclaimed, there is a corresponding manifestation of divine providence and power in mighty works, signs, and wonders. This powerful impact of the miraculous and proclamation is God's doing, who, through the apostles, proclaims and endorses the proclamation through mighty works. Where this happens in Acts, the miraculous transports the narrative audiences into the domain of God and his deeds. This is the definite role of the miraculous in Christian witnessing in Acts.

However, the narrative ploy in Acts is such that the numinous quality of the event possesses an inexplicable character for the observer-characters in the narrative. It is an astonishing event, an object of amazement, and, as a consequence, and taking into account its exceptional character, it is an object of inquiry. Therefore, the audiences ask, "*What does this mean?*" (e.g., 2:6-7,12; 3:11-12), or they misunderstand (2:13; 14:11). The audiences do not have the intuition to see the reality behind the miraculous occurrences apart from the versions and conceptual schemes given in and by the interpretation. Thus, the miraculous functions both as an attention-catcher and as a necessitator of an exposition of the event. In the Cornelius story, for instance, Cornelius is instructed in a vision to send for Peter (10:5). Similarly, the Spirit instructs Peter to go with Cornelius' delegates (10:19-20). However, the visions do not come with any inherent explanation as to why Cornelius must send for Peter and why Peter must go to Cornelius. But their obedience to these vision-directives leads to Peter's proclamation of the message of salvation (10:7-8, 20-24a, 34-43; 11:14) at the end of which, the Spirit comes on Cornelius' household as a symbol of their conversion (10:44). Thus, visions and their lack of self-explanation necessitate and make possible a speech that explains why visions occurred and their ultimate purpose (e.g., 10:34).

Moreover, although Luke presents the miraculous as occasionally capable of leading people to God on its own (e.g., 9:32-42), it also functions within certain constraints. First, in terms of audience *reaction*, most often it prompts reactions of wonder such as θάμβος and φόβος, as shown earlier. Luke shows the inadequacy of these reactions by juxtaposing them with the *responses* that the missionary speeches evoke, namely repentance, turning to God and believing in him. In this sense, the miraculous has its own limits. Secondly, Acts evinces (as also does Josephus) that the miraculous cannot always evoke a 'faith-response' in the audience (excepting Acts 9:32-42). In fact, we have shown that in Acts instead of leading to faith, miracle working in many instances has led to opposition and persecution and sometimes even to martyrdom (e.g., 4:3; 6:8; 7:58f.; 14:19).

Therefore, Luke suggests, it is not enough simply to be amazed and afraid. Such initial reactions need to be 'changed' into deeper responses, namely μετανοεῖν, ἐπιστρέφειν, and πιστεύειν, etc., by means of missionary expositions, which are qualitatively and teleologically different. It is not just a matter of recognising and discovering the meaning of the miraculous, but on the basis of this recognition and newly discovered Theological, Christological, and soteriological meaning embedded in the miraculous, a change in perception, viewpoint, and lifestyle is demanded of the narrative audience either explicitly (e.g., 2:38) or implicitly (e.g., 10:43). The end of such a hermeneutical exercise is repenting, believing, and turning to God.

Thus, the miraculous phenomena are important for Luke to transport the narrative audiences into the domain of God, to pave the way for the missionary speech, to demonstrate divine providence and power, and to confirm the word proclaimed as God's word. This, then, leads to the consideration of the cumulative functions of the missionary speeches.

THE IMPORTANCE OF THE (MISSIONARY) SPEECHES IN ACTS

In chapter 1 we also identified the texts where the missionary speeches are juxtaposed with the miraculous. Therefore, we asked what could be Luke's reason behind this juxtaposition and why are the speeches important for him. The study of Graeco-Roman speeches, of the OT, and of Josephus (chapter 4) showed that Graeco-Roman (Thucydidean) speeches are political debates about the policies that should govern inter-state affairs. By contrast, the few speeches in the OT (Deut. 1:6-30:20; Josh. 23; Judg. 6:8-10; 1 Sam. 12) are Theological in nature, emphasising the theme of divine retribution, which runs through the speeches, unifying them all together and providing a coherent perspective on God and his deeds. The speeches in Josephus, on the other hand, follow the Graeco-Roman speeches in form, in style, and in nature (political) as well.

By contrast, Luke's missionary speeches, adopting the Theocentric perspective of the OT speeches, focus primarily on God, and his works, particularly in and through the person of Jesus. This Theocentricity is Luke's basic frame of reference and, therefore, as maintained throughout the study, assuming such a Theocentric/Christocentric worldview is indispensable to understand and appreciate fully what Luke says in his missionary speeches.

To begin with, Luke interjects his narratives with his missionary discourses to enliven the otherwise drab progression of events, where the characters are mere mute participants in the action of the narrative. Luke's characters act as well as speak, but their action is significantly relative to and is always highlighted by their speech. By making his characters speak, Luke facilitates an active participation in the action of the story. In this sense, the speech itself becomes an action within the action of the narrative and thereby the speaking characters become the principal actors. The (missionary) speeches are essential in order to expose Luke's Theological/Christological position, since speeches reveal what the flow of events normally conceals. Consequently, Luke subordinates action to speeches. Without these speeches, Luke's narratives would be totally meaningless and lifeless.

Further, the limitations that Luke sets for the miraculous (the reactions it evokes, the opposition and persecution regardless of miracle-working, and its limited effectiveness in turning people to God) indicate his predilection to accord proclamation a functional primacy over the miraculous in Christian witnessing. Thus, Luke expects the converts in Acts not to build their Christian life entirely on sensational or spectacular events since the 'reactions' of wonder, astonishment, and fear that they evoke are inadequate to the Christian testimony. On the contrary, the responses demanded are repentance, faith, and turning to God, which issue, primarily, from hearing the word. His conclusion, therefore, is that the community of believers in Acts is sustained not primarily by sensational or spectacular events, but by the word of God. The post-conversion community life in 2:42 is evidence to this: "*They devoted themselves to the apostles' teaching and fellowship....*"

Luke, therefore, constructs his missionary discourses (e.g., 2:14-43; 3:12-26; 10:34-43; 11:1-17; 15:7-11, 13-21) not as simple addresses, but as proclamations. The narrative world created by the missionary speeches is, in some way, in an organic relationship to Luke's Theocentric convictional world. Therefore, their content and meaning could be understood better and appropriated only if the hearers share Luke's Theocentric convictions.

Within these parameters, miracles happen due to God's intervention but, because of their inherent inexplicable quality, they necessitate an interpretation. Therefore, Luke interposes his narrative with the missionary speeches to provide an exegesis of the miraculous phenomena and to put forth an alternative vision of reality that goes beyond the immediate perception of the narrative audiences. For instance, at Pentecost, after the interpretation, the phenomena stop being just wind and tongues of fire (2:1-13). They become visual symbols of the actual descent of the Spirit within the narrative. In the end, the audience gains a better grasp of the miraculous phenomena as a fulfilment of God's own promises (cf., 10:34). Missionary speeches, thus, make an event more comprehensible and intelligible.

Further, sometimes the missionary speeches do not simply interpret the event, but also expect the audiences to adopt a particular view of God, by interpreting the miraculous Theologically (e.g., 2:17-21; 3:13ff), Christologically (e.g., 2:22ff), and soteriologically (e.g., 16:31), so that in its light, the audiences would alter their perception and judgement about a past event and change their behaviour in the present in light of that altered perception. For example, Luke wants the Jews to adopt a revised perception, particularly vis-à-vis Jesus, and to make them see his crucifixion, which seemed like an absurdity, as actually the necessary prelude to his resurrection and exaltation. (e.g., 2:23ff., 36). Moreover, the word proclaimed possesses an inner dynamism that can appeal for a response from its hearers to repent, to believe, and turn to God. The aim of the Pentecost speech is, therefore, to revise their earlier perception and to change their lives in the present in terms of repentance (2:38; 3:19) and turn to God (3:19; cf. 14:15). Thus, the end of the speech becomes the main purpose of the speech.

Therefore, the audience asks, "*What should we do*?" (e.g., 2:37; cf. 16:30). The speeches, then, place before the audiences certain choices by exposing their true condition and suggesting a new comprehension of themselves (e.g., 2:37); they are judged by the choices they make (2:37-40; 3:19,23; 8:22-23; 14:15). In the system of values developed by the missionary speeches in Acts, the hearers are exhorted to choose the positive table of values.

Thus, both the miraculous phenomena and the missionary discourses originate from the same source—God. He is the operating subject of them both. Both involve interpretation—the miraculous necessitates it and the missionary speeches actually do it, in which process, the missionary speeches create a model of values in an attempt to modify the audience's perception, its viewpoint, and its value system. Ultimately, the interpretation does lead (therefore, should lead) to change. What causes this change is primarily the Theological and Christological contents of the missionary discourses.

At the end of the study of Luke's presentation of both the miraculous and missionary speeches in Acts, the readers might identify Luke's logic—sometimes explicit and sometimes implicit—behind the conversion stories where the miraculous and proclamation interface with each other, which the following diagram brings out clearly:

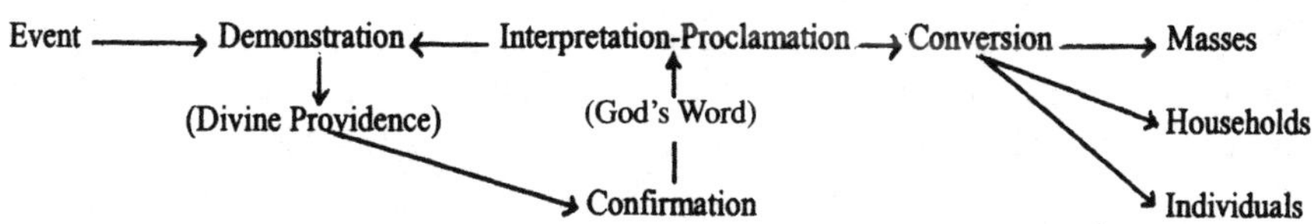

The diagram shows the complex interdependence and the interactive relationship that exists between the miraculous and proclamation. The numinous quality of an (extraordinary) event functions as an attraction; its inherent ineffability necessitates and anticipates interpretation, which confirms the event as a miraculous act of God, and as a manifestation of divine providence. In turn, the miraculous confirms the proclamation as God's word. Where there is such a complementarity and mutuality, there conversions happen in a grand scale—people are converted as masses, as households, and as individuals, which we have repeatedly shown in our study. Chapters 5 and 6 in the study demonstrate in detail the complex literary symbiosis and complementarity that exists between the miraculous and proclamation.

In the Pentecost account (chapter 5) the supernatural phenomena (wind, tongues of fire, and glossolalia: 2:2-4) attract the audience's attention and arouse amazement; therefore, they ask, "*What does this mean?*" (2:6,7,12). The interpretation declares that the phenomena are, indeed, God's doing and, therefore, miraculous (2:14ff.). Then, going beyond mere interpretation of the miraculous happenings, the missionary speech reveals their Theological (2:14-20) Christological (2:22-36), and soteriological (2:21) contents. That the word spoken is, indeed, God's word is implicitly demonstrated in the fact, that together with the miraculous, the missionary speech persuades the audience to a life-changing action—repentance (e.g., 2:38).

The same principle of complementarity between the miraculous and proclamation functions in much the same way in the Cornelius story too (chapter 6), but differently. Cornelius' story is replete with visions. The visions to Cornelius (10:3-6) and to Peter (10:9-16) initiate actions from Cornelius (to "*send...for Peter*": 10:5) and from Peter to go with Cornelius' delegates (19-20,23). Their obedience to the divine instructions leads to another action in the narrative—Peter's missionary speech (10:34-43). The visions and the missionary sermon in the narrative eventuate another supernatural event—the descent of the Spirit (10:44-47). What do the visions mean? What does the infusion of the Spirit mean? How does the latter relate to the former? The recapitulations in 11:1-18 and in 15:7-11, 14ff. reveal the Theological (11:18; 15:7-9,14), Christological (36-42), and the soteriological (10:43; 11:18; 15:11) contents embedded both in the visions and in the descent of the Spirit (10:44-47). The recapitulations reveal that the descent of the Spirit meant faith in the Lord Jesus Christ (11:17a), repentance that leads to life (11:18), cleansing of hearts by faith (15:8-9), and salvation through the grace of the Lord Jesus (15:11). This is Luke's demonstration of what he summarily states elsewhere: "*...the Lord...testified to the word of his grace by granting signs and wonders....*" (14:3).

WHY IS CONVERSION IMPORTANT TO LUKE?

In Luke's arrangement and presentation of his material in Acts and also in his notion of divine providence (chapter 2) we located his aim—to show that God's eternal purpose is to bring salvation in all its fullness to everyone without discrimination. The miraculous and the apostolic voices that speak on God's behalf anticipate this aim. Such a clarification of God's purpose provides a yardstick by which to ascertain who have oriented themselves fully around God's purpose. That is, those who obey the missionary programme outlined by Jesus in Acts 1:8 operate under the guidance and power of the Spirit. Since they follow God's plan, they are his authentic witnesses.

The Book of Acts thus highlights the centrality of God's purpose to bring salvation to all people regardless of all distinctions. The Christian witness is part of God's universal redemptive purpose. It is willed by God (11:21), envisioned by Jesus (1:8), empowered and guided by the Spirit (2:1-13), and implemented by Jesus' followers. Acts is Luke's own advocacy for the expansion of the Christian witness and a demonstration of his conviction that it demands nothing less than God's own intervention to fructify this. When God acts in this way, Luke shows, his salvific action includes those at the ends of the earth (11:1-18; 15; 21:1=26:32). Therefore, "*the ends of the earth*" in 1:8 is, as stated earlier, more a reference to the universal scope than to the geographical goal of the Christian mission in Acts.

Further, the conversion stories and the overall narrative of Acts suggest the juxtaposition of a triangular point-of-view: a) "Exclusivism": the Jewish reluctance to break geographical (implied by Acts 1:8) and ritual barriers (15:1) and, therefore, to restrict the growth of the believing community to Jerusalem—therefore, to the Jewish community (10:9-16; 11:2-3; 15:1); b) "Excludedness": the Gentiles as 'outsiders', and c) the divine δεῖ that questions and challenges all these assumptions. Within this dynamism in the narrative flow of Acts, the Christian witness moves from Jerusalem to Rome, incorporating Jews, Samaritans, and non-Jews. How was this possible? There must be some underlying logic or reason for this expansion. Within Luke's frame of reference in Acts, the only possible explanation is the 'supernatural explanation', i.e., this can only be God's doing, because in human terms this is impossible.

Acts is, therefore, Luke's demonstration that within God's providence there is no room for 'exclusivism' or 'excludedness' in any sense, but only for the expansion of God's worldwide believing community. The sole criterion for membership into this community of believers is "*Everyone who calls on the name of the Lord shall be saved*" (2:21; 4:12). Therefore, in the final analysis there are no Jew-Gentile distinctions, but the establishment of God's rule in its all-encompassing nature. Luke demonstrates the reality and the credibility of this criterion in the conversion of the *Jews* (3000: 2:41/ 5000: 4:4), a multitude of *Samaritans* (8:12), *Gentiles* (e.g., Cornelius, 10:44-48; the Philippian jailer, 16:33, etc) and the Ethiopian Eunuch (8:36-38). The important point here is that God's salvation is for everyone. The most effective means, as far as Luke can see, that make this possible, are the ways in which the miraculous and the proclamation, both originating from God, function together in a creative unity.

By relating his conversion stories to the divine δεῖ, Luke identifies the source (God), the means (witnessing through the miraculous and proclamation), the message (God and his deeds, particularly in and through the person of Jesus), and the agents (the apostles) of his conversion stories. What is Luke's motive behind all this? At the end of our study, we are able to identify that in Acts Christian witnessing through the miraculous and proclamation functions primarily in three related ways as follows:

a) *To confirm* the faith of the Christian witnesses in Acts by focusing on God and his deeds and his power to accomplish his plans. This offers a coherent interpretation of the worldwide mission of the early church. Amidst the vicissitudes of human situations and the different phases of Christian mission, God and his works remain constant.

b) *To encourage* the witnesses in Acts to fulfil their task as faithful witnesses of God, and especially to equip them for such a task, by widening the scope of their mission to the farthest ends of the earth by supernatural means, guidance, and power.

c) *To enable* the witnesses to defend their convictions in the face of any opposition, particularly the conviction that the Christian witness should reach all people, by tying it up with God's worldwide plan.

CONVERSION AND THE DEVELOPMENT OF ACTS

How, then, does Luke's theme of witnessing contribute to the narrative development of Acts as a whole? Since we have already shown the way Luke's conversion motif runs throughout Acts as an undercurrent, we will not repeat it here. However, at the end of our investigation, we may sum up our findings for reasons of emphasis.

In Acts, the risen Jesus himself defines the nature, the course, and the scope of the apostles' task in continuing his mission. He instructs the apostles: "*You will be my witnesses in Jerusalem, in all Judea and Samaria, and to the ends of the earth*" (1:8). Within the implementation of this mandate, Luke introduces both the miraculous and the Christian proclamation as originating from God himself and, thereby, provides Christian witnessing the divine sanction and an important strategy that it needs—a balance between the miraculous (to attract people and to confirm proclamation) and the word (to persuade and lead them to repentance, believing, and turning to God).

After stating that the disciples would and should be witnesses till "*...the ends of the earth*" (1:8), Luke shows the spread of the Christian witnesses outside Jerusalem. Remarkably, some missionary speeches are delivered at exactly those places in the progress of the apostolic witness indicated in 1:8. The first two speeches are given by Peter at Jerusalem, where the apostolic witness begins its course (2:14-40; 3:12-26); there is a summary form of Christian proclamation in Samaria by Philip (8:5,12); and then one at Caesarea, by Peter (10:32-43). Once Paul appears on the scene, he is set aside as "*an instrument...chosen to bring my name before Gentiles and kings and before the people of Israel*" (9:15). His subsequent mission demonstrates the dissemination of the Christian message into far-flung Gentile territories and the movement towards Rome, the precursor to the ends of the earth within Acts.

As the readers progress through the book of Acts, they might notice that Luke's focus in Acts is more on the universal relevance and expansion of the Christian mission than demonstrating its straightforward geographical growth. For instance, Cornelius, the Gentile, resides in Caesarea, which is geographically a part of Judea. In the scheme of Acts, as shown earlier, Cornelius' conversion is a point of transition towards Gentiles. In this sense, there is no neat geographical progression in Acts. The Ethiopian Eunuch's conversion also reinforces the same point. According to Graeco-Roman understanding, Ethiopia was at the end of the habitable earth.[4] Homer refers to Ethiopians as "the furthermost of men" (*Ody*., II.22-24).[5] If we accept these views, then Christian mission, anticipated in Acts 1:8 is over in Acts 8—even well before launching out. The point here is that the Christian witness appeals and is relevant to all

4 Martin Hengel, *Jesus and Paul: Studies in the Earliest History of Christianity*, (London: SCM, 1983), 111.

5 Ibid., 200, n.85. See also T.C.G. Thornton, "To the Ends of the Earth: Acts 1:8", *ExpTimes*, 89, (1977-78), 874-75.

kinds of people, and that nobody is outside the scope of God's offer of salvation. Geographical territories are only steps towards whatever Luke conceives as the "*end of the earth.*"

That Luke's interest is more universal than geographical progression is also seen in the way he leaves the identity of certain people groups ambiguous. We do not know how he wants us to understand the Samaritans and the Ethiopian Eunuch. All our present knowledge of the Samaritans and the Ethiopian Eunuch can only be subordinate to Luke's picture in Acts. In the scheme of Acts, the Samaritans and the Ethiopian Eunuch may function as liminal or fringe groups. Nevertheless, it really does not matter to Luke. He is concerned only to demonstrate the universal perspective and scope of his conversion motif.

Within this progression of the Christian witness, as shown earlier, each conversion story forms a significant turning point towards the final destination and shows the divine intervention in terms of the miraculous and proclamation. This is the synergy that pervades the conversion stories in the book of Acts. Together they spearhead the apostolic missionary endeavour. We have repeatedly shown that the convincing results of the Christian mission are due to this strategy.

The investigation of this core point in the conversion texts of Acts, directs our attention to various other possible implications. They are briefly pointed out here, more as issues for further exploration than as main concerns of this study.

POSSIBLE IMPLICATIONS

Acts as Prescriptive

One possible question that this study raises is that whether Acts should be read merely as a document of certain events or whether it is possible to read it as prescriptive, i.e., are the readers expected to find certain principles for their own lives from the text? In other words, "Is Acts just descriptive or are there certain models that can help readers in their *Sitz em Leben*? Does the text evoke just an aesthetic response or does it demand something deeper from the readers?" A close examination of the conversion stories brings out the following possible answers.

In chapter one, we showed that Luke's readers are already believers. Therefore, it may be, then, that while reading Jesus' commission to his disciples to go to the ends of the earth to be his witnesses, promising them the power from on high (1:8), at least *some* of Luke's *readers* might feel called for mission and, therefore, need to be endowed with power from God.[6] It is also possible that they too, in turn, would present this as a model to the audiences of their own mission. First, call to mission comes from God; secondly, since witnessing is God's work, it cannot be done in human strength; it needs heavenly power; thirdly, when God calls people to do his work, he gives them his power to accomplish it; fourthly, his mission is universal.

It is also possible that those of Luke's readers who are, perhaps, already involved in mission or who would want to be involved in mission, may find in Luke's Pentecost account a model for their own mission. In their own mission, after a powerful witnessing, when their audiences ask, "*What should we do?*" (cf. Acts 2:37), from the Pentecost account, they know exactly what answer they could give, "*Repent, and be baptized...in the name of Jesus Christ so that your sins may be forgiven; and you will receive the gift of the Holy Spirit*" (2:38).

At Pentecost, Peter declares that Pentecost was, in fact, the fulfilment of the prophecy that God would pour his Spirit upon "*all flesh*" (2:17). Within the narrative framework of Acts, Luke's readers know that Pentecost anticipates a limited fulfilment of this promise in terms of reaching out to the Samaritans (8:4-25), the Ethiopian Eunuch (8:26-40), and the Gentiles (e.g., 10:1-11:18). It might it be that at the end of Acts 28:31, Luke's readers would feel that the onus of carrying on the mission to the ends of the earth, that Pentecost has set on course, is transferred to them. Moreover, by demonstrating the overwhelming response of the narrative audiences to the apostolic mission in Acts, which integrates the miraculous and proclamation, it is possible that Luke would want his readers also to imbibe such a strategy in their own mission. Further, by according Christian proclamation a functional primacy in the apostolic mission, Luke puts forth for his readers a principle to follow in their own mission: The community of believers is sustained not by spectacular or sensational events, but by the word of God.

Further, the open ending of the book of Acts may offer some points for our discussion in this regard. Scholars suggest that the open ending of Acts indicates

---

6 Max Turner ("The 'Spirit of Prophecy' as the Power of Israel's Restoration and Witness" in I.H. Marshall & David Peterson (Eds.), *Witness to the Gospel*, 327-48) does not seem to think that such a possibility exists (pp.340ff.). Turner holds that the Spirit in Luke-Acts is the Spirit of prophecy and not of mission. See also Robert P. Menzies, *The Development of Early Christian Pneumatology with Special Reference to Luke-Acts*, (JSNTSup. 54; Sheffield: SAP, 1991), 43-48.

the ongoing nature of the progress of the word.[7] For instance, H.C. Kee suggests,

> "The important unfinished business in this situation is for the witness of the new community to press forward. Still to be accomplished in the contemporary life of the church is the divine intention...salvation to the uttermost parts of the earth.[8]

Similarly, Tannehill holds,

> "The narrative awakens other important expectations whose fulfilment cannot be reported. These include the completion of the mission 'to the end of the earth' and the judgment of the world in righteousness by Jesus (17:31; cf. 10:42). We are reminded of...the promise of salvation to the Jewish people. This expectation not only requires more time...Here lies the real openness of the ending of Acts...Because God is God, hope remains that God's comprehensive saving purpose will somehow be realized, but there is no indication of how that can happen...."[9]

L.T. Johnson similarly argues,

> "The ending of Acts is truly an opening to the continuing life of the messianic people, as it continues to preach the kingdom and teach the things concerning Jesus both boldly and without hindrance."[10]

What, then, is the narrative function of the ending of Acts? Rosner suggests,

> "Acts 28:30-31 belongs to a category of texts in the book that may be described as progress reports in which certain deeds and consequent growth are recounted. The function of such verses...was to act as transitions from one period of witness to the next...though the book has ended, the witness has not."[11]

Thus, scholars strongly argue that the open-ended ending of Acts portrays the ongoing progress of the word, and perhaps even to anticipate the inclusion of the readers in the continuing task of spreading the word and thus, prescribe certain models and strategies for effective Christian witnessing beyond Acts 28:31. Moreover, if we grant that characterisation is primarily for identification,

---

7 On different explanations about the ending of Acts, see C. Hemer, *Acts*, 83-87.

8 H.C. Kee, *Good News*, 107.

9 R.C. Tannehill, *Narrative Unity*, 2.356-57.

10 L.T. Johnson, *Acts*, 476.

11 B.S. Rosner, "Progress of the Word", 231.

as we showed earlier, then, through different characters, particularly the missionary characters, Luke apparently encourages his readers to act as missionaries themselves and be involved in advancing the Christian witness to the different ends of the earth.[12] Rosner concludes, "Acts...is about the spread of the gospel and it challenges its readers to press ahead with the unfinished task."[13]

To this extent, the text conditions both the reading and the response of the readers to the imperatives embedded in the text, either explicitly or implicitly. Therefore, it is likely that as far as Luke is concerned, under the circumstances, the ideal response of the readers is to continue the mission from where Acts leaves.

Conversion as a Promise to believers and as an Invitation to unbelievers

In chapter 1 we acknowledged that from literary critical point-of-view the readers envisaged for the book of Acts are the 'ideal implied readers' who are already believers, sharing Luke's Theocentric/Christocentric worldview. However, the concept of the 'ideal implied readers' suggested by literary criticism leads to certain unresolved tensions in the conversion texts, which become pronounced particularly in light of the soteriological sub-clauses in the conversion discourses as follows:

Call on the name of the Lord	Be saved (2:21)
Everyone who calls	Shall be saved (2:21; cf. 2:39)
Repent and be baptised	Forgiveness of sins and the coming of the Spirit (2:38)
Repent and turn to God	Sins may be wiped out (3:19) Times of refreshment (3:19) The appearance of Jesus, the Messiah (3:20)
Believe in him	Receive forgiveness of sins through his name (10:43)
Believe on the Lord	Be saved (16:31)

It is possible to read these soteriological sub-clauses as an encouragement to those who are already believers so that they may re-actualise their conversion

12 Ibid., 232.

13 Ibid., 233.

experience and re-appropriate the promises embedded in them and be strengthened in their faith. The conversion accounts and missionary discourses function as an opportunity for these believers to hear once again these salvific reassurances and to continue in their God-ward orientation.

This unavoidably raises the question whether the above-mentioned soteriological sub-clauses together with the references to 'everyone' can also function as an invitation to any unbeliever to respond in the way the text expects. The following are some of the examples:

2:21 Everyone (πᾶς ὅς ἄν) who calls on the name of the Lord shall be saved

2:39 Everyone (ὅσους ἄν) whom the Lord calls to himself

10:43 All (πάντα) who believe receive forgiveness of sins

These references show that anyone, who responds to the invitation of the text to call on the name of the Lord and believes, shall be saved. It is Luke's insistence on calling on the name of the Lord and believing in and turning to him that allows these soteriological sub-clauses to appeal to those who have not yet done so. Thus, apparently, the text itself presupposes, at least a section of non-believers among its readers, but this contradicts the concept of 'ideal implied readers' that literary criticism prescribes. For instance, there might be some readers, who, either have not called on the name of the Lord yet, or would read against the norms implicit in the text. That is why, it is possible to hold that Luke formulates his narrative strategy to revise these norms and presuppositions. If such readers subscribe to the positive table of values that the missionary speeches espouse, they will have extended themselves an invitation to adopt an alternative way of viewing things. In other words, the narrative holds potential for conversion.

Does Conversion presuppose Discontinuity from past religious loyalties?

In his missionary speeches to the Jews (2:14-40; 3:12-26, etc) Luke presents Jesus as someone who has been attested by God (2:22), raised from the dead (2:24; cf. 10:40), exalted as the Lord and Messiah (2:36; 3:13f.) and, therefore, whoever calls on him shall be saved (2:21; 4:12). This salvation does not come through mere observance of certain dietary laws (10:9-16; 11:2, etc) or through circumcision (15:1). If, then, Jesus is the final representative of God, the Messiah, the Lord of all, and the object of one's faith, then, according to Luke, he is the goal, the end, and the fulfilment of all Jewish messianic expectations.

Luke shows that this truth, far from becoming a Jewish monopoly, breaks down the barriers that separate people, particularly the barriers between Jews and non-Jews. Prior to conversion there was an obvious gap between the λάος and the ἔθνος due to the Law, which caused disunity and kept Jews and Gentiles apart (e.g., 15:1ff; 21:17-30). As the Christian witness moves into non-Jewish areas, it incorporates people considered so far by the Jews as 'outsiders'. We may cite Cornelius' story as one example to demonstrate that from God's point-of-view there are no such barriers. Inasmuch as the Jews are the λάος, τὰ ἔθνη are also the λάος. This becomes clear particularly in James' words in the external recapitulation of the Cornelius story (τὰ ἔθνη=λάος, 15:14).

Does this, then, mean that Jewish and Gentile Christians now forego their Jew-Gentile identity? Do they now cease to be 'Jewish' and 'Gentile' Christians?" Acts does not provide straightforward answers to these questions. However, for Luke, all those who have turned to God in response to the apostles' mission, both Jews and Gentiles, by believing in Jesus, are the μάθητα and ἀδελφοί. Luke records the presence of a new community of believers consisting of these μάθηται and the ἀδελφοί in many places, particularly as a consequence of what God has done by sending the Spirit (2:1-13; 10:44-48; 11:15ff.; 15:8), by granting the repentance that leads to life (11:18), and by cleansing the hearts by faith (15:8). This, as Luke himself shows, has rendered all ritual demarcations obsolete (Acts 11, 15). We have referred to this in chapter 2.

Does 'conversion to Christianity' then render Judaism obsolete in Jewish contexts, or that accepting Jesus somehow involves complete cessation from previous 'religious' loyalties? These questions arise out of Luke's own proclamation of Jesus as the fulfilment of the Jewish Scriptures, although this is not his main focus. These questions point to the relevance of this study to a multi-faith context in any part of the world. Let us illustrate this from the indian context.

Conversion and Multi-faith Contexts

According to tradition, the presence of Christianity in India dates back to A.D. 52 when St. Thomas, one of the 12 disciples of Jesus, is believed to have arrived in India to evangelise.[14] If this claim is credible, then Christian

[14] Of the many, see, for instance, George M. Moraes, *A History of Christianity in India from Early Times to St. Francis Xavier. A.D. 52-1542*, (Bombay: Manaktalas, 1964); Stephen Charles Neil, *A History of Christianity in India: The Beginnings to A.D. 1707*, (Cambridge: CUP, 1984).

missionary work of converting Indians, or the 'pagans' has started from 1st century CE. Since then, many missionary methods have been proposed, defended, modified, and innovated to convert Indians to Christianity, in the sense of, in L. Rambo's terms, "Tradition Transition"[15]—abandoning one's past religion and becoming a Christian (e.g., 14:15). The search for more effective means of conversion is still an ongoing one. The primary reason for this constant search for new methods of conversion is that just as there have been mass-conversions to Christianity[16], in recent times, there have also been mass-'conversions' to Islam and Buddhism.

The famous Meenakshipuram conversion to Islam[17] and the conversion of the Mahar community in Maharashtra under the leadership of B.R. Ambedkar, to Buddhism[18], and the print media reported 'reverse' conversions to Hinduism, are measures taken by others to combat the 'menace' of Christian conversions. More recently, on 5-11-2001, the Star News, broadcast from India, reported that a group of 3,000 *dalits*, or the untouchables, originally Hindus, 'converted' to Buddhism. In an email sent to millions all over the world prior to this event, Gospel For Asia (GFA) and the All India Christian Council (AICC)—two well-known Christian organisations in India—hoped that all these *dalits* (nearly one million of them) would become Christians, but they preferred Buddhism to Christianity, following the example of B.R. Ambedkar.

Thus, Christianity is forced to compete in the emerging religious market place in Indian society. Therefore, the need arises to make Christianity more attractive and if it is to attract more converts it has to offer them more benefits. This accounts for the proliferation of popular Christian movements in India, offering real benefits of all sorts, particularly healing. All the popular Christian movements are involved in healing campaigns (or 'Healing Crusades') in some form or another. Thus, miracle working is the most effective means of attracting

---

15 Rambo, *Religious Conversion*, 13.

16 For a descriptive study, see J.W. Pickett, *Christian Mass Movements in India*.

17 Mumtaz Ali Khan, *Mass-Conversions of Meenakshipuram: A Sociological Enquiry*, (Madras: Christian Literature Society, 1983).

18 See Balkrishna Govind Gokhale, "Dr. Bhimrao Ramji Ambedkar: Rebel Against Hindu Tradition", *JAAS*, 11, (1976), 13-23; A. Bopegamage, "Status Seekers in India: A Sociological Study of the Neo-Buddhist Movement", *AES*, 20, (1979), 19-39; S.L. Sharma, "Comparative Styles of Conversion on Major Religions in India", *JSR*, 11, (1968), 141-49; Arvind Sharma, "How and Why Did the Women in Ancient India Become Buddhist Nuns?", *SA*, 38, (1977), 239-51; India Bibliographic Centre, *Christianity and Conversion in India*, (Campbell, CA: Rishi Publications, 1999); Samuel Jeyakumar, *Dalit Consciousness and Christian Conversion*, (Oxford: Regnum International, 1999), etc.

'outsiders' to Christianity and this does *attract* tens of thousands of non-Christians from Hinduism and Islam.[19]

However, there are two real dangers here. First, when miracle working is used as a bait to attract non-Christians to Christianity, it creates a kind of 'dependency syndrome', that is, continued attraction to Christianity and its sustenance depends solely on continued performance of miracles, failing which, this attraction will begin to wane. In other words, sustained attraction to Christianity depends on sustained miracle working. Secondly, this *attraction* to Christianity does not mean conversion in terms of transition from another religion to Christianity. Non-Christians may continue to feel attracted to Christianity (for reasons of miracles), but may not leave their mother-religions—Hinduism or Islam—to fully become Christians.

Popular Christian movements stop at making Christianity only attractive; they are not able to sustain and nurture those non-Christians who are attracted to Christianity into becoming mature 'believers' precisely because of the lack or the absence of teaching of the word (e.g., Acts 2:42; 5:20-21; 13:43-44; 14:1,3,7,22a; 15:35; 16:32, etc). Where there is only miracle working, there, people are only attracted or awe-struck; but where there are both miracle working and proclamation, there is 'attraction', and more importantly, people believe and grow. We may recollect here the Lucan principle stated above that the community of believers in Acts is sustained not primarily by sensational or spectacular events, but by the word of God. This means that the results and the ramifications of this study can be tested particularly in contexts of religious pluralism.

---

19 Here we are reminded of Fiorenza's claim that miracle working was the way of attracting potential 'converts' to the church. See, Fiorenza, "Miracles, Mission", 12.

BIBLIOGRAPHY

Texts and Translations

Apuleius, *Metamorphoses*. Ed. & Trans. Arthur Hanson, (LCL; London Cambridge, Mass.: Harvard University Press, 1989).

Aristotle, "De Generatione Animalium" in Richard McKeon (Ed.), The *Basic Works of Aristotle*, (New York: Random House, 1941). *The Art of Rhetoric*. Trans H.C. Lawson-Tancred, (London NewYork: Penguin Books, 1991).

Cicero, *De Oratore*. Trans. E.W. Sutton, (LCL; London: William eineman/ Cambridge, Mass.: Harvard University Press, 1942).
De Divinatione. Trans. W.A. Falconer, (LCL; London/Cambridge, Mass.: Harvard University Press, 1996).

Dio Cassius, *Roman History*. Trans. Ernest Cary, (LCL; London: William Heinemann, 1914-27).

Diodorus Siculus, *The Library of History*. Trans. C.H. Oldfather, (LCL;Cambridge, Mass.: Harvard University Press, 1933-68).

Diogenes Laertius, *Lives of Eminent Philosophers*. Trans. R.D. Hicks, (LCL; London/Cambridge, Mass.: Harvard University Press, 2000).

Epictetus, *Discourses*. Trans. W.A. Oldfather, (LCL; London/New York: William Heinamann/G.P. Putnam's Sons, 1925).

Flavius Josephus, *The Works of Josephus*. Trans. William Whiston, (Peabody, MA: Hendrickson Publishers, 1999).

Herodotus, *History*. Trans. C. Hude, (Oxford: Clarendon, 1927).

Homer, *Illiad*. Trans. A.T. Murray, (LCL; London: William Heinemann, 1925).
Odyssey. Trans. A.T. Murray, (LCL; Cambridge, Mass.: Harvard University Press, 1995).

Lucian, *Alexander the False Prophet*. Trans. A. Harmon, (LCL; London: Heinemann, 1961).

Philopseudes. Trans. A.M. Harmon, (London: William Heinemann New York: G.P. Putnam's Sons, 1921).

Philo, *The Works of Philo*. Trans. C.D. Yonge, (Peabody, MA.: Hendrickson Publishers, 1997).

Philostratus, *The Life of Apollonius of Tyana*. Trans. F.C. Conybeare, (London: Harvard University Press/Cambridge, Mass.: William Heinemann,1912-1950).

Plato, *Republic*. Trans. C-D. Benjamin Jowett, (London: Encyclopedia Britannica, Inc., 1952).

Plutarch, *Lives*. Trans. Bernadotte Perrin, (LCL; London: William Heinemann, 1916.

Polybius, The Histories. Trans. W.R. Paton, (LCL; London/New York: William Heinamann/G.P. Putnam's Sons, 1922-27).

Seneca, *Hercules*. Trans. David R. Slavitt, (Baltimore: John Hopkins University Press,1995).

Tacitus, *Annals*. Trans. D.C.A. Shotter, (Warminster: Aris & Phillips, 1989).

The Histories. Trans. C.H. Moore, (LCL; London/Cambridge, Mass.: Harvard University Press, 1999).

Xenophon, *Cyropaedia*. Trans. Walter Miller, (London/New York: William Heinamann/The Macmillan, 1914).

Hellenica. Trans. Carlton L. Brownson, (London/New York: William Heinamann/G.P. Putnam's Sons, 1918).

Articles and Monographs

Achtemeier, Paul J. "The Lukan Perspective on the Miracles of Jesus: A Preliminary Sketch" in C.H. Talbert (Ed.), *Perspectives in Luke-Acts*, (Edinburgh: T&T Clark, 1978), 153-67. Reprinted from *JBL*, 94, (1975), 547-62.

Adams, M.M. "The Role of Miracles in the Structure of Luke-Acts" in E. Stump & T.P. Flint (Ed.), *Hermeneia and Athena: Biblical Exegesis and Philosophical Theology*, (Notre Dame, IN: University of Notre Dame, 1993), 235-72.

Adkins, Arthur W.H. *Merit and Responsibility: A Study in Greek Values*, (Oxford: Clarendon, 1960).

Alexander, L.C.A. "Acts and Ancient Intellectual Biography" in B.W. Winter & A.D. Clarke (Eds.), *The Book of Acts in Its First Century Setting I: Ancient Literary Setting*, (Grand Rapids: Eerdmans Carlisle: Paternoster, 1993), 31-63.

The Preface to Luke's Gospel: Literary Convention and Social Context in Luke 1:1-4 and Acts 1:1, (SNTSMS 78; Cambridge: CUP 1993).

"The Relevance of Greco-Roman Literature and Culture to New Testament Study" in Joel B. Green, (Ed.), *Hearing the New Testament: Strategies for Interpretation*, (Grand Rapids: Eerdmans Carlisle: Paternoster, 1995), 109-26.

Alter, Robert *The Art of Biblical Narrative*, (New York: Crossroad, 1981).

Alter, Robert & et al (Eds.). *The Literary Guide to the Bible*, (London: Collins, 1987).

Anderson, J.C. & S.T. Moore (Eds.) *Mark and Method*, (Minneapolis: Fortress, 1992).

Aune, David E. *The New Testament in Its Literary Environment*, (Cambridge: James Clarke, 1988).

Prophecy in Early Christianity and the Ancient Mediterranean World, (Grand Rapids: Eerdmans, 1983).

Barclay, William *Turning to God: A Study of Conversion in the Book of Acts and Today*, (Edinburgh: Saint Andrew Press, 1978).

Bar-Efrat, Shimon *Narrative Art in the Bible*, (Decatur, GA: Almond Press, 1992).

Barrett, C.K. *The Acts of the Apostles*, 2 Vols., (Ed., J.A. Emerton, et al. [CC; Edinburgh: T&T Clark, 1994/1998]).

Bauckham, Richard "Kerygmatic Summaries in the Speeches of Acts" in Ben Witherington (Ed.), *History, Literature, and Society in the Book of Acts*, (Cambridge: CUP, 1996), 185-217.

Bayly, Susan *Saints, Goddesses and Kings*, (Cambridge: CUP, 1989).

Beare, Frank W. "Speaking with Tongues: A Critical Survey of the New Testament Evidence", *JBL*, 83, (1964), 229-46.

Berger, Peter L. & Luckmann, Thomas *The Social Construction of Reality: A Treatise in the Sociology of Knowledge*, (Harmondsworth: Penguin Books, 1971).

Berlin, A. *Poetics and Interpretation of Biblical Narrative*, (Sheffield: Almond Press, 1983).

Blenkinsopp, J. "Prophecy and Priesthood in Josephus", *Journal of Jewish Studies*, 25, (1974), 253-54.

Bock, Darrell L. *Proclamation from Prophecy and Pattern: Lucan Old Testament Theology*, (JSNTSup. 12; Sheffield: JSOT, 1987).

"Scripture and the Realisation of God's Promises" in I.H. Marshall & David Peterson (Eds.), *Witness to the Gospel: The Theology of Acts*, (Grand Rapids/Cambridge, UK: Eerdmans, 1998), 49-62.

"The Use of the Old Testament in Luke-Acts" in D.J. Lull (Ed.), *SBLSP1990*, (Atlanta: Scholars, 1990), 494-511.

Booth, W. *The Rhetoric of Fiction*, (Harmondsworth: Peregrine Books, 1987).

Bopegamage, A. "Status Seekers in India: A Sociological Study of the NeoBuddhist Movement", *AES*, 20, (1979), 19-39.

Brawley, R.L. *Luke-Acts and the Jews: Conflict, Apology, and Conciliation*, (SBLMS 33; Atlanta: Scholars, 1987).

Brown, Colin *Miracles and the Critical Mind*, (Grand Rapids: Eerdmans Exeter: Paternoster, 1984).

Brown, Raymond E. *The Birth of the Messiah: A Commentary on the Infancy Narratives in the Gospels of Matthew and Luke*, (Rev. edn.; London: G.P. Chapman/New York: Doubleday, 1993).

The Epistles of John, (AB; Garden City, NY: Doubleday, 1982).

Brown, Schuyler "The Prologues of Luke-Acts in Their Relation to the Purpose of the Author" in G.W. MacRae (Ed.), *SBLSP 1975*, (Missoula, MT: Scholars, 1975), 1-14.

"The Role of the Prologues in Determining the Purpose of Luke-Acts" in C.H. Talbert (Ed.), *Perspectives on Luke-Acts*, (Edinburgh: T&T Clark, 1978), 99-111.

Bruce, F.F. *The Acts of the Apostles: The Greek Text with Introduction and Commentary*, (Rev. edn.; Grand Rapids: Eerdmans/Leicester: Apollos, 1990).

"The Acts of the Apostles. Historical Record or Theological Construction", *ANRW*, II, (1985), 256-603.

"Paul's Apologetic and the Purpose of Acts", *BJRL*, 69, (1987), 379-93.

Burridge, Richard *What Are the Gospels? A Comparison with Graeco-Roman Biography*, (SNTSMS 70; Cambridge: CUP, 1992).

Cadbury, Henry J. *The Book of Acts in History*, (New York: Harper & Bros., 1955).

"Four Features of Lucan Style" in L.E. Keck & J.L. Martyn (Eds.), *Studies in Luke-Acts: Essays Presented in Honor of Paul Schubert*, (Nashville: Abingdon, 1966), 87-102.

"The Greek and Jewish Traditions of Writing History", *Beginnings*, 7-29.

The Making of Luke-Acts, (New York: Macmillan, 1927).

"Some Foibles of New Testament Scholarship" *JBR*, 26, (1958).

"The Speeches in Acts", *Beginnings*, 402-27.

Caird, G.B. *Saint Luke*, (London: SCM, 1963).

Cassidy, Richard *Jesus, Politics, and Society: A Study of Luke's Gospel*, (Maryknoll, NY: Orbis Books, 1978).

Society and Politics in the Acts of the Apostles, (Maryknoll, NY: Orbis Books, 1988).

Chadwick, H. *The Circle and the Ellipse*, (Oxford: Clarendon, 1959).

Chatman, Seymour *Story and Discourse: Narrative Structure in Fiction and Film*, (Ithaca, NY: Cornell University Press, 1980).

Christ, Carol P. *Diving Deep and Surfacing*, (Boston: Beacon Press, 1980).

Clines, D.J.A. & et al (Eds.), *The Bible in Three Dimensions*, (JOSTSup. 87; Sheffield: JSOT Press, 1990).

Cogan, Marc *The Human Thing: The Speeches and Principles of Thucydides' History*, (Chicago/London: University of Chicago Press, 1981).

Conzelmann, Hans *Acts of the Apostles: A Commentary on the Acts of the Apostles*, (Trans. A.T. Kraabel James Limburg, Donald H. Juel; Ed. Eldon J. Epp; Hermeneia; Philadelphia: Fortress, 1987).

The Theology of St. Luke, (Tr. Geoffrey Buswell; London: Faber & Faber/Philadelphia: Fortress, 1960/1961).

Cosgrove, C.H. "The Divine Δει in Luke-Acts: Investigations into the Lukan Understanding of God's Providence" *NovT*, 26, (1984), 168-90.

Crehan, J.H. "The Purpose of Luke in Acts" *SE*, 2, (1964), 354-68.

Culpepper, Alan*The Anatomy of the Fourth Gospel: A Study in Literary Designs*, (Philadelphia: Fortress, 1983).

Dahl, N.A. "The Purpose of Luke-Acts" in *Jesus in the Memory of the Early Church*, (Minneapolis: Augsburg, 1976), 87-98.

Darr, John A. *On Character Building: The Reader Rhetoric of Characterization in Luke-Acts*, (Louisville: Westminster Press/John Knox, 1992).

Davies, J.G. "Pentecost and Glossolalia" *JTS*, 3, (1952), 228-31.

Derrett, J.D.M "Clean and Unclean Animals (Acts 10:15; 11:9): Peter's Pronouncing Power Observed" *Heythrop Journal*, 29, (1988), 205-21.

Dibelius, Martin "The Speeches in Acts and Ancient Historiography" in *Studies in the Acts of the Apostles*, (Ed. H. Greeven; Trans. M. Ling; London: SCM, 1956), 138-85.

Dillon, Richard J *From Eye-Witnesses to Ministers of the Word*, (AB; Rome: Biblical Institute Press, 1978).

"The Prophecy of Christ and His Witnesses According to the Discourses of Acts", *NTS*, 32, (1986), 544-56.

Dodd, C.H. *The Apostolic Preaching and Its Developments*, (London: Hodder & Stoughton, 1938).

Dunn, James D.G. *The Acts of the Apostles*, (Epworth Commentaries; Peterborough: Epworth Press, 1996).

Baptism in the Holy Spirit: A Reexamination of the New Testament Teaching on the Gift of the Spirit in Relation to Pentecostalism Today, (Napierville, IL: Allenson, 1970).

Jesus and the Spirit: A Study of the Religious and Charismatic Experience of Jesus and the First Christians as Reflected in the New Testament, (London: SCM, 1975).

The Partings of the Ways between Christianity and Judaism And their Significance for the Character of Christianity, (London: SCM/ Philadelphia: Trinity Press International, 1991).

Easton, B.S. *The Purpose of Acts*, ("Theology" Occasional Papers, 6; London: SPCK, 1936). Reprint, *Early Christianity: The Purpose of Acts and Other Papers*, (Greenwich, CT: Seabury, 1954; London: SPCK, 1955), 33-118.

Efrat—Shimor Bar *Narrative Art in the Bible*, (Decatur, GA: Almond Press, 1992).

Ellis, Earl E. *The Gospel of Luke*, (London: Oliphants, 1974).

"The Situation and Purpose of Acts", *Int.*, 28, (1974), 94-98.

Eltester, W. (Ed.) *Neutestamentaliche fur Rudolf Bultmann*, (Berlin: Alfred Topelmann, 1954).

Erhardt, A. "The Construction and Purpose of the Acts of the Apostles", *ST*, 12, (1958), 45-79. (Reprinted in *The Framework of the New Testament Stories*, [Cambridge: Harvard University Press, 1964], 64-102).

Esler, Philip F. *Community and Gospel in Luke-Acts: The Social and Political Motivations of Lucan Theology*, (SNTSMS 57; Cambridge: Cambridge University Press, 1987).

Evans, C.F. "Is Luke's View of the Jewish Rejection of Jesus Anti-Semitic?" in Dennis D. Sylva (Ed.), *Reimaging the Death of the Lukan Jesus*, (Frankfurt: Hain, 1990), 29-56.

Fears, J.R. "The Cult of Jupiter and Roman Imperial Ideology", *ANRW*, II, (1981), 3-141.

"The Cult of Virtues and Roman Imperial Ideology", *ANRW*, II, (1981),827-948.

Ferguson, J. *The Religions of the Roman Empire*, (London: Thames and Hudson, 1970).

Fiorenza, E.S. "Miracles, Mission, and Apologetics: An Introduction" in Elizabeth Schüssler Fiorenza (Ed.), *Aspects of Religious Propaganda in Judaism and Early Christianity*, (Notre Dame/London: University of Notre Dame Press, 1976), 1-16.

Fishbane, Michael *Biblical Text and Texture: A Literary Reading of Selected Texts*, (Oxford: One World Publications, 1998).

Fitzmyer, J.A. *The Acts of the Apostles: A New Translation with Introduction and Commentary*, (AB; New York/London, et al.: Doubleday, 1997).

"David, 'Being Therefore a Prophet...' (Acts 2:30)", *CBQ*, 34, (1972), 332-39.

The Gospel According to Luke, 2 Vols., (AB; Garden City, NY: Doubleday, 1979/1981).

Luke the Theologian. Aspects of His Teaching, (New York: Paulist, 1989).

Foerster, Werner "κύριος", *TDNT*, III.103-58.

Forster, E.M. *Aspects of the Novel*, (Harmondsworth: Penguin Books, 1971).

Fowler, Robert M. "Who Is 'the Reader' in Reader-Response Criticism?", *Semeia*, 31, (1985), 5-23.

Franklin, Eric *Christ the Lord: A Study in the Purpose and Theology of Luke-Acts*, (London: SPCK/Philadelphia: Westminster, 1975).

Funk, Robert W. *The Poetics of Biblical Narrative*, (Sonoma: Polebridge Press, 1988).

Gasque, W.W. *A History of the Criticism of the Acts of the Apostles*, (Tübingen: Mohr, 1975).

Gasque,W.W. & R.P. Martin (Eds.) *Apostolic History and the Gospel: Biblical and Historical Essays Presented to F.F. Bruce*, (Grand Rapids: Eerdmans, 1970).

Gaventa, B.R. *From Darkness to Light: Aspects of Conversion in the New Testament*, (Philadelphia: Fortress, 1986).

"'You will be my Witnesses': Aspects of Mission in the Acts of the Apostles", *Missiology*, 10, (1982), 413-25.

Gilmour, S. M. "The Christophany to More Than Five Hundren Brethren", *JBL*, 80, (1961), 248-52.

"Easter and Pentecost", *JBL*, 81, (1962), 62-66.

Gokhale, B.G. "Dr. Bhimrao Ramji Ambedkar: Rebel Against Hindu Tradition", *JAAS*, 11, (1976), 13-23.

Goulder, M.D. *Type and History in Acts*, (London: SPCK, 1964).

Green, Joel B *Hearing the New Testament: Strategies for Interpretation*, (Grand Rapids: Eerdmans/Carlisle: Paternoster, 1995).

"Salvation to the End of the Earth (Acts 13:47): God as Saviour in the Acts of the Apostles" in I.H. Marshall, et al (Eds.), *Witness to the Gospel: The Theology of Acts*, (Grand Rapids/Cambridge, UK: Eerdmans, 1998), 83-106.

Grundmann, Walter "Δει" *TDNT*, II.21-25.

Gundry, Robert H. "Ecstatic Utterance", *JTS*, 17, (1966), 299-307.

Hadas, M, & M. Smith *Heroes and Gods: Spiritual Biographies in Antiquity*, (New York: Harper & Row, 1963).

Haenchen, Ernst *The Acts of the Apostles: A Commentary*, (ET; Oxford: Basil Blackwell, 1971).

"The Book of Acts as Source Material for the History of Early Christianity" in L.E. Keck & J.L. Martyn (Eds.), *Studies in Luke-Acts*, (London: SPCK, 1968), 258-78.

Hanson, J.S. "Dreams and Visions in the Graeco-Roman World and Early Christianity", *ANRW*, II, 1395-427.

Hardon, J.A. "The Miracle Narratives in the Acts of the Apostles", *CBQ*, 16, (1954), 303-18.

Hartman, Lars *"Into the Name of the Lord Jesus": Baptism in the Early Church*, (Edinburgh: T & T Clark, 1997), 127-45.

Hemer, Colin J. *The Book of Acts in the Setting of Hellenistic History*, (Tübingen: Mohr Siebeck, 1989).

Hengel, Martin *Acts and the History of Earliest Christianity*, (Trans. John Bowden; Philadelphia: Fortress, 1979).

Jesus and Paul: Studies in the Earliest History of Christianity, (London: SCM, 1983).

Hickling, C.J.A."Baptism in the First-Century Churches: A Case for Caution" in David J.A. Clines, et al (Eds.), *The Bible in Three Dimensions*, (JSOTSup 87; Sheffield: JSOT Press, 1990), 249-67.

Hornblower, Simon *Thucydides*, (London: Duckworth, 1987).

Horton, R. "African Conversion", *Africa*, 41, (1971), 85-108.

Houston, Walter *Purity and Monotheism: Clean and Unclean Animals in Biblical Law*, (JSOTSup. 140; Sheffield: JSOT Press, 1993).

Humphrey, Edith M. "Collision of Modes?—Vision and Determining Argument in Acts 10:1-11:18" in Robert B. Robinson & Robert C. Culley (Eds.), *Textual Determinacy*, (Semeia 71; Atlanta: Scholars, 1995), 65-84.

Immerwahr, Henry R. "Pathology of Power and the Speeches in Thucydides" in Philip A. Stadter (Ed.), *The Speeches in Thucydides: A Collection of Original Studies with a Bibliography*, (Chapel Hill: University of North Carolina, 1973), 16-31.

India Bibliographical Centre, *Christianity and Conversion in India*, (Campbell, CA: Rishi Publications, 1999).

Iser, Wolfgang *The Act of Reading: A Theory of Aesthetic Response*, (Baltimore/London: Johns Hopkins University Press, 1978).

Jaeger, Werner, W. *Paideia: The Ideals of Greek Culture*, (Oxford: Basil Blackwell, 1946).

James, M.R. (Tr.) *The Apocryphal New Testament*, (Oxford: Clarendon, 1972).

James, William *The Varieties of Religious Experience*, (London: Longmans, 1902).

Jervell, J. "The Church of Jews and Godfearers" in J.B. Tyson (Ed.), *Luke-Acts and the Jewish People: Eight Critical Perspectives*, (Minneapolis: Augsburg, 1988), 11-20.

Luke and the People of God: A New Look at Luke-Acts, (Minneapolis: Augsburg, 1972).

Theology of the Acts of the Apostles, (Cambridge: Cambridge University Press, 1996).

The Unknown Paul: Essays on Luke-Acts and Early Christian History, (Minneapolis: Augsburg, 1984).

Jeyakumar, Samuel *Dalit Consciousness and Christian Conversion*, (Oxford: Regnum Publications, 1999).

Johnson, L.T. *The Acts of the Apostles*, (Sacra Pagina 5; Ed. Daniel J. Harrington; Collegeville, MN: Liturgical Press, 1992).

The Literary Function of Possessions in Luke-Acts, (Missoula: Scholars, 1977).

"The New Testament's Anti-Jewish Slander and the Convention of Ancient Polemic", *JBL*, 108, (1989), 419-41.

Karris, Robert J. *Luke: Artist and Theologian: Luke's Passion Accounts as Literature*, (New York: Paulist Press, 1985).

"Missionary Communities: A New Paradigm for the Study of Luke-Acts", *CBQ*, 41, (1979), 80-97.

Keathley, N.H. (Ed.) *With Steadfast Purpose: Essays on Acts in Honor of Henry Jackson Flanders*, Jr., (Waco: Baylor University Press, 1990).

Keck, L.E. & J.L. Martyn (Eds.) *Studies in Luke-Acts: Essays Presented in Honor of Paul Schubert*, (Nashville: Abingdon, 1966).

Kee, Howard Clark *Christian Origins in Sociological Perspective*, (London: SCM, 1980).

Good News to the Ends of the Earth: The Theology of Acts, (London: SCM, 1990).

Medicine, Miracle and Magic in New Testament Times, (Cambridge: Cambridge University Press, 1986).

Miracle in the Early Christian World: A Study in Sociohistorical Method, (New Haven: Yale University Press, 1983).

Kenan, Shlomith R. *Narrative of Fiction: Contemporary Poetics*, (London: Methuen, 1983).

Kennedy, George A. *Classical Rhetoric in Its Christian and Secular Tradition from Ancient to Modern Times*, (London: Croom Helm, 1980).

New Testament Interpretation through Rhetorical Criticism, (Chapel Hill: University of North Carolina Press, 1984).

Kessels, A.H.M. *Studies in the Dream in the Greek Literature*, (Utrecht: HES, 1978).

Khan, Mumtaz Ali *Mass-Conversions of Meenakshipuram: A Sociological Enquiry*, (Madras: Christian Literature Society, 1983).

Kilgallen, J.J. "The Unity of Peter's Pentecost Speech", *The Bible Today*, 82, (1976), 650-56.

Kingsbury, Jack D. "Reflections on 'the Reader' of Matthew's Gospel", *NTS*, 34, (1988), 442-60.

Knight, Jonathan *Luke's Gospel*, (New Testament Readings; London/New York: Routledge, 1998).

Kodell, J. "The Word of Grew: The Ecclesial Tendency of Logos in Acts 1:7; 12:24; 19:20", *Biblica*, 55, (1974), 505-19.

Kremer, J. (Ed.) *Les Actes Des Apôtres: Traditions, Rédaction, Théologie*, (Gembloux: J. Duculot/Leuven: Leuven University Press, 1979).

Krodel, Gerhard A. *Acts*,(ACNT;Minneapolis: Augsburg, 1986).

Kurz, William S. "Hellenistic Rhetoric in the Christological Proof of Luke-Acts", *CBQ*, 42, (1980), 171-95.

Reading Luke-Acts: Dynamics of Biblical Narrative, (Louisville, KY: Westminster/John Knox, 1993).

Lake, Kirsopp "The Gift of the Spirit on the Day of Pentecost", *Beginnings*, V.111-21.

Lampe, G.W.H. "Miracles and Early Christian Apologetic" in C.F.D. Moule (Ed.), *Miracles:Cambridge Studies in Their Philosophy and History*, (London: Mowbray, 1965), 205-18.

"Miracles in the Acts of the Apostles" in C.F.D. Moule (Ed.), *Miracles*, 65-78.

Lentz, John Clayton *Luke's Portrait of Paul*, (Cambridge: Cambridge University Press, 1993).

Lieshout, R.C.A. van *Greeks on the Dream*, (Utrecht: HES, 1980).

Lindars, B. "Elijah, Elisha and the Gospel Miracles" in C.F.D. Moule (Ed.), *Miracles: Cambridge Studies in Their Philosophy and History*, (London: Mowbray, 1965), 61-79.

Lindars B. & S.S. Smalley (Eds.) *Christ, Spirit in the New Testament: In Honour of C.F.D. Moule*, (Cambridge: Cambridge University Press, 1973).

Lofland, John & Stark, Rodney "Becoming a World-Saver: A Theory of Conversion to a Deviant Perspective" *ASR*, 30, (1965), 862-75.

Lofland, John & Norman Skonovd "Conversion Motifs", *JSSR*, 20, (1981), 373-85.

Longenecker, R.N. *Biblical Exegesis in the Apostolic Period*, (Grand Rapids: Eerdmans, 1975).

Loos, H. van der *The Miracles of Jesus*, (NovTSup.; Leiden: Brill, 1965).

Lothe, Jakob *Narrative in Fiction and Film: An Introduction*, (Oxford: Oxford University Press, 2000).

Lull, D.J. (Ed.) *Society of Biblical Literature Seminar Papers 1990*, (Atlanta: Scholars, 1990).

MacMullen, R. *Christianizing the Roman Empire (A.D. 100-400)*, (New Haven/London: Yale University Press, 1984).

Paganism in the Roman Empire, (New Haven, CT: Yale University Press, 1981).

Macovski, M. (Ed.) *Dialogue and Critical Discourse: Language, Culture, Critical Theory*, (New York/Oxford: Oxford University Press).

MacRae, G.W. "Miracles in the Antiquities of Josephus" in C.F.D. Moule (Ed.), *Miracles: Cambridge Studies in Their Philosophy and History*, (London: Mowbray, 1965), 127-47.

MacRae, G.W. (Ed.) *Society of Biblical Literature Seminar Papers 1975*, (Missoula, MT: Scholars, 1975).

Maddox, Robert *The Purpose of Luke-Acts*, (FRLANT; Göttingen: Vandenhoeck & Ruprecht, 1982).

Malbon, Elizabeth "Narrative Criticism: How Does the Story Mean," in Janice C. Anderson & S.T. Moore (Eds.), *Mark and Method*, (Minneapolis: Fortress, 1992), 23-49.

Malina, Bruce J. *The New Testament World: Insights from Cultural Anthropology*, (Atlanta: John Knox, 1981).

Maloney, L.M. *"All That God Had Done with Them": The Narration of the Works of God in the Early Christian Community as Described in the Acts of the Apostles*, (American University Studies 7.19; New York: Peter Lang, 1991).

Marcus, Laura "The Face of Autobiography" in Julia Swindells (Ed.), *The Uses of Autobiography*, (London: Taylor & Francis Ltd., 1995), 13-23.

Marguerat, Daniel. "Saul's Conversion (9,22,26) and the Multiplication of Narrative in Acts" in C.M. Tuckett (Ed.), *Luke's Literary Achievement: Collected Essays*, (Sheffield: Sheffield Academic Press, 1995), 125-55.

Marshall, I. Howard. *The Acts of the Apostles*, (Sheffield: JSOT Press, 1992).

"The Meaning of the Verb 'to Baptize'", *EQ*, 45, (1973), 130-40.

"The Significance of Pentecost", *SJT*, 30, (1977), 347-69.

Marshall, I.H & David Peterson (Eds.) *Witness to the Gospel: The Theology of Actsm*, (Grand Rapids/Cambridge, UK: Eerdmans, 1998).

Martin, I.J. "Glossolalia in the Apostolic Church", *JBL*, 63, (1944), 123-30.

Mason, Steve & Robert A. Kraft. "Josephus on Canon and Scripture" in Magne Sæbø (Ed.), *Hebrew Bible/Old Testament: The History of Its Interpretation*,(Göttingen: Vandenhoeck & Ruprecht, 1996), 217-35.

Matera, Frank M. "Responsibility for the Death of Jesus According to the Acts of the Apostles", *JSNT*, 39, (1990), 77-93.

Matson, David L. *Household Conversion Narratives in Acts: Pattern and Interpretation*, (JSNTSup. 123. Sheffield: Sheffield Academic Press, 1996.

Mattill, A.J. (Jr.) "The Good Samaritan and the Purpose of Luke-Acts: Halevy Reconsidered", *Encounter*, 33, (1972), 359-76.

"The Jesus-Paul Parallels and the Purpose of Luke-Acts: H.H. Evans Reconsidered", *NovT*, 17, (1975), 15-46.

"Naherwartung, Fernerwartung, and the Purpose of Luke-Acts: Weymouth Reconsidered", *CBQ*, 34, (1972), 276-93.

"The Purpose of Acts: Schneckenburger Reconsidered" in W.W. Gasque & R.P. Martin (Eds.), -, (Grand Rapids: Eerdmans, 1970), 108-22.

May, Rachel "The Power of Speech: Dialogue as History in the Russian Primary Chronicle" in Michael Macovski (Ed.), Dialogue and Critical Discourse: Language, Culture, Critical Theory, (New York/Oxford: Oxford University Press, 1997), 47-64.

McCormick, Scott Behold the Man: Re-reading Gospels, Re-humanizing Jesus, (New York: Continuing Publishing Company, 1994).

Menzies, Robert P. The Development of Early Christian Pneumatololgy with Special Reference to Luke-Acts, (JSNTSup. 54; Sheffield: Sheffield Academic Press, 1991).

Minear, P.S. "Dear Theo: The Kerygmatic Intention and Claim of the Book of Acts", Int., 27, (1973), 131-50.

Moehring, H.R. "Rationalization of Miracles in the Writings of Flavius Josephus", SE, 6, (1973), 373-86.

Moessner, David P. "The 'Leaven of the Pharisees' and 'This Generation': Israel's Rejection of Jesus According to Luke" in Dennis D. Sylva (Ed.), Reimaging the Death of the Lukan Jesus, (Frankfurt: Hain, 1990), 79-107.

Moore, Stephen D. Literary Criticism and the Gospels, (New Haven: Yale University Press, 1989).

Moraes, George M. A History of Christianity in India from Early Times to St. Francis Xavier. A.D. 52-1542, (Bombay: Manaktolas, 1964).

Moule, C.F.D. "The Christology of Acts" in L.E. Keck & J.L. Martyn (Eds.), Studies in Luke-Acts: Essays Presented in Honor of Paul Schubert, (London: SPCK, 1966), 159-85.

Moule, C.F.D. (Ed.) *Miracles: Cambridge Studies in their Philosophy and History*, (London: Mowbray, 1965).

Munck, Johannes *The Acts of the Apostles*, (New York: Doubleday, 1973).

Neil, Stephen *A History of Christianity in India: The Beginnings to A.D. 1707*, (Cambridge: CUP, 1984).

Neil, William *The Acts of the Apostles*, (London: Oliphants, 1973).

Neirynck, F. "The Miracle Stories in the Acts of the Apostles, an Introduction" in J. Kremer (Ed.), *Les Actes Des Apôtres: Traditions, Rédaction, Théologie*, (Gembloux: J. Duculot/Leuven: Leuven University Press, 1979), 169-213.

Nock, Arthur D.Conversion: *The Old and the New in Religion from Alexander the Great to Augustine of Hippo*, (Oxford: The Clarendon Press, 1933).

Neusner, J. & et al (Eds.) *The Social World of Formative Christianity and Judaism: Essays in Tribute of H.C. Kee*, (Philadelphia: Fortress, 1988).

Noth, Martin *The Deuteronomistic History*, (JSOTSup. 15. Sheffield: JSOT Press, 1981).

Oepke, A. "ὄναρ", *TWNT*, V.220-330.

Ogilvie, R.M. *The Romans and Their Gods in the Age of Augustus*, (London: Chatto & Windus, 1969).

O'Neill, J.C. *The Theology of Acts in Historical Setting*, (London: SPCK, 1961).

O'Reilly, Leo *Word and Sign in the Acts of the Apostles: A Study in Lucan Theology*, (Analecta Gregoriana 243; Roma: Editrice Pontificia Gregoriana, 1987).

O'Toole, Robert F. *The Unity of Luke's Theology: An Analysis of Luke-Acts*, (Wilmington, DE: Michael Glazier, 1984).

"Why Did Luke Write Acts (Luke-Acts)?", *BTB*, 7, (1977), 66-76.

Panagopoulos, J. *Prophetic Vocation in the New Testament and Today*, (NovTSup. 45. Leiden: Brill, 1977).

Parker, Robert *Athenian Religion: A History*, (Oxford: Clarendon, 1995).

Parsons, M.C. *The Departure of Jesus in Luke-Acts: The Ascension Narratives in Context*, ((JSNTSup. 21; Sheffield: JSOT Press, 1987).

" The Unity of the Lukan Writings: Rethinking the Opinio Communis" in Naymond H. Keathley (Ed.), *With Steadfast Purpose: Essays on Acts in Honor of Henry Jackson Flanders, Jr.*, (Waco: Baylor University Press, 1990).

Parsons, M.C. & Pervo Richard I. *Rethinking the Unity of Luke and Acts*, (Minneapolis: Fortress, 1993).

Pelling, Christopher *Literary Text and the Greek Historian*, (London/New York: Routledge, 2000).

Pervo, Richard I. *Luke's Story of Paul*, (Minneapolis: Fortress, 1990).

"Must Luke and Acts Belong to the Same Genre?" in D. Lull (Ed.), *SBLSP 28*, (Atlanta: Scholars, 1989), 309-16.

Peterson, David "The Motif of Fulfilment and the Purpose of Luke-Acts" in Bruce W. Winter, et al (Eds.), *The Book of Acts in Its First Century Setting*, Vol. 1: *The Book of Acts in Its Literary Setting*, (Grand Rapids: Eerdmans/Carlisle: Paternoster, 1993), 83-104.

Phipps, W.E. *Paul Against Supernaturalism: The Growth of the Miraculous in Christianity*, (New York: Philosophical Library, 1987).

Pickett, J.W. *Christian Mass Movements in India*, (Nashville: Abingdon, 1933).

Plunkett, M.A. "Ethnocentricity and Salvation History in the Cornelius Episode (Acts 10:1-11:18)" in K.H. Richards (Ed.), *Society of Biblical Literature Seminar Papers 1985*, (Atlanta: Scholars, 1985), 465-79.

Porter, Stanley E. *The Paul of Acts*, (WUNT 115; TŸbingen: Mohr, 1999).

Powell, Mark Allan *What Are They Saying About Luke?* (New York: Paulist, 1989).

What Is Narrative Criticism? (Minneapolis: Fortress, 1990).

Praeder, S. Marie "Jesus-Paul, Peter-Paul, and Jesus-Peter Parallelisms in Luke Acts: A History of Reader-Response" in K.H. Richards (Ed.), *SBLSP 1984*, (Chick, CA: Scholars, 1984), 23-39.

"Luke-Acts and Ancient Novel", *SBLSP 1984*, (Chico, CA: Scholars, 1981), 269-92.

Preminger, Alex, et al (Eds.) *Classical Literary Criticism: Translations and Interpretations*, (New York: Frederick Ungar Publishing Co., 1974).

Prier, Raymond A. *Thauma Idesthai: The Phenomenology of Sight and Appearance in Archaic Greek*, (Tallahassee: Floria State University Press, 1989).

Propp, Vladimir*Morphology of the Folktales*, (Austin: University of Austin Press, 1968).

Rambo, Lewis R. "Current Research on Religious Conversion", *RSR*, 8, (1982), 146-59.

Understanding Religious Conversion, (New Haven/London: Yale University Press, 1993).

Raubitschek, A.E. "The Speech of the Athenians at Sparta" in Philip A. Stadter (Ed.), *The Speeches in Thucydides: A Collection of Original Studies with a Bibliography*, (Chapel Hill: University of North Carolina, 1973), 32-48.

Remus, H. "Does Terminology Distinguish Early Christian from Pagan Miracles?", *JBL*, 101, (1982), 531-51.

Pagan-Christian Conflict over Miracle in the Second Century, (Patristic Monograph Series 10; Cambridge, Mass.: The Philadelphia Patristic Foundation Ltd., 1983).

Rengstorff, K.H. *A Complete Concordance to Flavius Josephus*, (Leiden: Brill, 1979).

Richards, K.H. (Ed.) *Society of Biblical Literature Seminar Papers 1984*, (Chick, CA: Scholars, 1984).

Society of Biblical Literature Seminar Papers 1985, (Atlanta: Scholars, 1985).

Rhoads, D. & Michie, D. *Mark as a Story: An Introduction to the Narrative of a Gospel*, (Philadelphia: Fortress, 1982).

Richardson, Neil *The Panorama of Luke: An Introduction to the Gospel of Luke and the Acts of the Apostles*, (London: Epworth, 1982).

Robinson, R.B. & Robert C.C. (Eds.) *Textual Determinacy*, (Semeia 71; Atlanta: Scholars, 1995).

Ropes, James H. "The Text of Acts", *Beginnings*, III.2.

Ross, J.P. "Some Notes on Miracle in the Old Testament" in C.F.D, Moule (Ed.), *Miracles: Cambridge Studies in Their Philosophy and History*, (London: Mowbray, 1965), 43-60.

Ryken, Leland *The New Testament in Literary Criticism*, (New York: Frederick Ungar Publishing Company, 1984).

Sæbø, Magne (Ed.) *Hebrew Bible/Old Testament: The History of its Interpretation*, (Göttingen: Vandenhoeck & Ruprecht, 1996).

Sanders, Jack T. *Charisma, Converts, Competitors: Societal and Sociological Factors in the Success of Early Christianity*, (London: SCM, 2000).

The Jews in Luke-Acts, (London: SCM/Philadelphia: Fortress, 1987).

"The Salvation of the Jews in Luke-Acts" in C.H. Talbert (Ed.), *Luke-Acts: New Perspectives from the SBL Seminar*, (New York: Crossroad, 1984), 104-28.

"Who Is a Jew and Who Is a Gentile in the Acts of the Apostles", *NTS*, 37, (1991), 434-55.

Sandnes, Karl Olav *A New Family: Conversion and Ecclesiology in the Early Church with Cross-Cultural Comparisons*, (Bern/Berlin: Peter Lang, 1994).

Schiering, S.P & Schiering M.J. "The Influence of the Ancient Romances on the Acts of the Apostles", *Classical Bulletin*, 54, (1978), 81-88.

Schmidt, K. Ludwig "ἔθνος in the New Testament" *TDNT*, II. 369-72.

Scholes, Robert, Robert Kellog *The Nature of Narrative*, (London/New York: Oxford University Press, 1968).

Schreuder, D. & G. Oddie, "'What is Conversion?' History, Christianity and Religious Change in Colonial Africa and South Asia", *Journ. Rel. Hist.*, 15, (1989), 496-518.

Schubert, Paul "The Final Cycle of Speeches in the Book of Acts", *JBL*, 87, (1968), 1-16.

"Structure and Significance of Luke 24" in *W. Eltester (Ed.), Neutestamentaliche fur Rudolf Bultmann*, (Berlin: Alfred Topelmann, 1954), 165-86.

Scott, James M. Paul and the Nations. *The Old Testament Background of Paul's Mission to the Nations with Special Reference to the Destination of Galatians*, (Tübingen: Mohr, 1995).

Scroggs, J.R. & W.G.T. Douglas "Issues in the Psychology of Religious Conversion", *JRH*, 6, (1967), 204-16.

Segal, Alan F. *Paul the Convert: The Apostolate and Apostasy of Saul the Pharisee*, (New Haven/London: Yale University Press, 1990).

Sharma, A. "How and Why did the Women in Ancient India Become Buddhist Nuns?", *SA*, 38, (1977), 239-51.

Sharma, S.L. "Comparative Styles of Conversion on Major Religions in India", *JSR*, 11, (1968), 141-49.

Shipley, Graham *The Greek World after Alexander, 323-30 B.C.*, (London/New York: Routledge, 2000).

Shuler, P.L. *A Genre for the Gospels: The Biographical Character of Matthew*, (Philadelphia: Fortress, 1982).

Shutt, R.J.H. "The Letter of Aristeas", *OTP*, 7-34.

Siegert, Folker "Early Jewish Interpretations in a Hellenistic Style" in Magne Sæbø, (Ed.), *Hebrew Bibld/Old Testament: The History of Its Interpretation*, (Göttingen: Vandenhoeck & Ruprecht, 1996), 162-89.

Sklba, Richard J. "The Call to New Beginnings: A Biblical Theology of Conversion", *BTB*, 11, (1981), 67-73.

Sleeper, C. Freeman "Pentecost and Resurrection", *JBL*, 84, (1965), 389-99.

Smalley, S.S. "The Christology in Acts Again" in B. Lindars & S.S. Smalley (Eds), *Christ, Spirit in the New Testament: In Honour of C.F.D. Moule*, (Cambridge: Cambridge University Press, 1973), 79-93.

Smith, Gail "Jewish Christian and Pagan Views of Miracle under the Flavian Emperors", *SBLSP 20*, (Chico: Scholars Press, 1981), 341-48.

Soards, Marion L. *The Speeches in Acts: Their Content, Context, and Concerns*, (Louisville: Westminster/John Knox, 1994).

Spencer, Scot F. *The Portrait of Philip in Acts. A Study of Roles and Relations*, (JSNTSup. 67; Sheffield: Sheffield Academic Press, 1992).

Squires, John T. *The Plan of God in Luke-Acts*, (SNTSMS 76; Cambridge: Cambridge University Press, 1993).

Stadter, P.A. (Ed.) *The Speeches in Thucydides: A Collection of Original Studies with a Bibliography*, (Chapel Hill: University of North Carolina, 1973).

Stendahl, K. "Call Rather Than Conversion", in *Paul among Jews and Gentiles and Other Essays*, (Philadelphia: Fortress, 1976), 7-23.

Sterling, Gregory E. *Historiography and Self-Definition: Josephos, Luke-Acts and Apologetic Historiography*, (Leiden/New York/Koln: Brill, 1992).

Sternberg, Meir *The Poetics of Biblical Narrative: Ideological Literature and Drama of Reading*, (Bloomington: Indiana University Press, 1985).

Stibbe, M.W.G. *John as Story Teller: Narrative Criticism and the Fourth Gospel*, (SNTSMS 73; Cambridge: Cambridge University Press, 1992).

Stonehouse, N.B. *The Witness of Luke to Christ*, (London: Tyndale Press, 1951).

Stone, G.P. & Harvey A.F. (Eds.) *Social Psychology through Symbolic Interactions*, (Waltham, Mass.: Ginn-Blaisdell, 1970).

Stump, E & T.P. Flint *Hermeneia and Athena: Biblical Exegesis and Philosophical Theology*, (Notre Dame: University of Notre Dame, 1993).

Swinburne, R. *The Concept of Miracle*, (London: Macmillan, 1970).

Swindells, Julia (Ed.). *The Uses of Autobiography*, (London: Taylor & Francis Ltd, 1995).

Sylva, D.D. (Ed.) *Reimaging the Death of the Lukan Jesus*, (Frankfurt: Hain, 1990).

Syrjänen, Seppo *In Search of Meaning and Identity: Conversion to Christianity in Pakistani Muslim Culture*, (Helsinki: The Finnish Society for Missiological Ecumenics, 1984).

Talbert, C.H. "An Anti-Gnostic Tendency in Lucan Christology", *NTS*, 14, (1967-68), 259-61.

"Biographies of Philosophers and Rulers as Instruments of Religious Propaganda in Mediterranean Antiquity" in C.H. Talbert (Ed.), *Luke-Acts: New Perspectives from the SBL Seminar*, (New York: Crossroad, 1984), 63-88.

Literary Patterns, Theological Themes, and the Genre of Luke-Acts,

(Missoula, MT: Scholars Press, 1977).

Luke and the Gnostics: An Examination of the Lucan Purpose, (Nashville: Abingdon, 1966).

"Promise and Fulfilment in Lukan Theology" in C.H. Talbert (Ed.), *Luke-Acts: New Perspectives from the Society of Biblical Literature Seminar*, (New York: Crossroad, 1984), 91-103.

Reading Luke: A Literary and Theological Commentary on the Third Gospel, (New York: Crossroad, 1982).

What Is a Gospel? The Genre of the Canonical Gospels, (Philadelphia: Fortress, 1977).

Talbert, C.H. (Ed.) *Luke-Acts: New Perspectives from the SBL Seminar*, New York: Crossroad, 1984), 91-103.

Perspectives in Luke-Acts, (Edinburgh: T&T Clark, 1978).

Tannehill, Robert C. "'Cornelius' and 'Tabitha' Encounter Luke's Jesus", *Int.*, 48, (1994), 347-56.

"The Functions of Peter's Mission Speeches in the Narrative of Acts", *NTS*, 37, (1997), 400-14.

"Israel in Luke-Acts: A Tragic Story", *JBL*, 104, (1985), 69-85.

The Narrative Unity of Luke-Acts: A Literary Interpretation, 2 Vols., (Philadelphia: Fortress, 1986/1990).

"Rejection by the Jews and Turning to the Gentiles: The Pattern of Paul's Mission in Acts" in J.B. Tyson, (Ed.), *Luke-Acts and the Jewish People*, (London: SCM, 1988), 83-101.

Theissen, Gerard. *The Miracle Stories of Early Christian Tradition*, (Trans. Francis McDonah; Ed. John Riches; Edinburgh: T & T Clark, 1983).

Thornton, T.C.G. "To the Ends of the Earth. Acts 1:8", *ExpTim*, 89,(1977-78), 874-75.

Throckmorton, B.H. "Σῴζειν in Luke-Acts", *SE*, 6, (1973), 515-26.

Tiede, David L. "Acts 11:1-18", *Int.*, 42, (1988), 175-80.

Charismatic Figure as Miracle Worker, (SBLDS 1; Missoula, MT: SBL, 1973).

"Glory to Thy People Israel: Luke-Acts and the Jews", in J. Neusner, et al (Eds.), *The Social World of Formative Christianity and Judaism: Essays in Tribute of H.C. Kee*, (Philadelphia: Fortress, 1988), 327-41.

Prophecy and History in Luke-Acts, (Philadelphia: Fortress, 1980).

Travisano, Richard "Alternation and Conversion as Qualitatively Different Transformations", in Gregory P. Stone & Harvey a. Farberman

(Eds.), *Social Psychology through Symbolic Interactions*, (Waltham, Mass.: Ginn-Blaisdell, 1970), 594-606.

Trites, Allison A. *The New Testament Concept of Witness*, (SNTSMS 31; Cambridge: Cambridge University Press, 1977).

Tuckett, C.M. *Luke*, (New Testament Guides; Sheffield: Sheffield Academic Press, 1996).

Tuckett, C.M. (Ed.) *Luke's Literary Achievement: Collected Essays*, (JSNTSup. 116; Sheffield: Sheffield Academic Press, 1995).

Turner, Max "The 'Spirit of Prophecy' as the Power of Israel's Restoration And Witness" in I.H. Marshall & David Peterson (Eds.),

Witness to the Gospel: The Theology of Acts, (Grand Rapids/Cambridge, UK: Eerdmans, 1998), 327-48.

Tyson, Joseph B. "The Gentile Mission and the Authority of Scripture in Acts", *NTS*, 33, (1987), 619-31.

"The Jewish Public in Luke-Acts", *NTS*, 30, (1984), 574-83.

Tyson, J. B. (Ed.) *Luke-Acts and the Jewish People: Eight Critical Perspectives*, (London: SCM, 1988).

Unnik, van W.C. "The Book of Acts: The Confirmation of the Gospel" in *Sparsa Collecta*, (Leiden: Brill, 1973), 340-73. Reprint from *NovT*, 4, (1960), 26-59.

"Luke-Acts, a Storm Center in Contemporary Scholarship" in L.E. Keck & J.L. Martyn (Eds.), *Studies in Luke-Acts*, (London: SPCK, 1968), 15-32.

"Luke's Second Book and the Rules of Hellenistic Historiography" in J. Kremer (Ed.), *Les Actes des Apôtres: Traditions, Rédaction, Théologie*, (Gembloux/Leuven: Duculot/Leuven University Press, 1979), 37-60.

Unsworth, Jane "Why Does an Author Who Apparently Draws So Much on Autobiography Seem Committed to Alienating the Reader?: A Reflection on Theories of Autobiography with Reference to the Work of Janet Frame", in Julia Swindells (Ed.), *The Uses of Autobiography*, (London: Taylor & Francis Ltd., 1995), 24-30.

Varneda, P Villalba I. *The Historical Method of Flavius Josephus*, (Leiden: Brill, 19860.

Votaw, C.W. "The Gospels and Contemporary Biographies", *AJT*, 19, (1915), 45-73, 217-49.

Walaskay, P.W. *"And So We Came to Rome": The Political Perspective of Luke*, (Cambridge: CUP, 1983).

Wall, R.W. "Peter, 'Son' of Jonah: The Conversion of Cornelius in the Context of the Canon", *JSNT*, 29, (1987), 70-79.

Warner, Rex *Thucydides. History of the Peloponnesian War*, (London: Penguin Books, 1972).

West, William C. "The Speeches in Thucydides: A Description and Listing", in Philip A. Stadter (Ed.), *The Speeches in Thucydides: A Collection of Original Studies with a Bibliography*, (Chapel Hill: University of North Carolina, 1973), 3-15.

Wilkenhauser, A. *The New Testament Introduction*, (ET; London: Nelson and Herder and Herder, 1958).

Wilson, Stephen G. *The Jewish and the Gentile Mission in Luke-Acts*, (London: Cambridge University Press, 1973).

Luke and the Law, (Cambridge: Cambridge University Press, 1983).

Winn, A.C. "Elusive Mystery: The Purpose of Acts", *Int.*, 13, (1959), 144-56.

Winter, B.W. & A.D. Clarke (Eds.) *The Book of Acts in its First Century Setting*, I: *Ancient Literary Setting*, (Grand Rapids: Eerdmans/Carlisle: Paternoster, 1993).

Witherington, B. (Ed.) *History, Literature, and Society in the Book of Acts*, (Cambridge: Cambridge University Press, 1996).

Witherup, Ronald D. "Cornelius over and over Again: 'Functional Redundancy' in the Acts of the Apostles", *JSNT*, 49, (1993), 45-66.

"Functional Redundancy in the Acts of the Apostles: A Case Study", *JSNT*, 48, (1992), 67-86.

Woodman, A.J. *Rhetoric in Classical Historiography*, (London/Portland: Croom Helm/Areopagitica Press, 1988).

Wright, R.B. "Psalms of Solomon", *OTP*, 639-70.

Zehnle, Richard F. *Peter's Pentecost Discourse: Tradition and Lukan Reinterpretation in Peter's Speeches of Acts 2 and 3*, (SBLMS 15; Nashville/New York: Abingdon, 1971).

Zwaan, J. de. "Was the Book of Acts a Posthumous Edition?", *HTR*, 17, (1924), 95-153.